The Frontiers of Literature

The Frontiers of Literature

Laurence Lerner

Basil Blackwell

Copyright © Laurence Lerner 1988

First published 1988

Basil Blackwell Ltd
108 Cowley Road, Oxford, OX4 1JF, UK

Basil Blackwell Inc.
432 Park Avenue South, Suite 1503
New York, NY 10016, USA

British Library Cataloguing in Publication Data

Lerner, Laurence
  The frontiers of literature.
  1. Criticism
  I. Title
  801′.95   PN81
  ISBN 0–631–14967–8

Library of Congress Cataloging in Publication Data

Lerner, Laurence
  The frontiers of literature.
  Includes index.
  1. English literature – History and criticism – Theory, etc.
  2. Literary form. I. Title.
  PR21.L47   1988   820′.9   87–35190
  ISBN 0–631–14967–8

Typeset in Bembo on 11/12pt
by Columns of Reading
Printed in Great Britain

Contents

Preface

Some of this book has already been published. Part of chapter 2 appeared as 'What is Confessional Poetry?' in *Critical Quarterly*, Summer 1987; chapter 5 (ii) was an essay in *Reconstructing Literature*, a collection edited by me for Basil Blackwell in 1983; chapter 5 (iv) was broadcast by the BBC under the title 'Murdering the Text', and an outline of the whole, based mainly on the introduction, chapter 1 (i) and chapter 4 was broadcast as a series of three talks with the same title as the book. Much of the rest has been delivered to patient and helpful audiences in lectures and seminars not only at my own universities (Sussex, Munich, Vanderbilt) but at many others that have been kind enough to invite me and listen to my work in progress – Wuerzburg, Passau, the Jagellonian University of Krakow, the Brazilian Association of Professors of English, The University of Tennessee, and others.

Literary criticism is a co-operative activity, and this book has profited not only from such official occasions but from the constant stimulus of conversations with (among others) Gabriel Josipovici, Stephen Medcalf, Bernard Harrison, Jonathan Dollimore, Vereen Bell, Manfred Pfister and Werner Sedlak. An even greater debt is owed to those who read and commented on some or all of the first draft, and showed me how badly it was, in places, expressed: John Burrow, Wayne Booth, Tony Thorlby and Tony Nuttall, to the last of whom I pay a small part of a large intellectual debt by dedicating this book to him.

According to Gerard Genette, the making of such acknowledgements is not an altogether disinterested act: 'un auteur qui a tant d'amis ne peut être absolument mauvais'. So I will say openly what he believes I have already said implicitly, that I hope you (colleague, student, thoughtful lover of literature) will read and enjoy this book, which I value highly and have struggled hard to make as clear and helpful as I can.

Laurence Lerner

To Tony Nuttall

Introduction: An Analogy

Sometimes a country has clear boundaries, such as a river or the ocean. Clear-cut national boundaries, however, are not the norm but the exception: only islands have clean edges, and even they may have internal territorial disputes, or other, smaller islands to which they lay claim. More characteristic are boundaries like Alsace-Lorraine, disputed territories (this one changed hands five times in a century) where there may be two languages spoken, each wrestling for a larger share of attention and prestige.

Now the dispute over Alsace-Lorraine does not, of itself, call into question the reality of France and Germany. Demarcation disputes are quite compatible with the existence of distinct territories – are, indeed, a consequence of their existence if, as I suggest, the typical national boundary is not an ocean shore but a strip of ambiguous land. But suppose the whole territory of Germany were surrounded by border disputes – with Switzerland, with Czechoslovakia, with Austria, with Poland, with Denmark, with Holland, with France (as much of it has been). Suppose these disputes were exacerbated to the point that there was no square inch of territory that was indisputably German (as has been the case with Poland). A German might be reluctant to admit this about his own country: he might insist on a heartland, which could include Heidelberg (the oldest university) or Teutoberger Wald (the legendary victory over a foreign invader) or Aachen (seat of Charlemagne and of an old and richly meaningful cathedral). Since these are geographically remote from each other, and one at least is near the frontier, it is not easy to locate the physical existence of the German heartland. In the conceptual country of literature, such a heartland is often postulated; it is equally difficult to find the actual novels, poems or plays which embody it.

To be committed to the idea of a heartland is (in contemporary parlance) to take an essentialist view of literature. To the essentialist, it is reductive to see literature (we might even say Literature) as serving any other purpose, to 'faire des Lettres une sort d'institution d'utilité publique . . . tournant en moyens d'éducation des instruments de plaisir spirituel', as Valéry complained.[1] If the essentialist overcomes his reluctance to pointing out the analogies between literature and other forms of discourse, he will only do so as a strategy for showing that what really matters is the difference, that literature is defined by not having public usefulness, poetry is defined by its untranslatability. He is the patriot who maintains that this piece of soil is wholly and exclusively, ineluctably German.

At the other extreme stands the view that exploration of the frontiers is important because it leads to the steady erosion of the whole territory. The difficulty of knowing whether Alsace-Lorraine is French or German is not a peripheral difficulty, but a paradigm of the very process of defining, a clue to the fact that once we examine closely we see that 'Germany' was a provisional concept, a logocentric entity: it crumbles as it is understood. 'Structure is perceived,' says Derrida, 'through the incidence of menace, at the moment when imminent danger concentrates our vision on the keystone of an institution.'[2] What we have called 'literature' is simply what we have chosen (probably for ideological reasons) to call literature, not for intrinsic qualities, but because of the way we have read it, a way that can change as we give place to (lose power to) a new group of readers.[3] I will call this the deconstructionist view.

This book is neither essentialist nor deconstructionist. Against the essentialist I would claim that Germany is much larger than any heartland, so that we need not pursue a notion of the literary that excludes all disputed territory. For such a notion would take us into a tiny area of pure poetry, excluding most of what as living breathing human beings we spend our time (and our literary reading) on. Valéry declared once to Mallarmé that though he would never be popular, there was in every town in France 'un jeune homme secret qui se ferait hâcher pour vos vers'.[4] He meant this, under the comic note, to count as the highest praise, but it can also be seen as showing the futility of feeling that all that ultimately matters is a pure essence of poetry. Even the gruesome image of being willing to be chopped into pieces may be more appropriate than Valéry noticed, for withdrawing to a heartland is what you do when you are losing a war. I postulate peace as the normal state of affairs, and in that case a country will have large areas which have much in common with contiguous lands, areas where people cross the border freely, speak two languages, carry two currencies in their wallets, but usually know whether they are German or French, German or Danish.

Against the deconstructionist, on the other hand, I want to claim that the conceptual insecurity of Germany (or of literature) need not make a great deal of difference to our national identity or our literary experience. Even if there is no heartland, even if every inch of Germany consists only of disputed territory, that does not deny the existence of Germany. Switzerland has three languages, each of which is spoken outside the country by a much larger number of people: the linguistic heartland of Switzerland consists only of Romansch (spoken by one per cent of the inhabitants) and the dialectal variations that distinguish Schweitzerdeutsch from Hochdeutsch. No Swiss will allow this fact to impugn the reality or importance of Switzerland. Nations are a valid way of dividing up the world, even, for some purposes, the most important.

This book is an attempt to explore how literature impinges on, and overlaps with, the contiguous territories. It is written in the belief that the boundaries are real, but that overlaps are nothing to be frightened of, indeed, that they are enriching. It draws the boundaries not by theoretical speculation, but by the examination of actual borderline cases. We are often told nowadays that literary criticism can no longer be practised by the theoretically innocent, that it is necessary to clarify the theoretical basis of what one is doing. Behind this book lies a partial acceptance of this. Theory is important, but so are instances: it is only through their embodiment in actual works of literature that literary theories take on meaning. To read without reflection, even to discuss without wider reflection, is like strolling through one's home town without wondering how it relates to the rest of the world. But to spend all one's time on the principles of demarcation is to be lost in methodology. What sort of a book would one write on Germany if one never learnt German, never visited Aachen or Heidelberg, let alone Cologne or Munich, never read Heine or met any Germans?

In order to give an outline of the book, I must now, clearly, name and describe the adjacent territories (readers who prefer to find out as they go along where they are being taken, are invited to skip the next four paragraphs). There are four, which I have named history, crying, persuading, and play. I have had to regard these territories as unproblematic, though no doubt there could be studies of history, of psycholinguistics, of moral philosophy and of children's games, that explored the problems raised by the frontiers of each of these territories, as I here explore those raised by 'literature'. But one can only write one book at a time, and I have had to put aside those hypothetical explorations, and operate with a stable conception of each.

1 History is the study of the past. Examples of historical statements are 'Edwin Chadwick's Report on the Sanitary Condition of the Labouring Classes was completed in 1841, and published by the Poor Law Commission in 1842', or 'Though Wesley wished to remain in the Church of England, the Methodists, soon after his death, were for all practical purposes a Dissenting sect'. The common element in history and literature is narrative, and the first chapter therefore compares historical and fictitious narrative. Since most novelists draw in their work on a blend of observation, memory and imagination, the discussion will be cleanest if we can isolate these from one another. I therefore begin with two limit cases: first, that in which the novelist draws on material to which no reader has any access (autobiographical fiction), and second, that in which the reader has, in principle, the same access to the material as the author (historical fiction). Since both these discussions deal with the portrayal of individuals, I then turn to what could be seen as the only proper concern of history, the portrayal of social movements, and here again there are two sections, both concerned with nineteenth-century England: one on the physical circumstances of life, the other on changing beliefs and attitudes.

2 The adjacent territory of chapter 2 is called 'crying', a conveniently ambiguous term for the discharge of emotion, verbal and non-verbal. Examples of cries are 'I hate you', 'It hurts', 'Oh Hell' or 'Oh frabjous day, callooh, callay'. As an example of material that seems to belong on both sides of the frontier I choose confession, and the subgenre of confessional poetry, so popular in the 1950s and 1960s. In asking whether the term 'confessional' should be extended to other poetry, taking us back in time to the Romantics and even before, I am led into a discussion about expression theory, and the ways in which it can be heuristically useful. Finally, I ask whether the structuralist decentring of the autonomous subject means that we must abandon expression theory.

3   Persuasion, or advocacy, is the attempt to cause others to act in a certain way: 'Vote Labour.' 'Believe and you shall be saved.' 'You'll never regret buying a Cortina.' Its overlap with literature is caused by the didactic theories that see the function of literature as exciting us to virtue. Didactic views of literature, which go back to the ancient world, dominated criticism for many centuries. Didacticism is now so widely rejected in aesthetics that we need to remind ourselves how many of our great writers claimed, almost as a matter of course, that their work was morally improving. In the two main areas of our social life, religion and politics, advocacy of one position and rejection of another has not and will not cease. This is an adjacent territory that continues to matter, and attempts to assimilate literature to it, either by surreptitious boundary shifts or by direct conquest, will therefore continue. This chapter compares religious advocacy in its commonest form, the sermon, with religious poetry (choosing Donne as the test case); and political advocacy with the political novel or poem.

4   We all play games; but the play element in literature has usually had a bad press. To speak of a poem as a word-game is usually dismissive. Taking the concept of the adjacent territory from Huizinga and Freud, I begin this chapter with the obvious presence of the play element in nursery rhymes and nonsense verse, then go on to suggest that form itself can be regarded as play. We are all too puritanical to leave play alone to enjoy itself, so I go on to discuss those theories that attribute to form not self-contained delight, but some wider function.

It is natural to ask whether I consider these four to be the only frontiers on to which literature abuts. I am sure the answer is no, if only because of the recurrent quirkiness of artists, trying to set themselves unprecedented tasks; but it could still be that these are the most important, and that I do believe, since exploring these frontiers seems to throw up most of the traditional arguments about the nature of literature. If we look for other contiguous territories that I could have explored, the strongest candidate would probably be systematic thinking, or the ordered exposition of knowledge: psychology, sociology, philosophy, even science. Essentialists often select as the defining quality of literature the subordination of part to whole, the claim that no detail can be considered apart from its contribution to the total effect: a claim often stated in organic language. The same claim can be made (but without the organic metaphor) for systematic knowledge, and a discussion of this frontier would have enabled us to explore the concepts of part and whole, and the uses of organicism. But in the end I was not convinced enough (or not fertile enough) to take on a fifth frontier.

But there is an alternative model of the territory of literature which I must pause to consider. It is possible to construct a frontier that is not taxonomic but evaluative, that sees in the territory beyond that frontier not history or verbal play, but bad novels, bad poems and bad plays.

At a first glance, this would seem to present no theoretical problem. Literature as taxonomic and as evaluative concept can each exist in its own discourse, and to say that bad novels are literature in one sense and not in the other seems a simple matter of being clear about the terminology. The complication arises when works of history or sermons or treatises in moral philosophy or autobiographies get raised, through their excellence, to the status of literature (it will clearly not be quite the same kind of excellence that makes them good history or good philosophy). If some of Plato's dialogues are regarded as literary masterpieces, this means that what began as philosophy can turn into poetry; but it clearly does not mean that all philosophy is aspiring to the condition of poetry, or that Leibnitz, Mill and Wittgenstein should be condemned because they do not show the same kind of imagination or verbal inventiveness. Dorothy Osborne's letters, which have given as much pleasure to later generations as they ever gave to William Temple, are often considered part of English literature, but if we had Temple's letters, and found them no more attractive than those of our great-uncle, we would not dismiss him as unworthy to be her husband. There is no ultimate justification for writing a novel unless it is a good one; but there is plenty of good reason for writing letters or sermons or history books which have no claim to be considered literature. It is possible to produce a work of literature by setting out to do so (in which case it might be good or bad) or by setting out to produce a different kind of writing and performing (without announcing that you are going to) one of the functions this book will be exploring.

But we must go further. Is it possible to separate the taxonomic from the evaluative? There have been schools of criticism (the Chicago Aristotelians, for example) who have firmly answered yes: both discussions are valid, but they are different, and the former must take place before we move to the latter. There have been others (the *Scrutiny* critics, for instance) who have answered no: it is impossible to have any meaningful discussion of a text unless we ask, all the time, about its quality of felt life, its imaginative vision, its ability to realise its concepts in images. More recently, there have been critics who want to rule out evaluation completely, on ideological grounds: that it 'privileges' some kinds of work over others, and thus some classes of readers over others, and is therefore elitist. Such a critic might also reject the taxonomic concept of literature, on the grounds that no taxonomy is value-free, that the concept of 'literature' is a way of highly valuing (or 'privileging') certain kinds of writing. In this way, F.R. Leavis and Terry Eagleton are at one:[5] both refuse to admit any neutral, non-evaluative way of answering the question, What is Literature? They differ in that for Leavis it is a reason for accepting, in Eagleton a reason for interrogating the concept.

I will try to indicate the position taken by this book about evaluation, but it will not be easy, since in contrast to those above, it is not a clear-cut position. First, it is necessary to point out that value judgements are inescapable for pragmatic purposes. Publishers must decide which books to publish, which to reject; reviewers, which ones to discuss, which to ignore; judges, which to award the prizes to; readers, which are worth their time and money. In a world in which there is more available than one man can ever read, such a sifting process is essential, but evaluation is even more central to literature than that, for the very process of literary composition involves value judgement. Choice is value judgement, and writing is a continual series of choices – include or delete that adjective in the sentence, that sentence in the story, that story in the volume. The choice may be conscious and agonized, or it may be made instantly and unreflectingly, but there is always choice. Everything in a book might have been different, and if the author (or the reader) is satisfied with what there is that means it might have been worse.

But all this applies to any form of writing: historians, too, make choices, readers of history, too, have limited time. There is a second, more central sense in which literature involves questions of value. This is because the very idea of literature involves valuing highly the experience of reading certain books, and thus implicitly rating others lower. It involves, that is, the idea of a canon. A canon is a set of sacred books, and the meaning has become secularized to refer to those works chosen by consensus as embodying what is truly valuable in a subject, so there will be a canon of works of literature, of great paintings, of works of philosophy. I know no discussion of the literary canon as perceptive as Richard Rorty's discussion of the philosophic canon, so I shall lean on that, and make the appropriate changes. In his essay on 'The Historiography of Philosophy', Rorty recognises four genres. The first two study individual texts, and are called reconstruction: historical reconstruction recaptures what the past philosopher said, in terms acceptable to him; rational reconstruction puts our questions to him, and can be called conversation with the re-educated dead. The first treats what E.D. Hirsch calls 'meaning', the second what he calls 'significance'.[6] Rorty claims that in order to do the first properly you need a good deal of the second, since to understand an argument is to know how far it answers the questions it does not put; and he therefore rejects Hirsch's claim that the study of meaning must precede that of significance. The other two genres deal not with individual works but with the general history of the subject, and here Rorty distinguishes *Geistesgeschichte*, which is concerned with canon formation, from 'intellectual history', which is concerned with all the thinking that was going on at any time. *Geistesgeschichte* cannot stay within the voacabulary of past texts, like historical reconstruction, but it equally cannot, like the history of science, settle the question of who belongs to the canon simply by appealing to modern practice. It is essentially a dialogue with the past, asking who are the great dead philosophers by asking what questions are important: the answer will keep changing, but not by mere subordination of past to present. There is an inferior version of *Geistesgeschichte* which Rorty calls doxography: this is the kind of history of philosophy which accepts an inherited canon, on to which it then imposes a problematic drawn up independently of it, and thus has to claim that certain continuing problems have always engaged the great philosophers, when they clearly haven't.

It is not difficult to shift this argument from philosophy to literature. The meaning/significance distinction was originally designed for literary study, and we can distinguish between the historical reconstruction of (say) *Julius Caesar* (using it to recapture what Elizabethans thought about Roman history, and their own politics), and its rational reconstruction (its contribution to understanding our political problems, its emotional impact on a twentieth-century audience). For intellectual history we would substitute the history of writing – all writing: letters, pamphlets, journals, novels good and bad, poems and pop songs, newspaper reports, advertisements. We would then single out from this mass of writing those works which are 'literature' in the honorific sense. If we did this by simply accepting from earlier generations a list of great writers, that would be doxography: if we regarded the canon as subject to change in response to the changes in modern literature (while also regarding modern literature as nourished by the great works of the past) that would be literary criticism, the equivalent to *Geistesgeschichte*.

If there is no *Geistesgeschichte*, and thus no canon, the same texts can still be studied – as part of intellectual history. Rorty attributes to 'the Foucaultians' the view that if we have the sort of complicated, thick intellectual history that is wary of canons, we have enough; that if we get rid of doxography (which Rorty would be glad to do), then it will take *Geistesgeschichte* with it. In reply, he asserts the necessity of canons,

because we cannot get along without heroes. We need mountain peaks to look up towards. We need to tell ourselves stories about the mighty dead in order to make our hopes of surpassing them concrete. We also need the idea that there is such a thing as 'philosophy' in the honorific sense – the idea that there are, had we but the wit to pose them, certain questions which everybody should have been asking.[7]

Similarly, if there is no literary canon, it will still be possible to study *Paradise Lost* and *Bleak House*. The historian will study them as examples of puritanism, of patriarchy, of belief in free will, or attitudes to industrialism or illegitimacy or the law; the linguist may study them as examples of particular sentence formations. The interest here will not lie in the intrinsic value of the works, but in the movement, the code or the rule that they exemplify or confirm: they will be selected for study not because they are outstanding but because they are representative. If literature disappears as a concept, individual works of literature can still be studied – but they will not be read. We call *Paradise Lost* and *Nostromo* 'literature' because generations of readers have found them moving, or beautiful, or that they speak to their condition, or keep children from play and old men from the chimney corner; readers read them for pleasure, for spiritual satisfaction, for kicks, for aesthetic experience (all these expressions are value judgements). Like Rorty I want to defend the case for canons, but in stronger form. It is not just that we need heroes: we need them because we value what they do. It is not enough to say 'we need the idea that there is such a thing as literature in the honorific sense'. What we need is *Macbeth* and *Julius Caesar*, *Bleak House* and the 'Ode to the West Wind', *Middlemarch* and 'Surprised by Joy' – not the idea of literature but actual works, not the belief that there are poems had we the wit to write them, but the knowledge that there *are* poems, and the heroes of the canon did have the wit to write them.

There are, then, two models of the literary territory, and two concepts of the frontier: taxonomic, and evaluative. We need both: the first, obviously, for clarity of thought, the second if works of literature are to be read by readers as well as studied by scholars. Now it has to be admitted that they cannot be kept completely separate, because the qualities which give Plato's philosophy a claim to be literature but not Wittgenstein's, Dorthy Osborne's letters but not yours or mine, have much in common with what distinguishes Tennyson from Tupper, and George Eliot from the pulp romance. In showing why Plato and Dorothy Osborne are part of literature (a question that is both evaluative and taxonomic), we use arguments that can apply to the purely evaluative question why *Middlemarch* is and *Heart-throbs* isn't 'literature'.

We cannot, then, entertain a concept of literature that completely excludes evaluation; but that does not mean that literary criticism should, or even can, be constantly evaluative, just as it does not mean there are no taxonomic questions. There is always much to say about a text that is only marginally evaluative, or not so at all: what it means, what genre it belongs to, how it relates to social and intellectual movements, how it relates to the author's other work, what codes it uses and how conscious these are, how its narrative devices and its syntactical structures relate to each other (if they do), what concept of God, of change, of woman, of work it operates with. These questions may be of enormous complexity (it may drift between several not wholly compatible concepts of God or of work), and an over-eager rush to say how good or how bad it is can easily interfere with our perception of just what it is doing. Furthermore, it is possible to conduct an argument about meaning, genre or narrative devices with far more rational control than an argument about literary merit, for there are more generally agreed criteria for settling the former. There is therefore a necessary paradox about literary evaluation: it is inescapable, but it cannot often be performed. If we did not think some books better than others, we could not value any books, but it is much more possible to decide whether *Middlemarch* is a *Bildungsroman*, and what changes are required when the hero of a *Bildungsroman* is female, than it is to discuss whether it is the greatest English novel (though I am equally convinced of the truth of both).

In this book, therefore, evaluation will never be the prime aim of a discussion, but in addressing taxonomic and interpretative questions we may throw up points that help us to understand what is good or bad in a work: and when this happens, they will be gratefully seized on. There may well be instances when a reader assents to the primary argument, but dissents from the evaluative corollary; when that happens I shall not of course know, but if I did, I would be disappointed but unprotesting.

We cannot, of course, begin with a definition of literature: that would anticipate, even preclude, the writing of the book. All we can begin with is ostensive definition. Literature is *David Copperfield* and *Bleak House*, 'Ode to the West Wind' and Donne's *Holy Sonnets*, *Le Rouge et le Noir* and 'Palmstroem'. Plato's *Symposium* can be seen as literature, but not Wittgenstein's *Philosophical Investigations*, not the sermon you heard last week, nor the letter you received yesterday from your solicitor, nor this book.

1

History

History and story: etymologically, the two words are the same, and only in English have they separated in this way. French *histoire* has an element of fiction in its possible meanings, Italian uses *storia* for what we call history, a short story in German is *Kurzgeschichte*, announcing its link with *Geschichte*, history. The link lies precisely in the fact of story. The frontier with history is arguably the most important of all because of the common element, narrative. In recent years the study of narratology has often looked at history and literature alike, and offered a common theory for both; even discussions of theory have been subsumed under the heading of narrative. The result of this has been to obliterate the distinction between history and literature.

Yet this frontier should, surely, be the easiest to draw, because we have a familiar concept to help us, that of fiction. Literature is fiction, history is fact: everyone knows that, but what everyone knows is not necessarily unproblematic. It is precisely this common-sense distinction that has been called into question by recent theorists, claiming that historical reality is a special case of fiction, as speech is a special case of writing, sexual intercourse a special case of masturbation, and nature a special case of culture. The 'central signified', in the now well-known Derridian argument, 'the original or transcendental signified', is never 'absolutely present' outside a system of differences.[1] And so if we read a life of Napoleon, who really lived, and a novel about Julien Sorel, who didn't, we can ignore that difference, and study the two discourses. If there is no transcendental signified, no originary source of the trace, then there is no realm in which Napoleon 'exists' and Julien doesn't, for such a realm would be the *hors-texte* which Derrida denies. Both characters are the signified of the texts on which they depend, and if we grant a different ontological status to Napoleon, that is because we handle his case in a different way. The historical is a special case of the fictional.[2] So runs the argument.

The novel emerged as a genre, within recorded literary history, from a coming together of various other genres, that included both fiction and fact – real-life adventure stories, spiritual autobiography, memoirs of criminals, religious allegory, and others. Defoe used his prefaces to assure his readers that 'this story differs from most of the modern performances of this kind . . . in this . . . that the foundation of this is laid in truth of fact',[3] and it is a moot point how far they believed him. Some of the immediate precursors of the novel (the news ballad, for instance) may have complicated the confusion of the real and the fictitious, and readers of the early novel may actually have recognized the new genre by a new kind of uncertainty about the distinction.[4] Today of course we are more sophisticated: we do not need to be assured that Julian Sorel never lived, and if doubts about the distinction between fact and fiction have resurfaced, it is for theoretical not practical reasons.

Choosing examples will be crucial in exploring this distinction. Most novels are made from a mixture of memory, introspection, observation and the use of documents: the novelist moves between what he once did and felt, what he feels at the moment, what he sees and hears and remembers seeing and hearing, and what he has chosen to find out by study. The critic may try to follow him in all these, panting after some access to the same material, in order to compare raw material with finished product. But we will never disentangle the farrago, and the only method possible is to isolate the extreme cases. On the one hand, there is the case in which the author has access to his material in a way no one else can, in principle, ever have; on the other hand, that in which the author has no more access than we have. The first is autobiography, where memory and introspection, unavailable to us, are the raw material: and the autobiographical novel therefore stands at one extreme. The second is the biography of a person the author never met (nor met anyone who knew her), where all the author has is documents that are equally available to us: and the re-creation of a historical figure in fiction stands at the other extreme. The first marks the limit of what comes only from within, the second of what comes only from without. Studying these two extremes should help us to draw some kind of map of the frontier.

Young David and Young Charles

In 1847 John Forster happened to ask his friend Charles Dickens a casual question about his childhood, and realized immediately that he had touched on a distressing subject; shortly afterwards, he was shown by Dickens a written account of the childhood experience in question. The financial embarrassments of Dickens's father had led to the son being taken out of school at the age of ten, and he was (as is now well known) sent to work in Warrens Blacking Factory, near the Strand, for six or seven shillings a week. It was an episode Dickens never forgot:

It is wonderful to me how I could have been so easily cast away at such an age. It is wonderful to me that, even after my descent into the poor little drudge I had been since we came to London, no-one had compassion enough on me – a child of singular abilities: quick, eager, delicate and soon hurt, bodily or mentally – to suggest that something might have been spared, as certainly it might have been, to place me at any common school.

This autobiographical fragment is written with the vivid accuracy of passion and resentment. The blacking warehouse was 'a crazy tumbledown old house, abutting . . . on the river, and literally overrun with rats'. Two or three other boys worked along with him: one of them, Bob Fagin, was kind to him, and Dickens gave him a shabby reward by using his name in *Oliver Twist*. Whatever the individual kindness he received, Dickens could not be reconciled to what was happening to him.

No words can express the secret agony of my soul as I sunk into this companionship; compared these everyday associates with those of my happier childhood; and felt my early hopes of growing up to be a learned and distinguished man crushed in my breast. . . My whole nature was so penetrated with the grief and humiliation of such considerations, that even now, famous and caressed and happy, I often forget in my dreams that I have a dear wife and children; even that I am a man; and wander desolately back to that time of my life.

The modern egalitarian reader, we can remark in passing, might observe that if it was so painful for Dickens to spend a year in that warehouse, it must have been worse for the boys who were condemned to it for life. It is a nice political issue, to ask which is worse, the plunge into poverty of a bright young lad brought up to something better, or the steady poverty of those who do not even think of escape. What we can certainly say is that the former holds the more obvious pathos, and this is felt in every line of Dickens's autobiographical sketch.

The story has a happy ending, of a kind. Dickens's father and the relative who had found Charles the job quarrelled, and he was dismissed.

I cried very much, partly because it was so sudden, and partly because in his anger he was violent about my father, though gentle to me. . . With a relief so strange that it was like oppression, I went home.

Then comes the fascinating twist:

My mother set herself to accommodate the quarrel, and did so next day. She brought home a request for me to return next morning, and a high character of me, which I am very sure I deserved. My father said I should go back no more, and should go to school. I do not write resentfully or angrily: for I know how all these things have worked together to make me what I am: but I never afterwards forgot, I never shall forget, I never can forget, that my mother was warm for my being sent back.[5]

It looks at first as if Mrs Dickens is to come better out of the story than her husband: she is the peacemaker, he the one who stands on his dignity. She has the traditional feminine virtues, and the mention of the child's tears looks like a preparation for her thoughtfulness and understanding, for her husband does not seem to have been interested in the child's grief. But that, we realize with a shock, is not how her son saw it: from where he was, it was she who was snatching away rescue, and with what looks like unconscious rhetorical cunning he rounds on her all the more fiercely for its unexpectedness.

Dickens wrote the fragment in 1847; a few months later he began *David Copperfield*, his most autobiographical novel, which even bears his own initials reversed in its title. He used this sketch in chapter XI ('I Begin Life on my own Account, and don't Like it'), in which David, like his creator, is sent to work in a warehouse with three or four other boys of his age. Because we have the original fragment, written before he had begun work on *David Copperfield*, and indeed intended as part of an autobiography that he abandoned once he had thought up the novel,[6] it is almost as if

Dickens had set up an experimental control for us. Here we have the perfect opportunity to compare the real and the fictional versions of the same life; and what we find, first of all, is that they are almost identical. Clearly the shift in status of the text did not of itself involve any fundamental shift on Dickens's part.

Chapter XI of the novel opens:

I know enough of the world now, to have almost lost the capacity of being much surprised by anything; but it is a matter of some surprise to me, even now, that I can have been so easily thrown away at such an age. A child of excellent abilities, and with strong powers of observation, quick, eager, delicate, and soon hurt bodily or mentally, it seems wonderful to me that nobody should have made any sign in my behalf.

Most of the changes here are trivial, a matter of stylistic polish or adjustment to the facts of the story. What is most striking is what has remained. In both texts, the paragraph is introduced by an indignant statement of astonishment. David like Charles finds it a matter of 'some surprise' that he 'can have been so easily thrown away at such an age'. If 'some surprise' looks at first like a toning down from 'it is wonderful to me', we soon realize, as we read on, that there has not been any toning down. There are still no words to express 'the secret agony of my soul', there is the same indignant astonishment at his clumsy, solitary dinners. The relation of adult narrator to child subject has simply been carried over from autobiography to novel. Now we are certainly not intended to think that the adult David, when he was living happily ever after with Agnes, forgot in his dreams (as his creator did) that he had a dear wife and children, even that he was a man. The indignation, and the fact that it is in the present tense, is a case of authorial intervention, an attempt to involve the reader in the moral comment. Why? Only two answers seem possible: one, that the author as craftsman is over-anxious, losing confidence in the power of his writing to produce the intended effect, or two, that the author as autobiographer is over-involved, unable to contain his own feelings on the matter. They are not David's feelings, but Dickens's.

One episode was taken almost (not quite) unchanged from the fragment:

I was such a child, and so little, that frequently when I went into the bar of a strange public-house for a glass of ale or porter, to moisten what I had

had for dinner, they were afraid to give it to me. I remember one hot evening I went into the bar of a public house, and said to the landlord:

'What is your best – your *very best* – ale a glass?' For it was a special occasion. I don't know what. It may have been my birthday.

'Twopence-halfpenny,' says the landlord, 'is the price of the Genuine Stunning ale.'

'Then,' says I, producing the money, 'just draw me a glass of the Genuine Stunning, if you please, with a good head to it.'

The landlord looked at me in return over the bar, from head to foot, with a strange smile on his face; and instead of drawing the beer, looked round the screen and said something to his wife. She came out from behind it, with her work in her hand, and joined him in surveying me. Here we stand, all three, before me now. The landlord in his shirt-sleeves, leaning against the bar window-frame; his wife looking over the little half-door; and I, in some confusion, looking up at them from outside the partition. They asked me a good many questions; as, what my name was, how old I was, where I lived, how I was employed, and how I came there. To all of which, that I might commit nobody, I invented, I am afraid, appropriate answers. They served me with the ale, though I suspect it was not the Genuine Stunning: and the landlord's wife, opening the little half-door of the bar, and bending down, gave me my money back, and gave me a kiss that was half-admiring, and half-compassionate, but all womanly and good, I am sure.[6]

Considered simply as part of the novel, this displays a wonderful combination of involvement and detachment. David is still the neglected child, but the mode has shifted to comedy. 'Here we stand, all three, before me now' is not authorial intrusion to insist on the sufferings of the child, but the composing of a scene, frozen in its diverting indecorousness: the explicitness, that is, serves an aesthetic purpose. It is indecorous because the child's attempt to fit the adult role he has been miscast in is both very successful and a total failure: he picks up the publican's advertising jargon, but he does not get the Genuine Stunning. The landlord and his wife staring at him testify to the failure, yet the child is more in command than they realize: 'to all of which . . . I invented, I am afraid, appropriate answers.' There is a double contest taking place: in the text, between David and the landlord, in the reader, between reading the scene as pathos and as comedy. In both cases, it is not easy to say who wins.

Now let us place next to this the same episode from the autobiography. That began, 'I was such a little fellow, with my poor white hat, little jacket and corduroy trousers.' Why did Dickens tame this vivid sentence, removing the description of the child's dress and (even more of a loss) the details of the dinner 'eaten in the street'? To compensate, he added two new touches of invention. Most brilliant, there is the phrase 'Genuine Stunning', raised above the status of the merely adjectival first by the capitalizing, then by its use as a substantive by David: the commercial, puffing habits of the landlord seen with a momentary, detached amusement. And then there is the fact that the landlady gives him his money back, and so emerges more fully from comedy into pathos than her husband does. The other changes are trivial.

Not all the important connections between novel and auto-biography can be perceived by juxtaposition of passages. Of the larger elements, the most striking is the invention of Mr Micawber, the volatile improvident with his parody of dignity, modelled, as everyone knows, on Dickens's father. When John Dickens was sent to the Marshalsea he announced histrionically that the sun was set on him for ever, though the famous Micawber arithmetic may owe more to his son than to him:

Annual income twenty pounds, annual expenditure twenty pounds ought and six, result misery. The blossom is blighted, the leaf is withered, the God of day goes down upon the dreary scene, and – and in short you are for ever floored. As I am.[7]

It would be fascinating to know what parental oration lies behind this, but the sharp change of register in the last dozen words surely derives, not from the original but from the stylistic brilliance of the author. That a novelist should base a comic personage on the father he regarded with a mixture of contempt, resentment and affection is not surprising; what is striking is that the figure is used as a bystander in David's humiliation. It was John Dickens's bankruptcy and imprisonment for debt that took his son out of school, it was John Dickens's easygoing nature that consented to his being sent to the warehouse; Mr Micawber is just as irresponsible and easygoing, he too is sent to a debtor's prison, but he is in no way the cause of David's miseries. It is as if Dickens had put Micawber into these chapters in order to draw attention to the fact that the substitute father is not guilty, as if he is saying to his father, 'Look, I'm not blaming you'. This would of course be a private message, inaccessible to the ordinary reader; what that reader notices is the fact that Micawber's improvidence is of the kind that could well visit his children with the same fate as David (a point never even hinted at in the book), and this could be seen as a rhetorical device to emphasize, by contrast, the much more positive cruelty of Mr Murdstone.

Young Ruddy

For a second example, it would be convenient to take a case in which we have rather more independent evidence. In 1871 the six-year-old Rudyard Kipling, and his sister Trix, then aged three, were left by their parents with Captain and Mrs Holloway in Southsea. The parents then returned to India, and the children did not see them for six years. This was not all that unusual among Anglo-Indians at a time when child mortality was high in tropical climates, but it is clear that the experience was painful to Mrs Kipling and traumatic for young Ruddy. Captain Holloway had been a midshipman at the battle of Navarino, and when he took the lad for walks he would reminisce about his youth; he died in 1874, and the children were left with Mrs Holloway and her son, about six years older than Ruddy. Mrs Holloway was pious and evangelical, and clearly preferred Trix to her brother. Though the children did not see their parents all that time, they spent the summers with their maternal aunts, especially at the Burne-Joneses, where Ruddy passed a happy month each year. Ruddy had eye trouble which went undiagnosed until shortly before the mother's return, of which the immediate cause was a letter from her sister saying that the child was unhappy and seemed sadly changed.

We have two versions of this story. This time the fictional version is the earlier, a story called 'Baa Baa Black Sheep', written in 1888. At the very end of his life, Kipling told it again in his autobiography, *Something of Myself.* Here he insisted that Mrs Holloway had been cruel to him, and her son a bully:

It was an establishment run with the full vigour of the Evangelical as revealed to the Woman. I had never heard of Hell, so I was introduced to it in all its terrors. . . I was regularly beaten. The Woman had an only son of twelve or thirteen as religious as she. I was a real joy to him, for when his mother had finished with me for the day he (we slept in the same room) took me on and roasted the other side. . .
I can but admire the infernal laborious ingenuity of it all. *Exempli gratia.* Coming out of church once I smiled. The Devil-boy demanded why. I

said I didn't know, which was child's truth. He replied that I *must* know. People didn't laugh for nothing. Heaven knows what explanation I put forward; but it was duly reported to the Woman as a 'lie'. Result, afternoon upstairs with the Collect to learn. I learned most of the Collects that way, and a good deal of the Bible. The son after three or four years went into a Bank, and was generally too tired on his return to torture me, unless things had gone wrong with him. I learned to know what was coming from his step into the house.

One lurid detail sounds as if it came from Victorian fiction. Ruddy threw away a school report, was found out, and 'was well beaten and sent through the streets of Southsea with the placard "Liar" between my shoulders'. And one particularly moving touch, which is very briefly related, concerns his mother's return:

Then – I do not remember that I had any warning – the Mother returned from India. She told me afterwards that when she first came up to my room to kiss me good-night, I flung up an arm to guard off the cuff that I had been trained to expect.[8]

Kipling's biographers have questioned some of this, and we have more independent evidence than we had in the case of Warrens Blacking. Carrington is sceptical about the placard, and Trix's reminiscences as an old woman (after her brother's death) do not altogether square with his. And we know that she continued at the Holloways, on and off, for the next three years, so there cannot have been any really terrible revelations.[9]

'Baa Baa Black Sheep' relates the same facts, with a few additions and deletions. All mention of the Burne-Joneses and the Macdonalds, the relatives where Ruddy spent his happy summers, is removed. Very little that is completely new is added about the child's torments, and though the fictional version is rather fuller, it is very much in the spirit of the autobiography. (Terms like 'added' and 'deleted' are clearly not to be taken literally, because of the order of composition of the two versions.) There is much more about Captain Holloway, who becomes the child's ally. His kindness is built up as prominently as the cruelty of his wife and son, and in fact produces further trouble for the boy, culminating in the brilliant scene of his death:

That night Black Sheep woke with a start. Harry was not in the room, and there was a sound of sobbing on the next floor. Then the voice of

Uncle Harry, singing the song of the Battle of Navarino, came through the darkness:–
Our vanship was the *Asia* –
The *Albion* and *Genoa*!
'He's getting well,' thought Black Sheep, who knew the song through all its seventeen verses. But the blood froze at his little heart as he thought. The voice leapt an octave, and ran shrill as a boatswain's pipe:–
And next came on the lovely *Rose*,
The *Philomel*, her fire-ship, closed,
And the little *Brisk* was sore exposed
That day at Navarino.
'That day at Navarino, Uncle Harry' shouted Black Sheep, half wild with excitement and fear of he knew not what. A door opened, and Aunty Rosa screamed up the staircase: 'Hush! For god's sake hush, you little devil! Uncle Harry is *dead*!'[10]

The most telling touch here is 'little devil', which both betrays Aunty Rosa's cruelty, and yet is clearly sincere: at this point, the child's singing would indeed have seemed devilish to her. Aunty Rosa is quite as cruel as the original Mrs Holloway, and the effect of this on the child is presented very bluntly. In the autobiography, it is related to his subsequent career as a novelist:

If you cross-examine a child of seven or eight on his day's doings (especially when he wants to go to sleep) he will contradict himself very satisfactorily. If each contradiction be set down as a lie and retailed at breakfast, life is not easy. . . Yet it made me give attention to the lies I soon found it necessary to tell; and this, I presume, is the foundation of literary effect.[11]

In the story, the effect is seen more in terms of immediate survival, and Black Sheep is not presented as a future writer, so the long-term benefit to his imagination is irrelevant: he learns to lie and to fight back, and becomes chillingly good at it:

Then the placard was procured. Aunty Rosa stitched it between his shoulders and bade him go for a walk with it upon him.
   'If you make me do that,' said Black Sheep very quietly, 'I shall burn this house down, and perhaps I'll kill you. I don't know whether I *can* kill you – you're so bony – but I'll try.'
   No punishment followed this blasphemy, though Black Sheep held himself ready to work his way to Aunty Rosa's withered throat, and grip

there till he was beaten off. Perhaps Aunty Rosa was afraid, for Black Sheep, having reached the Nadir of Sin, bore himself with a new recklessness.[12]

Fiction and Autobiography

What, now, can we learn from these two examples about the use of autobiographical material in fiction? In both cases, we are dealing with intense feeling in the writer, most apparent in the earlier piece – the autobiography in the case of Dickens, the story in that of Kipling. Exploring this emotional involvement enables us to notice (as I have already tried to show) elements in the fiction that seem to be there for some private reason which the uninformed reader would need to guess at. A natural next step is to go on from that and look for explanations of artistic success and failure, asking whether such involvement is an advantage or a disadvantage aesthetically.

Both authors have made considerable attempts at detachment, inserting into the fictitious narrative several details that cause us to stand back and watch the child from outside. In the case of Dickens it is tempting to say that these details provide the artistic success, and the involvement provides the failure. Can anything, for instance, justify the sentimentality of the final account of the landlady, and above all of the last eight words, 'all womanly and good, I am sure'? The landlady was there as part of the comic tableau; this earnest reassurance that she was womanly and good is the sentimentalist's reassurance that he does not take too low a view of human nature, and whether the sentimentality is David's or (as here seems to be the case) Dickens's, it reads like an intrusion. In contrast to this, the cool comedy of the tableau, and of the Genuine Stunning, seems to provide clear evidence of the advantages of detachment.

But this may be too simple, for the good reason that it is easier for us to notice the detachment. The comic touches are explicit and striking, as is the nature of comic touches; the explicit sentimental touch that mars the end may not come from personal involvement at all, but from the conventional expectations, shared by Dickens, that the warm-heartedness of a motherly figure must be underlined to the point of overinsistence. The form taken by personal involvement may be more pervasive, less immediately visible: only because we have the autobiography do we know that it is so powerfully there. And it may, in a manner that analysis of details cannot show, provide a great deal of the power of the writing.

In the case of Kipling, the emotional intensity is unmistakeable, and it does seem to lead to some of the most powerful details (the children going down to the sea to find the parents who they can't imagine have deserted them, and finding 'nothing but sand and mud for miles and miles'), but also to a sentimentalizing very like Dickens's. At the end of the story, when the mother returns, warm feeling appears more overtly than at the end of the autobiographical version. 'Was it possible that by fondling she wanted to get anything out of Black Sheep? Only all his love and confidence; but that Black Sheep did not know': the step out of the child's consciousness in that second sentence is not in the direction of cool distancing, but rather towards a reassurance of the warmth of the mother's love, perhaps even (since that individual mother is not the story's concern) a reassurance that we live in a world of loving mothers: an exact parallel, then, to Dickens's seeing the landlord's wife as loving and motherly.

(Though we can notice that the sentimentalizing is much less strong than at the end of 'His Majesty the King', the adjacent story in *Wee Willie Winkie*. The child's viewpoint there is a device for telling a story about the adults (the *What Maisie Knew* technique) – a story of marital crisis and reconciliation that is trite and even melodramatic, so that the interest resides largely in the indirect narration, in the extent to which it really is a story about a child. In 'Baa Baa Black Sheep' invention is entirely in the service of the autobiographical material, undisturbed by a conventional tale. The closeness of the story to autobiography has in this case been greatly to its advantage.)

Detachment is achieved by establishing a distance between the child's consciousness and the narrating voice. In the autobiography Kipling achieves this through the contrast between the reminiscent adult and the suffering child, and the two are never confused, though the first person is used. In the story, where emotional intensity is greater, so that we are led to identify more deeply with the child, the third person is used, so that we are also held at arm's length from him. More important still is the renaming of the children. From the beginning they are known as Punch and Judy. Can these be their real names? Well, Judy might be: Punch sounds like a comic nickname, as if the sister's name was the stimulus to seeing him as ridiculous. But since he is not ridiculous, the effect is a kind of arbitrary detachment, a reminder that even a suffering child is made fun of. Then his name changes to 'Black Sheep', the nickname furnished by the bullying Harry. That name is obviously unfair, yet it is used by the narrative not only to name him but to provide the structure of the story ('One Bag Full', etc.), as if in imitation of the unfairness of Punch's world, as if the authorial voice accepted that unfairness is inevitable.

Childhood

I move now to a point so obvious that to state it may seem a truism, but it will turn out to be important. Both these autobiographical stories deal with childhood, for it is in childhood that fiction and autobiography are most likely to meet. The association of childhood with emotional intensity may have had a fitful existence from as long ago as Augustine, and has become a commonplace since Wordsworth. It entered English fiction with *Jane Eyre*, and autobiography with Dickens's fragment. It is memorably stated by George Eliot:

These bitter sorrows of childhood! When sorrow is all new and strange, when hope has not yet got wings to fly beyond the days and weeks, and the space from summer to summer seems measureless. . . There is no better reason for preferring this elderberry bush than that it stirs an early memory – that it is no novelty in my life, speaking to me merely through my present sensibilities to form and colour, but the long companion of my existence, that wove itself into my joys when joys were vivid.[13]

After that, childhood is an available subject for fiction, offering both a perspective on and an intensely simplified version of the adult passions. For autobiography it becomes not just a possible but the central subject, so that C.S. Lewis, ending his at the age of seventeen, observes that he has never read an autobiography that did not fall off in interest once childhood was over.[14]

Fiction and autobiography, then, will meet in childhood with greater closeness than elsewhere, to the point where the distinction may threaten to disappear altogether. To explore this, let us juxtapose a professed autobiography and a professed work of fiction.

I was set down from the carrier's cart at the age of three; and there, with a sense of bewilderment and terror, my life in the village began.

The June grass, amongst which I stood, was taller than I was, and I wept. I had never been so close to grass before. It towered above me and all around me, each blade tattooed with tiger-skins of sunlight. It was knife-edged, dark, and a wicked green, thick as a forest and alive with grasshoppers that chirped and chattered and leapt through the air like monkeys.

I was lost and didn't know where to move. A tropic heat oozed up from the ground, rank with sharp odours of roots and nettles. Snow-clouds of elder-blossom banked in the sky, showering upon me the fumes and flakes of their sweet and giddy suffocation. High overhead ran frenzied larks, screaming as though the sky were tearing apart.

There was nowhere like that farmyard in all the slapdash county, nowhere so poor and grand and dirty as that square of mud and rubbish and bad wood and falling stone, where a bucketful of old and bedraggled hens scratched and laid small eggs. A duck quacked out of the trough in one deserted sty. Now a young man and a curly boy stood staring and sniffing over a wall at a sow, with its tits on the mud, giving suck.[15]

Both the opening of Laurie Lee's autobiography, *Cider with Rosie*, and the paragraph from Dylan Thomas's story 'The Peaches', are concerned with rendering the sensuous excitement of childhood. The sharpness of Lee's metaphors is an attempt to recapture the vividness with which the child sees and feels. Of course there is a paradox here, for no child has the articulateness to describe what he is perceiving; an adult presence is therefore inescapable.

This presence exists on several levels. The first and most general springs from the child's inability to write at all, so that even the words 'I was set down' may exceed the powers of the three-year-old; this is the most obvious and least interesting level, since the convention it demands is obvious to anyone. At the other extreme come moments when the child's vision is dropped and we step back to see him from outside. This is common in Thomas, and is explicit in the last sentence of the passage just quoted: 'now a young man and a curly boy. . .' Even there, however, the curly boy has inserted himself into the diction ('with its tits on the mud'): young Dylan, older than young Laurie, can contribute his adolescent vocabulary to the flavour of the whole. And no example of stepping back to see himself from the outside is more vivid than the account of young Laurie sitting amid the muddle while his big sisters darted into the kitchen to

cram my great mouth with handfuls of squashed berries, and run out again. And the more I got, the more I called out for more. It was like feeding a fat young cuckoo.

The two poles, then, are that in which the consciousness is that of the child, and the adult contributes only articulateness; and that in which we step outside the child altogether, and see him from outside. The most interesting cases of adult presence fall between these two extremes; the cases where adult language is specifically in the service of childhood awareness: 'snow-clouds of elder-blossom banked in the sky, showering upon me the fumes and flakes of their sweet and giddy suffocation'. Here we are looking upwards, like the child; we confuse the elder tree and the clouds, as the child might; we are delighted and a bit frightened by the heady smell, as the child might be. Yet the carefully crafted sentence is a totally adult achievement, based on an implicit claim that such an image-laden, even eccentric style departs from everyday language in a way that is equivalent to childhood perception departing from everyday dull observation. (There may be a parallel with impressionist painting here, where the blurring is an equivalent to preconceptual, innocent-eye seeing, though the painter is not himself an innocent.)

Much the same point can be made about Thomas, but here the adult presence is more prominent and more individual. For Thomas was a stylist to the point of eccentricity, and he wrote poems about childhood memory. The farm to which the young lad is taken in 'The Peaches' is the same as the farm celebrated in the poem 'Fern Hill', and readers of the latter will easily notice its seeds in the prose of the story. There is less metaphor than in Laurie Lee, but there is a use of parallel structure that impresses itself almost as a trick of style: 'nowhere so poor and grand and dirty', 'that square of mud and rubbish and bad wood'. Such accumulation of lists is like the prose equivalent of metre, a patterning by repetition of equal units, and the reader who knows 'Fern Hill' can begin to hear 'as I was green and carefree' or 'My wishes raced through the house high hay'.

Thomas's stylishness, and the fact that his protagonist is older, accounts for many of the differences, but what really matters to us is how similar the two books are. Both attempt to capture a way of perceiving the world, sometimes as an oblique commentary on adult goings-on, but more often for its own sake. One book is offered as a series of stories, the other as an autobiography, but this difference is not important. Some of the stories in *Portrait* ('The Fight', or 'A Visit to Grandpa's') have very little plot, and some of the episodes in *Cider with Rosia* ('Grannies in the Wainscot' or the story of Vincent) are carefully structured and as rich in incident as any story. Should the following passage, for instance, be read as fiction or autobiography?

Blushing, I turned to answer Mr Jenkyn, who was asking me how old I was. I told him, but added one year. Why did I lie then? I wondered. If I lost my cap and found it in my bedroom, and my mother asked me where I had found it, I would say 'In the attic', or 'Under the hall stand'. It was exciting to have to keep wary all the time in case I contradicted myself, to make up the story of a film I pretended to have seen, and put Jack Holt in Richard Dix's place.[16]

The speaker here is called Thomas, and the episode takes place at the house of his new friend Dan Jenkyn, called Warmley. This was the name of the house of Dan Jones, whose version of the schoolboy friendship is almost as close to this story as Kipling's autobiography is to 'Baa Baa Black Sheep'.[17] One point of contact with Kipling is particularly interesting: they give precisely opposite accounts of how childhood experience led to writing. Kipling, as we have seen, claimed that the bullying made him 'give attention' to the necessary lying, 'and this, I presume, is the foundation of literary effect'; whereas Thomas's youthful lies resulted not from self-defence but from a delight in risk-taking. Kipling learnt fiction from lying; Thomas practised lying because of his interest in fiction. Is it an accident that we are told the first in a memoir, the second in a story?

The more carefully we look at these childhood tales, the more superficial the distinction between fiction and autobiography seems to become. Almost everything of importance (the relation between sensibility and articulateness; the development of the child; the kinds of awareness offered of the world) is independent of the ontological status of the text.

Everything is Fiction: Nothing is Fiction

That fiction and autobiography overlap is well known, and confirmed by the very existence of the term 'autobiographical novel'; and I have suggested that the overlap is particularly important in the case of childhood experience. When two countries overlap, there is always the possibility of territorial aggrandizement, that one will invade and take over part of the other, even the whole of the other, claiming that it really owns it already. This can take place in either direction.

So on the one hand there is the view that nothing is fiction: that the only way to create is to make the experience your own, to identify with the protagonist to the point that you share all his

feelings. Every successful poem or novel is therefore an autobiography.

And on the other hand there is the view that everything is fiction:
for to write is to impose the conventions of language upon
experience, and escape into the *hors-texte* is not possible. All texts,
whatever truth claims they make, exist in a prison house of
language, and are in the profoundest sense fictions.

I shall call these two apparently contradictory views respectively
the Romantic and the structuralist.[18] It may seem absurd to claim
that both can be true, yet once we ask what each enables us to
understand it becomes possible to accept each for what it can do.
The Romantic view has to be normative: it has to be an attempt to
say what gives life to a work of literature, so that the good novel is
autobiographical in a sense in which the run-of-the-mill novel isn't.
We have already seen, in discussing *David Copperfield*, that so
simple a formula will not do. This Romantic view is a version of
the expression theory, and its strength and limitations will concern
us in chapter 3.

As for the view that everything is fiction, it would mean that the
distinction between raw material and invention must be abandoned.
There are only texts, systems of difference out of which no
transcendental signified can escape: to call something 'raw material'
is to claim that it exists independent of interpretation, independent
of a system of differences, but nothing does.

Is this view tenable? It depends, I suggest, on where we are
standing. For the writer, it cannot be tenable: he is aware of the
clear distinction between what was given to him, extra-textually,
and what was not. Why did Dickens, in the autobiographical
fragment, place the public house in Parliament Street? The answer
is that it actually was in Parliament Street, and he had found it
there. When he wrote the novel, he removed that information,
because referring the reader to a specific extra-textual location is less
appropriate in fiction. He might have decided to place it in Cannon
Row, or even – to tease the reader, by giving him an autobiographical wink – to keep it in Parliament Street, but we could
still have said that the fictitious public house is not 'really' in any
street. But why on the other hand did Dickens place
Mr Micawber's lodging in Windsor Terrace, City Road? There
really is a Windsor Terrace off City Road, but not even the fact that
the next street is now called Micawber Street can remove the fact
that Mr Micawber never lived there, for Mr Micawber never lived
anywhere in real time and space. On this point the text of the

autobiographical fragment does, and that of *David Copperfield* does not, derive from a particular fact, and Dickens was well aware of the difference.

That is easy, because it concerns the physical world. When it comes to inner experience the distinction is less clear-cut, but we can still say that the childhood fears and hatreds that both Dickens and Kipling wrote about were experiences that they remembered having; whereas the frail courage of Wee Willie Winkie, rescuing Miss Allardyce, was not, in the same sense, a memory of Kipling's, and the terror of Pip when seized by the convict was not a memory of Dickens's. That courage, that fear, did not enter the fiction from the memory of a particular experience.

To deny this distinction is absurd (though there are theorists who deny it); but I have immediately to say that as a distinction it is not worth much to us as readers. For we have no independent access to either the situation of the public house, the fears of Kipling, or the resentments of Dickens. The first we might, in principle, have, but in fact haven't; the other two we cannot, in principle, have. Even if we possessed, say, a version of the Warrens Blacking episode written by John Dickens, or by his wife, or by the relative who owned the warehouse, we would have to measure it against Dickens's version by interpreting both. Whatever we then learnt about the original experience would be the result of our act of interpretation: for us, there is no raw material. To the reader, there are two texts: they are written according to different rules of evidence, and they make different ontological claims, but what they relate to cannot, for us, have an extra-textual status. The view that everything is fiction, that there is no distinction between raw material and invention because there is no such thing as raw material, is true for the reader but false for the writer.

The Famous Mr Joseph Addison

And now I turn to the opposite extreme: a character in fiction based on material to which we have the same access as the author.

Joeph Addison was born in Miltson, Wiltshire, the son of the Rev Lancelot Addison, and Jane, née Gulston. He went to school at Charterhouse, where he met Richard Steele; after that to Queen's College, Oxford. In 1689 he was elected Demy (a sort of senior scholar) at Magdalen College, and in 1698 he became a fellow. He began publishing poems in the 1690's, set off on the Grand Tour in

1699, spent about six months at Blois in order (successfully) to learn French. He published *The Campaign*, a poem about Marlborough's victories, in 1704: it was written at the request of Lord Godolphin, the Lord Treasurer, and Addison was rewarded with a number of public offices, including the sinecure of being under-secretary to Sir Charles Hedges in 1705. In the same year he published his Travels, and went to Hanover on a diplomatic mission with Lord Halifax. Halifax continued to be his patron until his death in 1715.

And so on. The story could be continued in the same (or greater) detail down to Addison's death on 17 June 1719. It would record the details of his literary career (his opera *Rosamund* a flop in 1707, his tragedy *Cato* a great success in 1713, *The Tatler* begun by Steele when Addison was in Ireland, 1709, *The Spectator* begun in 1711) and of his political career (elected to Parliament in 1708, secretary to the Lord Lieutenant of Ireland in 1708, and culminating in the post of Secretary of State in 1717, and his resignation less than a year later because of ill-health), and a few family details could be added (his father's death in 1703, his marriage to the widowed Countess of Warwick in 1716, the birth of his daughter Charlotte in 1719). All good undisputed facts.

I call them undisputed because they all come from *The Life of Joseph Addison* by Peter Smithers, an admirably reliable biography published by the Oxford University Press.[1] There are several reasons for feeling confident about Smithers's reliability. He offers footnotes telling us (for instance) that Charlotte's birth is recorded in St Martin-in-the-Fields baptismal register. Why should anyone want to falsify a detail like that? And if there were a dispute – if Smithers were accused of carelessness in reading the register – we know quite clearly how it could be settled. A few of Smithers's assertions, for instance that Halifax continued to be his patron or that *Cato* was a great success, are summaries of a series of events, but it would not be difficult to split them into discrete units, and find the evidence for each.

Now in contrast let us look at Addison in fiction. One Sunday afternoon Henry Esmond was walking down Germain Street with his friend Dick Steele, when

Dick all of a sudden left his companion's arm, and ran after a gentleman who was poring over a folio volume at the book-shop near to S James's Church. He was a fair, tall man in a snuff-coloured suit, with a plain sword, very sober, and almost shabby in appearance.

The gentleman turns out to be the famous Mr Joseph Addison, who is introduced to Esmond, and invites them both to his apartment, 'which was indeed a shabby one, though no grandee of the land could receive his guests with a more perfect and courtly grace than this gentleman.' Addison explains that he is writing a poem on the campaign which Colonel Esmond has just taken part in, and shows them some of the verses; Esmond in turn supplies him with details about the battle of Blenheim, and with some sharp comments on the Duke of Marlborough, whom he admires as a general but does not trust as a man.

'There were brave men on that field,' says Mr Esmond (who never could be made to love the Duke of Marlborough, nor to forget those stories which he used to hear in his youth regarding that great chief's selfishness and treachery – 'there were men at Blenheim as good as the leader, whom neither knights nor senators applauded, nor voices plebeian or patrician favoured, and who lie there forgotten under the clods. What poet is there to sing them?'

This leads to a discussion about whether poetry should celebrate generals only, or the rank and file as well. 'Would you celebrate them all?' asks Addison.

If I may venture to question anything in such an admirable work, the catalogue of ships in Homer hath always appeared to me as somewhat wearisome; what had the poem been, supposing the writer had chronicled the names of captains, lieutenants, rank and file? . . . You say he hath no pity; no more have the gods, who are above it, and superhuman. The fainting battle gathers strength at his aspect; and, wherever he rides, victory charges with him.

    A couple of days after, when Mr Esmond revisited his poetic friend, he found this thought, struck out in the fervour of conversation, improved and shaped into those famous lines, which are in truth the noblest in the poem of the 'Campaign.'[2]

The lines are not as famous today as they once were, so it is necessary for me (as it was not for Thackeray) to quote them:

So when an Angel by divine command
With rising Tempests shakes a guilty land,
Such as of late o'er pale Brittania past,
Calm and serene he drives the furious blast;

And, pleas'd th'Almighty's orders to perform,
Rides in the whirlwind, and directs the storm.[3]

At that point Addison is visited by 'a gentleman in fine laced clothes', who inquires how his *magnum opus* is going on, and when the yet unfinished poem is read to him both he and Esmond are filled with enthusiasm at the lines describing the angel, which Addison reads with great animation, 'looking at Esmond, as much as to say, "You know where that simile came from – from our talk, and our bottle of Burgundy, the other day." ' Within a month of that the poem is published, and all the town is in an uproar of admiration over it. Addison is made Commissioner of Excise, and from then on his prosperity was scarce ever interrupted. 'But I doubt,' reflects Esmond, 'whether he was not happier in his garret in the Haymarket than ever he was in his splendid palace at Kensington.'

Now if we wished to dispute this version of Addison, there could not be any such straightforward appeal to evidence. It is quite certain that Steele never introduced Addison to his friend Esmond in Germain Street, and that the simile of the angel was not struck out in the course of a discussion with Esmond: for Henry Esmond is a fictitious character. About other negatives we cannot be so certain. Mr Boyle (who was Chancellor of the Exchequer) may well have called at Addison's garrett in the Haymarket to inquire how the poem was going on, since we know (Smithers, p. 92) that he had called there to commission the poem, and we know too that Godolphin saw the poem when yet unfinished, and was delighted with the simile of the angel. Thackeray knew the evidence about Addison's life, and used it with care.

But if we want to maintain, as I certainly do, that *Henry Esmond* will tell us more of what really matters about Addison than Smithers's meticulous biography, it is not mainly because of the care with which Thackeray has handled the evidence. That is a necessary but not a sufficient condition of his achievement. More important (though not the most important) is the use Thackeray has made of Addison's own writings, since his view that epic poetry should deal with great men and great deeds was held by Addison, as it was held by all eighteenth-century critics. We can easily find in *The Spectator* assertions that Homer's characters have 'a certain dignity as well as novelty, which adapts them in a more peculiar manner to the nature of an heroic poem' (no. 273), or that the greatest heroic poets 'celebrate persons and actions which do honour to their country' (no. 70) – though as it happens the one detail that Thackeray has invented, the cautious dismissal of the catalogue of ships, is at odds with what Addison actually wrote on the subject:

Had Homer or Virgil only told us in two or three lines before their fights, that there were forty thousand of each side, our imagination could not possibly have been so affected, as when we see every Leader singled out, and every Regiment in a manner drawn up before our eyes.[4]

Yet this is an inconsistency we can imagine a man committing and even defending: for in this passage, the singling out is a way of building up the greatness of the action, and thus of the leader. I think it not impossible that Thackeray had seen this note, and decided, perhaps even because of it, to give Addison this hesitant statement of the apparently opposite opinion (the hesitation then would be a delicate transfer of tone from the author to his character). Certainly he has got the tone right: just the same modest hesitation comes in *The Spectator* no. 267, where Addison writes, 'I will not presume to say, that the Book of Games in the *Aeneid*, or that in the *Iliad*, are not of this nature (ie great), nor to reprehend Virgil's simile of the Top, and many other of the same kind in the *Iliad*, as liable to any censure in this particular; but. . .'[5] Modest hesitation? Perhaps I should rather say 'Just hint a fault, and hesitate dislike.'

If Thackeray had merely quoted or paraphrased the critical opinions of *The Spectator* he would have taught us nothing we could not have learned from the original: he would then have been, not a biographer nor a novelist, but an editor. His freer treatment of the material enables him to draw further conclusions about Addison's position and, more interesting still, to go on to relate his critical position to his behaviour. What is really interesting in Thackeray's Addison, in this episode, is the connexion between his no doubt sincere conviction that epic poetry should deal with heroes, not common men, and his own self-advancement: the fact that his celebration of Marlborough led to 'his ticket coming up a prize in the prodigious lottery of life.' Earlier, before he has met Addison (though writing, clearly, with hindsight) Esmond is blunter. He has been describing the battle of Vigo, and the killing and plunder it led to. It was 'a bad business,' though Mr Addison did sing its praises in Latin. That honest gentleman's muse had an eye to the main chance; and I doubt whether she saw much inspiration in the losing side.[6]

The richest detail here is 'honest', a complex word on which an Empsonian equation could be offered. The social condescension in 'honest' ('Honest Joseph' is Lovelace's way of beginning a letter to his manservant)[7] is here both straight and ironic. Addison is Esmond's social superior, but only because of the success of his Muse, so it is not altogether honest of him to have risen in the world; yet Addison did really believe in what he was writing, holding the views he held about epic poetry, so he was genuinely honest; yet poetry, when it comes to celebrating war, is a pack of lies, and anyone who honestly believes in it is so unaware of reality that he deserves the patronising use of the term: 'honest Joseph'.

Then there is Addison's contentment. He enjoys entertaining his friends over a bottle, and the fact that it takes place in a garret does not matter – is indeed an advantage, since there are no elaborate forms to interfere with what matters, talking and drinking. Addison is a man divided against himself, for he is ambitious and wishes to rise, yet what he really enjoys is more easily achieved in his garret: a point hinted at in the last glimpse we get of him in the novel, when Esmond meets him one night walking to his cottage in Fulham. In a not altogether sober voice he invites Esmond home for a drink and a reminiscence about old times, and when Esmond refuses he turns round to walk back with him, 'and very likely Mr Under-Secretary would have stepped in and taken t'other bottle at the Colonel's lodging, had the latter invited him, but Esmond's mood was none of the gayest, and he bade his friend an inhospitable good-night at the door.'[8] The suggestion of a snub, and the obvious wish by Addison to be convivial, leave us with a touch of melancholy: this is Addison at the height of his success, but there is a suggestion that he regrets it, even that he envies Esmond (of whose political intrigues on behalf of the Pretender he knows nothing, just as Esmond may know nothing of the fact that the 'real' Addison – Thackeray does not mention this, but would surely expect his well-informed readers to know – was at that moment heavily involved in bringing the Elector of Hanover across to England). 'I doubt whether he was not happier in his garret in the Haymarket.'

By now Addison is a coherent character to us: what he now does follows understandably from what we already know about him. If he surprises us (this is a commonplace of fiction criticism) the surprise turns out on reflection to be quite explicable. Now I must point out that the character of Thackeray's Addision is dominated by one thing, the fact that we never see him direct, but only through the eyes of the narrator, Henry Esmond; and since it is essentially Esmond's story, what we learn about Addison is what mattered to Esmond. This is true to a much greater extent than we might at first notice. The emphasis on Addison's Whig politics, for instance, is not only a foil to Esmond's Toryism, it is a constant reminder of the view that Esmond ought to have held. Thackeray's own position is Whig, and the book not only offers reasons for accepting the Glorious Revolution of 1689, but is also a study in the way that 'with people that take a side in politics, 'tis men rather than principles that commonly bind them'. The family tradition of the Castlewoods, and the kindness of Father Holt the Jesuit to young Harry, had made it almost impossible for him to reject the Jacobite case, but writing in his mature years he comes to admit that Addison's politics were in the right, which adds a further touch of poignancy to Esmond's refusal to drink another bottle with him at their last meeting, when each is involved in his own political intrigue.

More important is the question of war. Just as Esmond is a Whig whom circumstances have made a Tory, so he is a peace-lover whom circumstances have made a soldier. His wry awareness of what great victories are really like contributes to the melancholy of his character, and is central to the meaning of the novel. The opening paragraph expresses the wish that History should be familiar rather than heroic, and announces a wish to 'pull off her periwig'; and of all the heroic ceremonies which the Muse of History encumbers herself with, none is more striking, than the celebration of war. Addison's poem on 'The Campaign' is so important because it represents the kind of history which *Henry Esmond* is trying not to be, written by a man whom Esmond likes and values, and who has far more literary talent than he (indeed, who serves as a model for what literary talent Esmond has, as we see in the mock Spectator paper he writes). A conception of literary talent itself is being called in question:

Why does the Muse of History, that delights in describing the valour of heroes and the grandeur of conquest, leave out these scenes, so brutal, mean and degrading, that yet form by far the greater part of the drama of war? You, gentlemen of England, who live at home at ease, and compliment yourselves in the songs of triumph with which our chieftains are bepraised – you pretty maidens that come tumbling down the stairs when the fife and drum call you, and huzza for the British Grenadiers – do you take account that these items go to make up the amount of the triumph you admire, and form part of the duties of the heroes you fondle?[9]

Style here operates as a comment on content. The stately Muse naturally uses the high style, and its register does not include such locutions as 'come tumbling down the stairs', or 'fondle'. These belong to the everyday life of those who like to be lifted above themselves by heroic poetry: we are being invited not to emerge from the world of 'hot red-faced women' and 'litle wrinkled old men' when we read of heroic exploits, but to require instead that war should be treated as common experience. The Addison who writes – and defends – 'The Campaign', we are to realize, is both an honest man and a timserver. He really does believe that heroic poetry should generalize and uplift and leave out the catalogue of ships; but in believing this he has committed himself to a communal act of bad faith. The honesty of Thackeray's Addison does not extend to questioning the hierarchy of writing that puts on periwigs, any more than Smithers's Addison is willing to question the social hierarchy: after having indicated to the Duke of Somerset that he would be conferring rather than receiving a favour if he accepted the post of tutor to his son, and then suffering a furious rebuke and the loss of the post, 'Addison,' says Smithers, 'is never again recorded as offending one so far his social superior.'

Addison is a foil to Esmond in a more general sense still. He is convivial, when Esmond is morose; he is contented when Esmond questions his lot; he marries a wealthy countess in middle-age, when Esmond is eating his heart out for love of Beatrix. Does this not lend a note of satisfaction to Esmond's belief in the rumours about the Countess of Warwick?: 'I believe the fortune that came to him in the shape of the countess his wife was no better than a shrew and a vixen.'

What effect does this transmission through the medium of Esmond have on Thackeray's picture of Addison? The technical skill of *Henry Esmond* as a historical novel has often been remarked on: the fact that it does not contain a sentence that could not have been written in the eighteenth century. Just as the narrating voice is locked up in its age, so it is also locked up in the point of view of the hero: it is an extreme example of a first person novel, containing nothing but what the narrator could have known (the fact that much of it is technically in the third person is a rhetorical device that underlines this, so that when the story shifts from third person to first we notice that that is really where we have been all along, that everything we have been told comes only from Colonel Esmond, who died long before Thackeray was born). We are being taken into a past culture, and nothing is allowed into the book that could not have been perceived, thought or said within that culture.

This is the exact opposite to the method used by John Fowles in *The French Lieutenant's Woman*. That novel too is intensely concerned with the limits of the cultural universe depicted, but Fowles draws them to our attention quite explicitly, by means of a narrator who situates himself in the twentieth century, and comments freely on the thoughts that are not available to his characters. Both Fowles and Thackeray show an awareness of how the inhabitants of their chosen period thought and spoke which is virtually flawless, and both, though by opposite techniques, invite us to step outside the depicted world into a perspective that can be called anthropological.

By locking us so firmly into Esmond's consciousness, Thackeray is able to portray Addison much more effectively than he could otherwise. Esmond after all was in a better position to know Addison than his creator, since he had met him and drunk with him, and Thackeray never had. An absurd argument, surely: Esmond had only met Addison in Thackeray's pages. Tweedledum and Tweedledee showed Alice the Red King lying asleep and told her 'He's dreaming about you. And if he left off dreaming about you, where do you suppose you'd be?'. She was most distressed when they claimed that she (and indeed they too) would be nowhere, since 'you're only a sort of thing in his dream. . . You know very well you're not real'.[10] If Thackeray dreamt Esmond, then Esmond's knowledge of Addison is no more real than Alice's tears; he cannot know anything that Thackeray doesn't know.

Absurd or not, I want to defend the argument. Henry Esmond represents that element in Thackerary's sensibility that best understands the world of Queen Anne's England. At one point in the novel Esmond composes an essay on women and passes it off, for a joke, as a genuine Spectator essay: it is indeed a remarkable piece of pastiche.[11] This *tour de force* on Esmond's part is a mark for the different and more important *tour de force* on Thackeray's part, of passing the whole book off as a piece of genuine eighteenth century. Writing as Esmond is Thackeray's heuristic device for entering the past, and understanding Addison.

Events

Smithers on Addison: Thackeray on Addison. Two different ways of conveying the past to us, yet not incompatible with each other. What conclusions can we now begin to draw from the comparison? To do this, we shall need two fresh elements: a theoretical element, that will provide the necessary concepts, and a comparative element, that will provide other attempts at biography falling somewhere between these two extremes.

The concept we need is that of an event, which I take from Collingwood.

The historian, investigating any event in the past, makes a distinction between what may be called the outside and the inside of an event. By the outside of an event I mean everything belonging to it which can be described in terms of bodies and their movements: the passage of Caesar, accompanied by certain men, across a river called the Rubicon at one date, or the spilling of his blood on the floor of the senate-house at another. By the inside of the event I mean that in it which can only be described in terms of thought: Caesar's defiance of Republican law, or the clash of constitutional policy between himself and his assassins. The historian is never concerned with either of these to the exclusion of the other. . . His work may begin by discovering the outside of an event, but it can never end there; he must always remember that the event was an action, and that his main task is to think himself into this action to discern the thought of his agent.[12]

When we see only the outside, we are dealing with an event; when we are concerned with the inside as well, we treat it as volitional, as brought about by one or more human beings, and Collingwood's term for events seen from the inside is 'actions'.

I must pause briefly to defend the term 'thought'. We can of course describe actions as having been brought about thoughtlessly, or unwittingly, or in passion, or as the result of unconscious motives, or of the 'List der Vernunft', and if 'thought' is used to contrast with these other psychic processes then it is too narrow a term to indicate the inside of an event. But since we have no convenient wider term – intention, purpose and even consciousness are subject to similar objections – I will continue to use Collinghwood's, noting that it is intended to bear the widest possible meaning.

Now it is clear that Smithers devotes a good deal of his book to the outside of events, and most of his skill to getting them right. What does he tell us about their inside? He confines himself almost entirely to two things: in the first place, he passes on the comments of Swift, Pope and others about Addison's character, and in the second place he tells us that he cannot tell us. He quotes letters in which Swift describes the cooling of his friendship with Addison, highly interesting letters in which Swift often seems to mean more than he is willing to say; Smithers however guarantees nothing except that Swift wrote them. To quote a document in this way is to treat it as an event: it only becomes an action when interpreted, and that Smithers prefers to leave to us.

One controversy in which Smithers involves himself raises very sharply the distinction between event and action: that concerning Addison's last words. The anecdote is well known: Addison called his stepson, Lord Warwick, to his bedside, and said to him 'See in what peace a Christian can die'. The story has been treated with scepticism since the eighteenth century: Horace Walpole ('not supported by evidence') wrote 'unluckily he died of brandy – nothing makes a Christian die in peace like being maudlin', but Smithers assures us that he entertains no doubt that it is true.[13]

Now establishing the truth of this story is not quite as simple as checking the parish register. The evidence is a passage in Young's *Conjectures on Original Composition*:

With his hopes of life he dismissed not his concern for the living; but sent for a youth nearly related and finely accomplished, yet not above being the better for good impressions from a dying friend. . . Forcibly grasping the youth's hand, he softly said, 'See in what peace a Christian can die.' He spoke with difficulty, and soon expired.[14]

Young claimed to have got the story from Thomas Tickell, Addison's young protégé, who was present. Now for the sake of the discussion I will give the anecdote the benefit of all incidental doubts, ruling out the possibility that Young, or Tickell, was lying; I will accept that both Lord Warwick and Tickell and even the physician agreed about Addison's dying words. Dying words are a well-known genre: they are meant to be clear, important and uplifting. Our diminished taste for uplift in the twentieth century has sent them out of fashion (it is tempting to ask if the scapegrace Lord Warwick received them with proto-modern cynicism). The noise which might overlay the choice phrasing (a gasp of pain; a request to move the pillow; a half-suppressed irritation that

Warwick had taken so long; subsequent, more trivial remarks before the actual moment of death) must be eliminated. The elimination could take place at various points: by the speaker himself, before speaking; by the hearers, in the act of perception; by their subsequent memory; quite deliberately, in the process of recording them. When Smithers declares his confidence in the truth of the story, what is he claiming? That there was no noise? This is unlikely, and we can never know it. That it does not matter at what point it was eliminated? This is a defensible position, but it means that what matters about the words is the way they belong to the genre, and that is an unSmitherslike claim: it suggests not the positivist historian but the epic poet, the heroic dramatist or the hagiographer (not the novelist, who might be particularly attentive to the noise).

Once we get beyond the outside of events, what are we looking for in the past? To answer this complicated question, we need as example a biographer more exploratory than Smithers, but who conceives of himself as not writing fiction. Addison has had his share of such biographers, and I choose Macaulay as the example.

As a man, he may not have deserved the adoration which he received from those who, bewitched by his fascinating society, and indebted for all the comforts of life to his generous and dedicated friendship, worshipped him nightly in his favourite temple at Button's. But after full inquiry and impartial reflection, we have long been convinced that he deserved as much love and esteem as can be justly claimed by any of our infirm and erring race. . .

He became a little too fond of seeing himself surrounded by a small circle of admirers, to whom he was as a king, or rather as a god. . . He was at perfect ease in their company; he was grateful for their devoted attachment; and he loaded them with benefits. . . But it must in candour be admitted that he contracted some of the faults which can scarcely be avoided by any person who is so unfortunate as to be the oracle of a small literary coterie.[15]

This very typical passage shows us how many different things are going on in what we call biography. There is the biographer's self-presentation ('after full inquiry and impartial reflection'); there are a few general reflections on humanity (also perhaps a form of self-presentation, indicating one's ripe wisdom); there is a moral judgement on Addison's character; and there is a summary of the actions of Addison's friends. None of this sounds like an account of

Addison's thoughts. Does that mean Macaulay too is not offering us the inside of events? Let us look at the statement 'He was at perfect ease in their company'. What kind of assertion is it? It doesn't look like the inside of an event, for where is the outside? There are two ways we could describe it. We can call it a summary, that is, a generalization based on a number of specific details which could, in principle, be listed (he often lit his pipe when speaking to Budgell; he would loosen his collar if it was warm; he was seldom known to raise his voice; etc.); or we can call it an account of Addison's character or sentiments. By sentiment we would then mean not the inside of an event but the inside of a person, i.e. thoughts and feelings which do not directly issue in words and deeds. There is very little sentiment, of this kind, in Thackeray's Addison (though there is plenty in Thackeray's Esmond), and the comparison shows us one difference between fiction and biography, perhaps to the advantage of fiction. Thackeray may have invented some of his events, but Macaulay's lack of invention does not mean he is closer to evidence (Thackeray is rather scrupulous about this) or more able to describe Addison's thoughts. It simply means that when he does offer thoughts, he has a less vivid sense of the words and deeds of which they are the inside.

We are now in a position to ask what the biographer does. I suggest that we divide his task into four. First is the editorial function, that of giving us the evidence as it is. It could be said that this is not, strictly, part of biography, but it can be the most valuable of all.

Addision was very vain. When somebody was speaking to him of Budgell's epilogue to the *Distrest Mother*, and said they wondered how so silly a fellow could blunder upon so good a thing, Addison said, 'O sir, 'twas quite another thing when first it was shown to me!'[16]

Perhaps we owe more to Spence for passing on this anecdote than we do to Macaulay for anything in his *Life*. Spence is merely a editor here: he is not telling us that the event took place, merely that Pope said it did. If he had gone on to inquire whether Addison really did say that, he would have performed the second function of the biographer, which is to establish events: a task that is often painstaking but need not be controversial.

Even less does Spence tell us how to interpret the anecdote. Is it an example of Addison's smooth gentility, or of Pope's deep dislike of Addison? This takes us to the third function of the biographer, which is to rediscover the thoughts of his subject. It is this that can make the second task controversial. The fact that Mr Boyle climbed the stairs to Addison's garret and commissioned him to write 'The Campaign' can be taken as showing the political power of literature, or the gullibility of Godolphin, or the dependence of authors on patronage, and a biographer who felt strongly on one of these might have special reasons for wanting to believe, or disbelieve, the anecdote.

Fiction differs most clearly from biography in this second function: it has no rules of evidence for establishing the outside of events. In the case of a wholly fictitious character, it would clearly be meaningless to ask if he really did this or that; and in the case of a historical character, his presence in a novel licenses the author to invent. Mr Boyle is allowed to pay a second visit to Addison in the pages of *Henry Esmond*.

I said that there are four tasks in biography, and have so far named only three. This is because the third should really be divided into two. If we are dealing with thoughts, we can relate them either to the outside of events, or to other thoughts. In the first case, we are said to be interpreting evidence; in the second we are building up a general view of the subject's character. We relate Addison's pleasure in writing 'The Campaign', in presiding at a meeting at Button's and making snide comments on Budgell, in marrying the Countess of Warwick, in drinking wine, in meeting Dick Steele, to one another, and to other occasions on which he took pleasure. This general view of his character will include opinions about his sentiments (that is, thoughts that did not issue in actions). If we add to our list Addison's pleasure at showing Esmond his part in the creation of the angel simile (a way of paying Esmond a compliment, but implying an even greater compliment to himself), or at meeting Esmond in the street when in slightly drunken need of companionship – or at opening the door of his lodgings to find a gentleman in fine laced clothes – we are not in any way altering our procedure. Pursuing Addison's character in this way is no different from pursuing Esmond's character, for the criterion here employed is not correspondence but coherence. Though we may call this the fourth function of biography, we must realize that the overlap with fiction is here complete. Whether we are offered a coherent picture of anyone's character is the same question whether the person is real, or fictitious, and will be answered in the same way: is that the sort of thing we would expect Addison – either Addison – to do?

Fact or Fiction?

The argument of this section ends here, and so could the section; but one postscript will (I hope) enrich the discussion. In comparing historical novel with biography, do we encounter any ontological traps? Are there, in other words, problems about distinguishing fact from fiction?

At one level, clearly not. The leading characters in *Henry Esmond*, as in all novels, are fictitious, and it is clearly no use asking for evidence about Henry's legitimacy, the quarrel with Rachel, the accidents that kept Beatrix unmarried, or the death of Francis, Lord Castlewood. No use, because they never happened; but the last must give us pause, for Viscount Castlewood is killed by Lord Henry Mohun – a character who did really live, who was a notorious and unscrupulous fighter (the Dictionary of National Biography actually heads its entry 'duellist'),[17] and who later fought a duel with the Duke of Hamilton in which both of them were killed. This duel takes place in the novel, correctly dated in 1712, when the widowed Duke is about to go to France as ambassador (documented) and is engaged to Beatrix (fictitious). The striking nastiness of the duel in the novel ('Mohun having his death-wound, and my Lord Duke lying by him, Macartney came up and stabbed his Grace as he lay on the ground') is also documented.

The mixture of fact and fiction here is very intricate, but not difficult, in principle, to disentangle – until we ask ourselves whether Lord Mohun is a real or a fictitious character. 'Thackeray's Lord Mohun,' says the DNB sternly, 'has little in common with the historical character' – an opinion in which it was anticipated by Thackeray himself, who remarks with a twinkle in a footnote to *The English Humourists of the Eighteenth Century*, 'the amiable baron's name was Charles, and not Harry, as a recent novelist has christened him.'[18] Thackeray changed the christian name in order to bring about the misunderstanding in Book I chapter 13, when Castlewood tells his wife, 'Here's poor Harry killed, my dear,' and she thinks he means Esmond. This touch of documentable inaccuracy may be the main basis for the disdainful complaint of the DNB. Thackeray's Mohun has the life style of Charles Mohun, and the fact that he is given fictitious adventures with the fictitious Viscount Castlewood is not likely to confuse anyone. The DNB author, I suggest, cared above all for the use of evidence. To such a historian, turning a real into a fictitious character is probably in itself distasteful, so that when he finds what seems an actual error he is eager to pounce.

If Charles Mohun or Joseph Addison could have read *Henry Esmond*, they would have had little difficulty in distinguishing the true from the fictitious: Addison would have known whether Boyle called on him more than once. And if he, or Boyle, had forgotten or misremembered, they would have had to do what the biographer does, appeal to documents (biographers often tell us that it is best to do this even when the subject claims to remember accurately): 'But Mr Addison, I called and you were out, so you kindly sent the MS by a messenger – stay, I have the note here.' Which may lead to a counter-appeal to other documents: 'But my Lord, I mentioned it in a letter to my mother, which I was glancing at only the other day.'

This is speculation. But speculation can enter a text, and the delicate balance between the true and the fictitious may itself become a strategy in the writing. Most of all this will be the case in satire, where the identifiability of the victim may become an urgent moral issue, even (when it comes to duels or libel actions) a very practical one. And the most famous of all literary portraits of Addison, Pope's character of Atticus, is a satire.

Pope's view of Addison comes to us in two forms: through Spence's *Anecdotes*, and through these celebrated lines. The *Anecdotes* tell us, over and over, that Addison was charming, was good company, but – Macaulay, who obviously knew them well, seems to have drawn much of his picture of Addison from such remarks as this:

Addison was perfect good company with intimates, and had something more charming in his conversation than I ever knew in any other man. But with any mixture of strangers, and sometimes with only one or with any man he was too jealous of, he seemed to preserve his dignity much, with a stiff sort of silence.[19]

The 'but' here is not greatly to Addison's discredit, but the structure resembles that of the much more savage portrait of Atticus:

Peace to all such! But were there one whose fires
True Genius kindles, and fair Fame inspires,
Blest with each Talent and each Art to please,
And born to write, converse, and live with ease:

Should such a man, too fond to rule alone,
Bear, like the Turk, no brother near the throne,
View him with scornful, yet with jealous eyes,
And hate for Arts that caused himself to rise;
Damn with faint praise, assent with civil leer,
And without sneering, teach the rest to sneer;
Willing to wound, and yet afraid to strike,
Just hint a fault, and hesitate dislike;
Alike reserv'd to blame, or to commend,
A tim'rous foe, and a suspicious friend,
Dreading ev'n fools, by Flatterers besieg'd,
And so obliging that he ne'er oblig'd;
Like Cato, give his little Senate laws,
And sit attentive to his own applause.
While Wits and Templars ev'ry sentence raise,
And wonder with a foolish face of praise.
Who but must laugh, if such a man there be?
Who would not weep, if Atticus were he![20]

There is one crucial difference here, the fact that Addison is not named. When chatting to Spence (off the record) Pope named names. When he wrote for publication, he sometimes used initials, sometimes nicknames, and frequently inserted discussions of whether it was right to identify his victims:

Spare then the person, and expose the vice.
– How sir! Not damn the sharper but the dice?[21]

But is this crucial? The disguise surely would not stand up for a moment in a libel case. The phonetic resemblance between 'Addison' and 'Atticus' and the reference to Cato are unmistakable; and to this we can add a number of points marginal to the text: that Pope sent the lines to Addison in a moment of pique, that Pope made one of the same points in a letter that clearly refers to Addison ('we have it seems a great Turk in poetry, who can never bear a brother on the throne' – though the authenticity of the letter is not unquestioned), and above all the fact that earlier versions of the lines actually concluded 'If Addison were he'.[22] In a court of law, these points would be unanswerable; but the effect of the lines as poetry depends not on our not knowing who Atticus is, but on our uncertainty about what we are doing when we perform the identification. By so ostentatiously not concealing the fact that the passage is 'about' Addison, can they be showing us the sense in which it is not about him? The near-confession of identity makes it clear that if the lines describe any living individual, Addison is the man; but the clearer this is, the more we must be struck by the fact that we're not told it. In the very letter in which Pope told Spence that he had sent the passage to Addison, he designated it as 'what has since been called my satire on Addison'. There is no disguise which says 'Not him but another', only a 'disguise' that says 'If anyone, him'.

There is another oddity to the lines, one I have never seen remarked on: this is the syntax. Take one of the most brilliantly poised couplets:

Damn with faint praise, assent with civil leer,
And, without sneering, teach the rest to sneer.

Taken in isolation, the grammatical form of these verbs is uncertain. They could be imperatives (this is what you must do to be an Atticus), infinitives (that's the technique), indicative plurals (that's what such people do). In fact, they are infinitives governed by the modal auxiliary 'should', as is the whole passage: it is one long hypothetical clause, though by the time we reach 'praise' we have forgotten this. 'Should . . . should . . . should' (in the sense of 'if . . . if . . . if') culminates finally in the main clause:

Who but must laugh, if such a one there be?
Who would not weep, if Atticus were he?

Rhetorically, this is designed so that the proper name shall come as a climax. But logically? If there is such a man, we laugh; if it's Atticus, we weep. What does that mean? I can only find one meaning that makes sense: that the portrait itself is comic, the act of attaching it to an individual is cause for tears. The passage, in other words, ends by calling attention to the issue of identification. It is a satiric portrait, we have been told, a portrait of near-hypocrisy; and it could be applied to you-know-who. This is very like telling us that the real is a special case of the fictional.

The Condition of England

But is any of this history? A widespread view claims that the life of an individual has no historical significance unless we see it as typical of, or caused by, or causing, some wider social movement. So I now turn, in deference to this view, from individual to society; and I will begin at the bottom, with the material basis of life. In the 1840s in England this was decidedly unattractive.

The Texts

The inhabitants of open streets can hardly conceive the complicated turnings, the narrow inlets, the close parallels of houses, and the high barriers of light and air, which are the common characteristics of our courts and alleys, and which give an additional noxiousness even to their cesspools and their filth. . . A man of ordinary dimensions almost hesitates, lest he should immovably wedge himself, with whomsoever he may meet, in the low and narrow crevice which is called the entrance to some such court or alley; and, having passed that ordeal, he finds himself as in a well, with little light, with less ventilation, amid a dense mass of human beings, with an atmosphere hardly respirable from its closeness and pollution. The stranger, during his visits, feels his breathing constrained, as though he were in a diving bell and experiences afterwards a sensible and immediate relief as he emerges again into the comparatively open street. . . Our friends were not dainty, but even they picked their way, till they got to some steps leading down to a small area, where a person standing would have his head about one foot below the level of the street, and might at the same time, without the least motion of his body, touch the window of the cellar and the damp muddy wall right opposite. You went down one step even from the foul area into the cellar in which a family of human beings lived. It was very dark inside. The window-panes, many of them, were broken and stuffed with rags, which was reason enough for the dusky light that pervaded the place even at mid-day. After the account I have given of the state of the street, no one can be surprised that on going into the cellar inhabited by Davenport, the smell was so foetid as almost to knock the two men down.

Is this visit to Victorian slums history or fiction? There are none of the obvious markers: we do not know the town, we do not know who Davenport is, and we do not know whether the strangers picking their way are sanitary inspectors or characters in a story.

The style is plain (only one figure of speech), and we are invited to think about the signified (the cramped passages, the highly non-verbal smell) rather than the behaviour of the signifiers (that is what plain style means). The one oddity that might strike the attentive reader is the change of tense half-way through. This could simply mark a shift from general observations to a particular visit, but in fact it is a shift from the present tense of the social investigator to the preterite of narrative; for I have here joined (I now confess) one of the reports of Dr John Simon, medical officer of health to the City of London, to an extract from Elizabeth Gaskell's novel *Mary Barton*, in order to show the overlap.[1]

Dirt and disease were not the only pains of slum life, as the Victorians never tired of pointing out:

If the noxious particles that rise from vitiated air were palpable to the sight, we should see them lowering in a dense black cloud above such haunts, and rolling slowly on to corrupt the better portions of a town. But if the moral pestilence that rises with them, and in the eternal laws of outraged Nature is inseparable from them, could be made discernible too, how terrible the revelation! Then should we see depravity, impiety, drunkeness, theft murder, and a long train of nameless sins against the natural affections and repulsions of mankind, overhanging the devoted spots, and creeping on, to blight the innocent and spread contagion among the pure. But I have to deal with the matter only as it relates to physical health. Whatever is morally hideous and savage in the scene – whatever contrast it offers to the superficial magnificence of the metropolis – whatever profligacy it implies and continues – whatever recklessness and obscene brutality arises from it – whatever keen injury it inflicts on the community – whatever debasement or abolition of God's image in men's hearts is tokened by it – these matters belong not to my office, nor would it become me to dwell on them.[2]

This time our composite author turns his attention from physical to moral squalor, and in doing so has heightened his rhetoric. The sentences are longer and more exclamatory, there are more abstract nouns, there is an extended *praeteritio* (it 'would not become' him to dwell on what he has just dwelt on). There is no convenient change of tense this time, to mark the break between the two authors, though there is something of a scientific blunder in the first sentence which could betray that this time I began with the novelist: disease is not carried by particles; but since bacteria and viruses were not known to the early Victorians, this is not conclusive evidence, and Dickens's error might well have been committed by Dr Simon as well. The break occurs after 'pure', and I added an editorial 'but' to smooth the transition. The rhetorical figure, we may note, comes from the medical man, just as it was he who provided the only simile in the previous passage.

If we use Paul de Man's criterion, that literature is writing that is aware of its own fictive or rhetorical status,[3] there is no sign of the literary in these extracts. The most prominent way in which writing can convey such awareness is through style, and the stylistic contrast between the two composite passages is greater than that within either. The plain style, where awareness of fictive status is at a minimum, is perfectly at home in *Mary Barton,* and the high-sounding rhetoric of the second passage is a mark not of the literary but of the fact that the subject-matter has shifted to morality. Both halves of it offer a list of various forms of moral degradation (Dickens leaning the more heavily on abstract nouns) and both show awareness that the item in the list which will arouse most emotion in their readers is sex, which is mentioned in vaguer terms than the others (again Dickens is the more embarrassed and the more evasive). The heightened style has nothing to do with the fact that he is writing fiction, but derives from this embarrassment, along with the high-minded conviction that these matters are more important than physical health: it is the style of sermons, of moral treatises, of authorial intervention (whether into a medical report or into a novel). And it leaves modern readers uncomfortable: I have little doubt that readers will have preferred the first passage.

That example was very simple. To see more of the complexities of overlap, we need passages that interpret as well as describe the slum landscape. Since each passage from now on will raise enough complexities on its own, there will (I promise) be no more composites.

The town itself is peculiarly built, so that a person may live in it for years, and go in and out daily without coming into contact with a working-people's quarter or even with workers, that is, so long as he confines himself to his business or to pleasure walks. This arises chiefly from the fact that by unconscious tacit agreement, as well as with outspoken conscious determination, the working people's quarters are sharply separated from the sections of the city reserved for the middle-class. . .

Right and left a multitude of covered passages lead from the main street into numerous courts, and he who turns in thither gets into a filth and disgusting grime, the equal of which is not to be found – especially in the courts which lead down into the Irk, and which contain unqualifiedly the most horrible dwellings which I have yet beheld. In one of these courts there stands directly at the entrance, at the end of the covered passage, a privy without a door, so dirty that the inhabitants can pass into and out of this court only by passing through foul pools of stagnant urine and excrement. . .

I have seen many a cottage . . . whose outer walls were but one-half brick thick, the bricks lying not sidewise but lengthwise, their narrow ends touching. The object of this is to spare material, but there is also another reason for it; namely, the fact that the contractors never own the land, but lease it, according to the English custom, for twenty, thirty, forty, fifty or ninety-nine years, at the expiration of which time it falls, with everything upon it, back into the possession of the original holder, who pays nothing in return for improvements upon it. The improvements are therefore so calculated by the lessee as to be worth as little as possible at the expiration of the stipulated term.[4]

It is necessary to quote at some length from Engels's *Condition of the Working Class in England in 1844*, not because anything less than the full text lessens the impact of its cumulative account of the horrors of urban poverty (it does: but there is no avoiding that) but also to show at least something of the range of his analysis. The three paragraphs here quoted show us four aspects of the text. First, the explanation of the physical layout of Manchester, a kind of wheel, with the business district in the centre, and the roads like spokes enabling the middle class to reach their dwellings on the rim without passing through the slums; and the implicit assertion that this mixture of tacit assumption and conscious determination is an example of the Hegelian cunning of history, the *List der Vernunft* that transcends individual motivation. Second, the long description of dirt, disease and starvation that makes the book so fierce and unanswerable an indictment of early industrial capitalism. There are two methods of describing this, illustrated respectively by each of the two sentences of the second paragraph: indignation and superlatives on the one hand (one very easily runs out of both) and blunt individual facts, noted without comment, on the other. That privy, with its open door, beckons us, after we have supped full with horrors, with the plain eloquence of particularity. Finally, the third paragraph offers economic explanation. Engels believes that the slums are due to the institutions of capitalism, and the way these encourage greed in the entrepreneur and discourage thrift in the workers, and this detail of why landlords don't improve properly is part of a much larger argument. The first and third paragraphs make it clear that the book is not simply descriptive but also political.

And now, in juxtaposition to Engels, two novels which treat the same subject-matter.

Advancing more and more into the shadow of this mournful place, its dark, depressing influence stole upon their spirits, and filled them with a dismal gloom. On every side, and far as the eye could see into the heavy distance, tall chimneys, crowding on each other, and presenting that endless repetition of the same dull, ugly form which is the horror of oppressive dreams, poured out their plague of smoke, obscured the light, and made foul the melancholy air. On mounds of ashes by the wayside, sheltered only by a few rough boards or rotten pent-house roofs, strange engines spun and writhed like tortured creatures, clanking their iron chains, shrieking in their rapid whirl from time to time as though in torment unendurable, and making the ground tremble with their agonies. Dismantled houses here and there appeared tottering to the earth, propped up by fragments of others that had fallen down, unroofed, windowless, blackened, desolate, but yet inhabited. Men, women and children, wan in their looks and ragged in attire, tended the engines, fed their tributary fires, begged upon the road, or scowled half-naked from the doorless houses. Then came more of the wrathful monsters, whose like they almost seemed to be in their wildness and their untamed air, screeching and turning round and round again; and still, before, behind, and to the right and left, was the same interminable perspective of brick towers, never ceasing in their black vomit, blasting all things living or inanimate, shutting out the face of day, and closing in on all these horrors with a dense dark cloud.[5]

Coketown, to which Messrs Bounderby and Gradgrind now walked, was a triumph of fact; it had no greater taint of fancy in it than Mrs Gradgrind herself. Let us strike the key-note, Coketown, before pursuing our tune.

It was a town of red brick, or of brick that would have been red if the smoke and ashes had allowed it; but as matters stood, it was a town of unnatural red and black like the painted face of a savage.

It was a town of machinery and tall chimneys, out of which interminable serpents of smoke trained themselves for ever and ever, and never got uncoiled.

It had a black canal in it, and a river that ran purple with ill-smelling dye, and vast piles of building full of windows where the piston of the steam-engine worked monotonously up and down like the head of an elephant in a state of melancholy madness. It contained several large streets all very like one another, and many small streets still more like one another, which all went in and out at the same hours, with the same sound upon the same pavements, to do the same work, and to whom every day was the same as yesterday and tomorrow, and every year the counterpart of the last and the next. . .

A town so sacred to fact, and so triumphant in its assertion, of course got on well? Why no, not quite well. No? Dear me! . .

Is it possible, I wonder, that there was any analogy between the case of the Coketown population and the case of the little Gradgrinds. Surely, none of us in our sober senses and acquainted with figures, are to be told at this time of day, that one of the foremost elements in the existence of the Coketown working-people had been for scores of years deliberately set at naught?[6]

The industrial landscape to which Nell and her grandfather come, in chapter 45 of *The Old Curiosity Shop*, is presented with conscientious horror. The attitude is one of simple repulsion, and the language is consequently predictable. The gloom is 'dismal', the form of the chimneys is 'dull' and 'ugly', the smoke 'made foul the melancholy air'. The extended simile, by which the engines 'writhe like tortured creatures' (and shortly after are called 'monsters') manages to force a brief frenetic life – or imitation of life – into the language. The list of adjectives attached to the houses is undistinguished in itself, but for those who have read Engels it sums up his long, appalling account of inhabiting the uninhabitable (reducing, one might say, his factual horrors to the mild antithesis of 'but yet inhabited'). In some ways the most interesting – and revealing – word in the passage is 'scowled'. The outsider looking in on such scenes of dirt and poverty is tempted to assume that the people there are his enemies, that their expression is a kind of sub-human animosity. This is exactly the response that Engels and Gaskell, interested in what it must be like to live there, managed to avoid.

Coketown is the same landscape, but how different. There is nothing conscientious about this lively prose, which bears the Dickensian hallmark from the first ludicrous image of the painted face of the savage. There is nothing monotonous about its rendering of monotony: the exaggerated repetition of 'like one antoher' or of 'same pavements . . . same work . . . same as' is a mimesis of the monotony of Coketown but the very process of describing it generates a perkiness, both in sentence structure and in the images. How the interminable serpents and the grotesque alliterative elephant would have enlivened the first landscape. For here we have real satire, filled with the central satiric delight in what can be done, in the writing, with the object of dislike. (Yet before the chapter is over, *Hard Times* has dropped into a moralizing at least as pondeorus as that of *The Old Curiosity Shop*. I have included only a glimpse of this, beginning with the laboured sarcasm of 'Why, no, not quite well' and going on, with a nudge and a wink, to offer us as a discovery the connection which Dickens had himself planted in the text.)

This chapter is not about Dickens *per se*, but in common justice we can pause to ask if this picture of him as opposed to industrialization is a true one; and indeed, asking it may throw some light on the two passages. When Dickens died, Ruskin remarked that the literary loss was much greater than the political, since

Dickens was a pure modernist – a leader of the steam-whistle party par excellence. . . His hero is essentially the ironmaster; in spite of *Hard Times*, he has advanced by his influence every principle that makes them harder – the love of excitement, in all classes, and the fury of business competition.[7]

It is clear that to *Hard Times* we must add *The Old Curiosity Shop*, but in general Ruskin is right: the ironmaster *is* a kind of hero in *Bleak House*, albeit a marginal hero. Industrial capitalism represents a possible new start for the England that the Doodles and the Dedlocks have made such a mess of, just as Daniel Doyce the inventor is a marginal hero in *Little Dorritt*.[8] In much of Dickens's writing, too, there is an unmistakeable delight in speed and mechanical processes.

Ding, Clash, Dong, BANG, Boom, Rattle, Clash, BANG, Clank, BANG, Dong, BANG, Clatter, BANG BANG *BANG*! What on earth is this? This is, or soon will be, the Achilles, iron armour-plated ship. Twelve hundred men are working at her now. . . Twelve hundred hammerers, measurers, caulkers, armourers, forgers, smiths, shipwrights; twelve hundred dingers, clashers, dongers, rattlers, clinkers, bangers bangers bangers!

In this essay on Chatham Dockyard, Dickens's style plays happy verbal games to show its delight in bustle and mechanical activity, making up words to show that there is no real precedent for all this fascinating ingenuity. Then, turning to the machine that pierces iron plates for rivets, he uses the same image as in *The Old Curiosity Shop*:

'Obedient monster, please to bite this mass of iron through and through, at equal distances, where these regular chalk-marks are, all round.' Monster looks at its work, and lifting his ponderous head, replies, 'I don't particularly want to do it; but if it must be done –!' The solid metal wriggles out, hot from the monster's crunching tooth, and it *is* done. 'Dutiful monster, observe this other mass of iron. It is required to be pared away, according to this delicately lessening and arbitrary line, which please to look at.' Monster (who has been in a reverie) brings down its blunt head, and, much in the manner of Doctor Johnson, closely looks along the line – very closely, being somewhat near-sighted. 'I don't particularly want to do it; but if it must be done –!' Monster takes another near-sighted look, takes aim, and the tortured piece writhes off, and falls, a hot tight-twisted snake, among the ashes.[9]

Monster, snake, writhing: all the previous images are here. How little the vehicle of a metaphor matters, since the effect is so different from the horror and repetition of *The Old Curiosity Shop*, and of Coketown. These three pieces of Dickens, placed together, can be divided by two criteria. The one is aesthetic: is Dickens's imagination active, or is he following familiar stereotypes to produce clichés? Here Coketown and 'Chatham Dockyard' go together, in contrast to the conventional horrors of *The Old Curiosity Shop* (and also the moralizing about Coketown). The other is ideological: is Dickens a 'modernist'? Here *Hard Times* and *The Old Curiosity Shop* go together, since both show fear and dislike of industrialism, in contrast to the steam-whistle enthusiasm of 'Chatham Dockyard' (and most other Dickens).

My final extract is from an account, in the first person, of growing up in the slums:

But when I was just turned of thirteen, an altogether new fairy-land was opened to me by some missionary tracts and journals, which were lent to my mother by the ministers. Pacific coral islands and volcanos, cocoanut groves and bananas, graceful savages with paint and feather – what an El Dorado! How I devoured them, and dreamed of them, and went there in fancy, and preached small sermons as I lay in my bed at night to Tahitians and New Zealanders, though I confess my spiritual eyes were, just as my physical eyes would have been, far more busy with the scenery than with the souls of my audience. However, that was the place for me, I saw clearly. And one day, I recollect it well, in the little dingy, foul, reeking, twelve foot square back yard, where huge smoky party-walls shut out every breath of air and almost all the light of heaven, I had climbed up between the water-butt and the angle of the wall for the purpose of fishing out of the dirty fluid which lay there crusted with soot and alive with insects, to be renewed only three times in the seven days, some of the great larvae and kicking monsters which made up a large item in my list of wonders: all of a sudden the horror of the place came over me; those grim prison-walls above, with their canopy of lurid smoke; the dreary, sloppy, broken pavement; the horrible stench of the stagnant cesspools; the utter want of form, colour, life, in the whole place, crushed me down, without my being able to analyse my feelings as I can now; and then came over me that dream of Pacific Islands, and the free, open sea; and I slid down from my perch, and bursting into tears threw myself upon my knees in the court, and prayed aloud to God to let me be a missionary.[10]

The fact that this passage is in the first person must not be brushed aside as a mere technicality: now slum life is being described from the point of view of the slum-dweller, and there is little question of neutrality in the description. And the dirty and ugliness can no longer be contrasted automatically with an implied norm of clean, varied, spacious houses (as they are, with differing explicitness, by Engels, Simon and Gaskell). Now the contrast has to be supplied by the narrator, and this can only be done by his seeing better housing (walking, say, into suburbia) or by his imagining an escape, as is so brilliantly done here.

Point of view alone would not be enough to produce the power of this writing: the dreary sloppy broken pavement has to be as real as possible to engender that final cry, it has to be free of rhetoric and moralizing and compassion, placed before us in its quality of sheer ineluctable existence, in order to give full imaginative force to the escapism. There is nothing else in *Alton Locke*, little else in the whole work of Charles Kingsley, to equal this bluntness.

Three authors: Engels, Dickens, Kingsley. We must not assume that the most important difference between them is that between fact and fiction. It will be better to begin by asking what kinds of discussion of the differences between them is possible. I suggest that there are three: the first asks about their ideology, the second looks at their strategies of writing, the third relates them to social reality.

Ideology

It is not difficult to perceive an ideological purpose shaping the choice and presentation of material in all three. In Engels it is quite open: the book is an indictment, and some of the sentences have the commitment and pithiness of *The Communist Manifesto*: 'Money is the god of this world; the bourgeois takes the proletarian's money from him, and so makes a practical atheist of him.'[11] Since it was written before Engels met Marx, much of the ideological interest for us will consist in seing how far the main concepts of Marxism are already forming in the author's mind. For instance, the concept of alienation:

Londoners have been forced to sacrifice the best qualities of their human nature, to bring to pass all the marvels of civilisation which crowd their city. . . This isolation of the individual, this narrow self-seeking is the fundamental principle of our society everywhere. . . The dissolution of mankind into monads of which each one has a separate principle and a separate purpose, the world of atoms, is here carried out to its utmost extreme.[12]

Alienation, as used by Marx, results from two things: the monotony and purposelessness of machine work, and the lack of control over his life of the man who has nothing but his labour power. The two were inseparable during the early Industrial Revolution, though in principle they are separable, as Engels has realized in the last sentence. All the material for the concept is here, including the alternatives before the proletariat: submission, drunkeness ('in both cases they are brutes') and defiance.[13] At almost exactly the same time, Marx was sitting in Paris developing the concept in more abstract terms, but without any of the sense that we have here of the idea actually being forged from the realities of human experience. *The Condition* is a more powerful work than the Economic and Political Manuscripts because abstract thought intermeshes with the presentation of social experience, that is, because Engels has the qualities of historian and novelist, out of which the philosopher is struggling to emerge.

The ideology behind the Dickens extracts has already been explored, though a really full discussion of *Hard Times* would have to consider not only its hostility to industrialism but also its treatment of class relationships, utilitarianism and trade unions, and ask how far its hostility to industrialism led to a different position on these matters from the Dickens of the steam-whistle party. This is too large a question to treat here, but I will offer one tangential contact with it. Bounderby's relation to his workers is indicated in his insistence that any complaint on their part is evidence that they want to eat turtle soup and venison; the Ironmaster's in the fact that a stranger arriving in the town and inquiring for Rouncewell's is met with ' "Why master," quoth the workman, "do I know my own name?" ' In Coketown the capitalist treats his workers with scorn; in the industrial town of *Bleak House* he has established (as Sir Leicester Dedlock the traditional landlord has not) a sense of community. There is the ideological shift.[14]

The ideology of the extract from *Alton Locke* is particularly interesting. 'Religion is the sigh of the oppressed creature, the sentiment of a heartless world, and the soul of soulless conditions':[15] that seems not only a summary of what it is saying, it could almost be a sentence from *Alton Locke* itself. Even the next, famous sentence, 'It is the opium of the people', could be from Kingsley, who wrote at much the same time, 'We have used the Bible as if it was a constable's handbook – an opium-dose for keeping beasts of burden patient while they are being overloaded'.[16] But close as the two are verbally, the difference between them is enormous. Marx does not mean that slum life may betray us into forgetting the reality of the soul; he means that we *create* the very concept of a soul as a projection from the misery of our urban life, for his argument, following Feuerbach, is that 'man makes religion, religion does not make man'. If the Reverend Charles Kingsley had read that, or if he had read the suggestion that Romantic poetry was the quickest way out of a London slum, he would have turned in distaste from such clever, cynical ideas. Yet what else is Kingsley's own passage telling us? The intensity of the boy's longing for romance is a reaction from the grim prison walls; his spurious religious zeal has a ring of dreadful authenticity.[17]

Strategies of Writing

The second form of analysis treats the passages as examples of writing, and looks at their verbal strategies to see what this can tell us about the way in which they enable us to see the subject matter. We have an impressive example of this in Steven Marcus's study of

The Condition of the Working Class in England in 1844.[18]

Marcus analyses *The Condition* as an act of reading (reading Manchester) produced by an individual sensibility. Using the phrasing of a literary critic, Marcus describes the book as 'the best single thing that Engels wrote', and claims that for a worthy comparison one has to go to the later Dickens; he sees the writing as an intolerable struggle with words and meanings, and treats Engels as a writer in whose hands the language broke down; he disinters the underlying conceit when he claims that Engels sees the shopfronts along the main thoroughfares as 'Manchester's Potemkin Villages'. Manchester told a particular story in the nineteenth century, which Engels had the wit to read. That reading shaped his book.

There may seem an oddity in using this type of analysis on Engels's text, for it is an analysis that usually looks at the particularities of language, at that cumulative effect of verbal details that we call style; and Engels's style is less distinctive than Kingsley's, and very much less distinctive than Dickens's. As a result, Marcus has to report that Engels's language does not easily offer itself to the kind of discussion he is engaged in: 'the language itself is giving out on him'.[19] The inadequacy of language in the face of appalling experience is itself a linguistic strategy that can be used to great effect – by Conrad, for instance – but Engels does not appear to have the kind of self-consciousness that makes deliberate use of such a point. (If he did, the fact that we are dealing with a translation would grow more important.) The verbal strategies appropriate to the reading of Manchester often seem, in Marcus's discussion, to come from him rather than from Engels: it is he, after all, who provides the brilliant image of the Potemkin villages.

Discussion of style yields more in the case of Kingsley, whose prose controls our reponse by its shift from the exclamatory syntax and relaxed rhythms of the opening to the hammer blows of the long list of adjectives attached to the back yard, then to the mounting series of parallel phrases that govern 'crushed me down', and finally to the three insistent preterites, 'slid', 'threw' and 'prayed'. It is elaborate and skilful writing, worth fuller anlaysis than I can give here. Dickens's prose I have already commented on, and contrasted the elaborate predictableness of *The Old Curiosity Shop* with the liveliness of *Hard Times* and 'Chatham Dockyard'. Finding that Dickens drops into cliché when writing of class conflict, and that his prose crackles with life when he writes of the delights of machinery and progress, is interesting ideologically, since it confirms Ruskin's case in a way Ruskin might not have welcomed. Enthusiasm for industrialization tended to go with a belief in the harmony of interests between classes, and this makes Dickens more than ever a member of the progress and steam-whistle party. Of course this does not prove that the party of progress was right, not even that Dickens believed it to be right, for Dickens's opinions are not always well illustrated by his fiction; it proves only that Dickens's imagination was of that party without always knowing it.

Literary criticism necessarily interests itself in style, in the effects of metaphor and other figures of speech, or repetition, syntactic oddities, changes of rhythm and of register, unusual diction and the thousand other verbal devices that modify meaning. Now all these devices seem to assume a norm of ordinary usage from which they depart: how do we treat writing which sticks to that norm? Do we say that it has no style, that it uses language as a transparent medium, giving us access to extra-linguistic reality (the *hors-texte*)? Or do we say that the plain style is a style like any other, that it too imposes interpretation on otherwise inaccessible reality, and that there is no transparent language?

I postpone discussion of the *hors-texte*, a question that will concern us when we come to treat of the relation to social reality; but the question of the norm must be addressed here, since not only Engels but also Simon and Gaskell are clearly using the plain style. What enables us to perceive and talk about stylistic differences? The answer surely is that whatever its epistemological validity, we have to assume a norm of plainness. How can we discuss the impact of Dickens's elephant except by saying that everyone is aware of the many ways in which a steam-engine is nothing like an elephant – let alone one in a state of melancholy madness, which none of us has ever seen. A conceit is a violent departure from a norm: it makes it clear that all images are to some extent departures from the norm of the literal. We need to operate on the belief that the plain style is, in an important sense, no style.

The plain style can be found in history or in fiction. The departure from it that we found in Simon ('as though he were in a diving bell') was very mild, and so we naturally ask whether literature can bear greater departures from plainness than history. Most historians, suspicious of fine writing, will say yes: so let us turn to a historian who does write finely. When Carlyle describes the fall of the Bastille, he says: 'For four hours now has the World-Bedlam roared: call it the World-Chimera, blowing fire'.[20] One could imagine an ensuing discussion on the difference between these two capitalized abstractions, and whether World-Bedlam can blow fire as well. It could form part of a discussion on metaphor, or on Carlyle, but it is hard to see how to fit it into a discussion of the French Revolution. If a staunch Carlylean maintains that the distinction does tell us something about mob violence, then he is claiming that the sentence still belongs to history. But it seems to mark out the book as one that will not be willing to disappear.

Text and Reality

I introduce the idea of the disappearance of the book in order to move to the third form of possible discussion of the passages, that which relates them to social reality. On this there will be more to say.

The very title of *The Condition of the Working Classes in England in 1844* invites us to relate it to housing and sanitary conditions, population growth and factory work, crime statistics (and the difficulty of knowing them), and all the research subsequent to its publication. If the book is a contribution to economic and social history, this is how historians will treat it; and if they do so, their aim is to make it disappear. Their object of study is the past, and they will wish to retain the true facts and the valid analysis, confirmed by the work of others, and throw away the rest. When the wheat has been sorted from the chaff, the original ear of corn has been destroyed.

Such an approach clearly believes that the past is knowable. We no longer believe, now, that such knowing is unproblematic: the days of positivist history, of *wie es eigentlich geschehen*, are now over, and it has become a commonplace to argue that history cannot give us direct access to objective facts, since the ideology and the verbal strategies of the historian will determine what he chooses to notice and how he describes it, to say nothing of the connections between events that he then establishes. In fact, the reaction against positivism is now so strong that we are often told that to regard a text like *The Condition* as a response to the society it purports to be describing is outmoded and naive, for history is simply the result of the writing and (even more) the ideology of the historian. This would mean that the past is unknowable. Since what happened a moment ago belongs to the past, it is hard to credit that such an extreme view is tenable, yet it is often stated. The following is one example among scores of a view that can be heard at innumerable academic conferences:

Enough of the past is lost, and looks in any case so different from different points of vantage, for history itself to be regarded as no more (and indeed, no less) than a present fiction which must be constructed obliquely or directly according to the often only half-apprehended order of contemporary needs and struggles.[21]

The same doctrine is asserted more playfully by Malcolm Bradbury in the Author's Note to *The History Man*, whcih describes his novel as 'a total invention with delusory approximations to historical reality, just as is history itself'.[22] If the past (including the writings of the past) simply provides raw material for the ideologically motivated writings of historians, as Francis Barker appears to be here maintaining, and thus is not in itself knowable, it must also be the case that historians' writings, which belong to the past as soon as they are written, are not knowable either, and we are faced with an infinite regress: even Barker's own statement would result from contemporary needs and struggles, so that it would not be possible to know whether it is true.

The basis of Barker's position is stated in more general terms by Terence Hawkes:

The world does not consist of independently existing objects, whose concrete features can be perceived clearly and individually, and whose nature can be classified accordingly. In fact, every perceiver's *method* of perceiving can be shown to contain an inherent bias which affects what is perceived to a significant degree. A wholly objective perception of individual entities is therefore not possible: any observer is bound to *create* something of what he observes. Accordingly, the *relationship* between observer and observed achieves a kind of primacy. It becomes the only thing that can be observed.[23]

After asserting the great structuralist insight that unmediated perception of objects is impossible, he shifts to asserting that no perception of objects is possible, claiming (for instance) that a kinship system, when seen as a language, involves 'no reference (sic) to a "reality" or "nature" beyond itself'.[24] After showing the untenability of naive empiricism, Hawkes has swung to the opposite extreme of naïve scepticism. But if perception is not wholly objective, it does not follow that it must be wholly subjective: that would be to ignore the more complex possibility that it results from an interaction between the external world and our method of perceiving.

I have claimed that any text can be related to at least three contexts: its ideology, its strategies of writing, and social reality. To eliminate any of these completely is a dogmatic oversimplification; and a total rejection of positivism would be as naïve – and as fanatical – as its total acceptance.

Steven Marcus, it should be added, believes that the past is knowable. He shows no wish to brush aside the reality of nineteenth-century Manchester, and we do not need to point out to him, as we might to some, that when Engels writes 'it is almost impossible to get from the main streets a real viewing of the working class districts themselves',[25] he means *real*: his purpose is to convey knowledge of an extra-textual referent. It is most important to say that Engels himself would favour the approach that causes his book to disappear: though since his purpose is political first and scholarly second, the disappearance he would most favour would be that resulting not from the acceptance of his findings by other historians, but from the disappearance of Manchester's slums after the socialist revolution.

Dickens, Kingsley and Elizabeth Gaskell would all have rejected indignantly the charge that they were not interested in the condition of England, and that everything in their books was made up. They – and their readers – would have had no difficulty in distinguishing, in principle, the fictitious elements – the invented characters and incidents – from the account of slum conditions or (this is less straightforward) of Chartism and trade unionism. All of them showed concern, outside the boundaries of their fictional text, for the truth of their depiction. Kingsley wrote two prefaces to *Alton Locke*, one to the Working Men of Great Britain, and the other to the undergraduates of Cambridge, in which he admitted without hesitation the political purpose of his novel, and at the same time assumed that it dealt with social reality, remarking, for instance, that his disappointments with working-class movements since its appearance 'have strengthened my conviction that this book, in the main, speaks the truth'.[26] Dickens never hesitated to cite his own novels when making political speeches, trampling down the difference of genre with far less scruple than I am trying to display.[27] Elizabeth Gaskell defended *Mary Barton* by saying 'Some say the masters are very sore, but I'm sure I *believe* I wrote truth', or claiming 'that some of the men do view the subject in the way I have tried to represent I have personal evidence'.[28] These modest claims to truth refer to the controversial politics of the novel; *a fortiori* it would have seemed to her obvious that the descriptions of slum life were 'true'.

It is necessary to state the obvious. Fiction differs from history in not making a claim to truth. If Engels or Simon or a modern economic historian tells us something that can be refuted by evidence, he has broken faith, and will be censured by professionals. But to sign a contract is not the same as to carry it out: the historian, who undertakes to tell the truth, may be careless, or ignorant, or a liar, and the novelist, who does not undertake it, may be scrupulous. It is perfectly possible to maintain that the best historians of the condition of England in the 1840s were the novelists – as long as the claim is settled by historical and not by aesthetic criteria. The novelists would then be carrying out a contract they had not subscribed to.

Collingwood on History

The best account I know of the relation between history and fiction is that of Collingwood. In developing his central concept of the historical imagination, Collingwood compares it to 'the pure or free but by no means arbitrary imagination of the novelist': 'Each of them makes it his business to construct a picture which is partly a narrative of events, partly a description of situations, exhibition of motives, analysis of characters.' What then is the difference? Collingwood begins his answer with what to the structuralist will seem a question-begging naïvety: 'the historian's picture is meant to be true' – not even putting the term in the now fashionable quotation marks – but this turns out to be the beginning of a careful examination of the consequences of this claim. In doing this, I suggest, he anticipates and uses all that is valuable in the structuralist case, without driving it to the extreme of an untenable scepticism.[29]

The consequences flow from the fact that history tries to be true. First, the historians's picture 'must be localised in space and time': in contrast, Collingwood congratulates Hardy on the 'sure instinct' that led him in his novels to replace Oxford by Christminster, Wantage by Alfredson, and so on in 'what should be a purely imaginary world'. This is on the right lines, but a trifle crude. The world of fiction is not *purely* imaginary, but overlaps with the world of history; in the case of realistic fiction, the overlap is especially large, and welcomed. The fact that Elizabeth Gaskell locates *Mary Barton* in Mancheter and *North and South* in 'Milton' is in the end trivial: in every important sense, they are the same town. Hardy's careful alteration of the place names of Wessex is the result of aesthetic rather than epistemological considerations.

Second, 'all history must be consistent with itself . . . ; there is only one historical world'. Here we need a distinction similar to that drawn in the previous section, where I proposed that to the writer of autobiography there is an *hors-texte*, but not to the reader. To the responsible historian, there is only one historical world; if there were not, disagreements with other historians would simply be alternative, and compatible, constructs. But to us, as we read historians of differing schools, it often grows painfully obvious that they have not succeeded in adjusting their constructs to one another. Ideological difference leads historians to select from and even to observe the past so differently that the patent nonfulfilment of this aim lends to the Barker–Hawkes point what degree of plausibility it has.

Third, 'the historian's picture stands in relation to something called evidence'. This is the crucial difference, though there are occasions (as we saw with Addison) on which the novelist uses evidence too. But whereas the novelist uses evidence only in particular cases, the historian must always use it. Now Collingwood makes it quite clear that evidence is not something extra-textual – or, as he puts it, 'there is nothing other than historical thought itself, by appeal to which its conclusions may be verified'. It is obvious that historical inquiry could never proceed if the historian stopped to question the validity of every piece of evidence he had; in practice, he works from data. But what this means is that

for the purposes of a particular piece of work there are certain historical problems relevant to that work which for the present he proposes to treat as settled; though if they are settled, it is only because historical thinking has settled them in the past, and they remain settled only until he or some one else decides to reopen them.[30]

There is, in another words, no *hors-texte* for the historian, except provisionally. But Collingwood does not use this as an argument for scepticism, for denying that there is any difference between history and fiction. Instead, he draws a crucial distinction between the critic and the sceptic. The former is willing to re-enact the historian's thoughts, 'to see if they have been well done': he it is who may query the data, that is, reopen a problem which the first historian had accepted as settled. But he will do this because he has reason to suspect the settling: which clearly implies that he is willing to leave other data standing, if he has no good reason to question them. The sceptic gives himself a much easier task: without taking the trouble to examine which solutions to problems can stand and which must be reopened, he makes the general observation that since any of them could be reopened, none can ever be regarded as settled, and therefore there is no knowledge of the past. It is his refusal of this glib scepticism that leads Collingwood to say (without inverted commas) that history strives to be true, and then to go on to discuss the difficulties entailed by that attempt. Next to this careful thinking, how superficial the sceptic appears.

Realism

All this is connected with an issue internal to literature, the question of realism. The novelists we have discussed all see themselves as realists, and there is a close parallel between the structuralist criticism of realism, and the theory just cited that history is a form of fiction. As a starting point for investigating realism, I will choose an observation of Stendhal's:

Pour être intelligible . . . j'aurais du diminuer les faits. C'est à quoi je n'aurais pas manqué, si j'avais eu le dessein un seul instant d'écrire un livre généralement agréable. Mais le ciel m'ayant refusé le talent littéraire, j'ai uniquement pensé à décrire avec toute la maussaderie de la science, mais aussi avec toute son exactitude, certains faits.[31]

(In order to be intelligible I should have modified the facts. And I would not have failed to do this if I had had the slightest intention of writing a book that would be found charming. But heaven having refused me all literary talent, my only thought was to describe, with all the sombre gloom of science, but also with all its precision, certain facts.)

To make one's book generally acceptable, one needs to follow certain stereotypes which have little to do with reality itself. The faculty that enables us to do that is 'talent littéraire', and Stendhal will have none of it.

Now Barthes attacks realism on the grounds that 'le vraisemblable' simply corresponds to what the public believes possible, that the 'va-sans-dire' is simply the imposition (the violent imposition, he weirdly claims) of a set of conventions that society pretends are natural in order to constrain our thinking.[32]

The resemblance between this defence of realism and this attack on realism is surely very striking: in both cases, what is being pleaded for is the undermining and rejection of stereotypes. In *Adam Bede*, for instance, George Eliot interrogates the stereotype of the pretty tender-hearted milkmaid. Hetty Sorrel, with whom both young men in the novel fall in love, has walked straight out of a ballad, a rustic idyll or a pastoral etching. 'Ah, what a prize the man gets who wins a sweet bride like Hetty! . . . the dear, young, round, soft flexible thing! Her heart must be just as soft, her temper just as free from angles.' That is the version of Hetty we can call *vraisemblable*; to show her like that requires only *talent littéraire*. George Eliot sets out to subvert this picture, to show that Adam and Arthur really know very little about Hetty, to suggest that the reader (and the self-mocking persona of the narrator) also 'find it impossible not to expect some depth of soul behind a deep grey eye with a long dark eyelash'. But the purpose of this is not to show that we cannot know one another, cannot escape from the stereotypes we use in seeing, it is to tell us that Hetty was not like that at all. One ruthless sentence disposes of her: 'Hetty did not understand how anybody could be very fond of middle-aged people' – though I have had to extract that icy statement from a long moralizing paragraph (this is early George Eliot). Molly the housemaid, we are told, 'was really a tender-hearted girl, and as Mrs Poyser said, a jewel to look after the poultry, but her stolid face showed nothing of this'.[33]

The negative programme of George Eliot is exactly that of Barthes, but her positive aim is something like the opposite. For he regards *le vraisemblable* as a device for concealing from us our inability to attain real knowledge of the extra-textual world. Literature should therefore cease to strive for mimesis, and should become semiosis, 'an adventure of the linguistically impossible',[34] freeing itself from the tyranny of the referent. Her aim, however, is to replace worn-out mimesis by a truer version, just as Stendhal wished to replace *agrément* by *les faits*. They set out to free literature from the tyranny of the signifier.

To claim that realism simply replaces one set of conventions by another is to deny the central point of what George Eliot is doing. Realism is the claim that in the interaction between convention and observation that lies behind every piece of writing, a shift ought to take place, reducing the role of convention, and increasing that of observation. The structuralist who dismisses this does so because he does not really believe in observation. There is a parallel here between the rejection of realism and the denial that history gives us real knowledge of the past. Just as George Eliot is committed to the possibility of helping us to see milkmaids more shrewdly, so Engels is committed to the possibility of learning about Manchester. Knowledge of the extra-textual world is the result of an interaction between that world and our methods of perceiving it (including our language); the fact that the realist cannot get rid of language, cannot offer us naked objects untouched by our categories, is important, and explains the error of the simple-minded scholars of Laputa; but it need not lead us to abandon the possibility of observation.

The weakness of realism as a theory has always been that it does not show what is specific to art. Stendhal, offering us 'facts', and describing them wth 'toute la maussaderie de la science', appears to be announcing that he is deserting literature for sociology; and indeed *De l'Amour*, written before Stendhal had become a novelist, is a kind of study in sociology and psychology, as we would laboriously say nowadays. The case of Zola is even more notorious: defining the novelist as a mixture of 'l'observateur' and 'l'experimentateur', he sums up the writing of fiction as follows:

En somme, toute l'operation consiste à prendre les faits dans la nature, puis à étudier le mécanisme des faits, en agissant sur eux par la modification des circonstances et des milieux, sans jamais s'écarter des lois de la nature.[35]

(In sum, the whole operation consists in taking one's facts from nature, then in studying the mechanism of facts, by modifying circumstances and environment to produce an effect on them, without ever departing from the laws of nature.)

It is easy to see why Zola was accused of reducing the task of the novelist to that of the mere social scientist (he virtually says as much himself). Yet this weakness is the obverse of a strength: no one could accuse Stendhal and Zola of not taking seriously the social world they are studying and representing. The view that accepts an overlap between fiction and history is likely to accept realism too, for that is a literary doctrine designed to encourage literature to step over the frontier.

The condition-of-England novels were a response to what was

happening in English society, to the feeling that 'the condition and disposition of the Working Classes is a rather ominous matter at present; that something ought to be said, something ought to be done, in regard to it'.[36] Those parts of the novels that render this condition and disposition to us ought not to be dismissed as 'background' or as local colouring. They mattered to the novelist, and they matter in the novel. Their style is plain, their method realistic, their aim is truth. They are continuous at one edge with the fictitious elements of the novel, at the other with the work of historians.

Evangelicalism

Was the condition of England simply the condition of its bricks and mortar, its drinking water and lack of floor boards? No one is naïve enough to think these don't matter, but they are not usually the main concern of the historian. So now we must turn to the inside of events, and take an example that any historian, of any school, would regard as history. An example that deals not with individuals but with social forces, not with houses but with thoughts, not with a single moment but with change.

My example will be the Evangelical movement: the protestant regeneration of English religious life in the eighteenth and nineteenth centuries. This will include the rise of Methodism, the history of the older Dissenting sects, and Evangelicalism strictly speaking (that is, within the Anglican Church). There is a small initial problem of terminology: one movement was clearly at work in both Church and sects, and to give it one label we have either to extend the term 'Methodism' to include the movement inside the Established Church (a usage not unknown to contemporaries, and befitting after all the lifelong wish of Wesley not to found a separate sect), or, as I have preferred to do, to extend 'Evangelicalism' to cover the spirit of religious enthusiasm when found outside as well as inside the Church. The most important element in the movement was the stress on individual consciousness of sin and redemption, but it reached into many aspects of life: theology (arguments about predestination, justification by faith alone, particular and general redemption), ecclesiastical authority (the danger and wickedness of popery, the validity of ordination, the independence of individual congregations from a central body), worship, both individual and communal (importance and sufficiency of the Bible, extempore versus written prayer, ritual, music in church, missionary work), and much of social life (sabbatarianism, teetotalism, dress) as well as political issues such as Catholic emancipation or slavery.

Evangelicalism and the Historians

Both historians and novelists have written at length about this movement. I begin with the historians, of whom I have chosen four: Elie Halévy, E.P. Thompson, Owen Chadwick and Edward Quinlan.[1] What do they tell us?

What they tell us is complex and richly varied, and any attempt to classify it will oversimplify; but the attempt must be made, and I therefore begin with two distinctions – that between studying the history of religion in isolation and relating it to other institutions, and that between narrative and analysis. Chadwick's *The Victorian Church* is the most straightforward of our four historical studies: it does not appear to advance any unifying thesis, and though it contains a good deal of social and political history, it does not seek explanations of one area of human activity (here, the religious) in terms of another (say the economic), and is therefore not reductive in method.

Like all history, it consists of narrative and analysis. We can divide the narrative into, roughly, three kinds. First, anecdotes: particular events involving individuals. These are authentic (a source is given) and chosen because they are representative. Why are we told about the dedication of Dr Lant Carpenter's *Apostolical Harmony* to Queen Victoria in 1838? First, because it shows the importance of the numerically small Unitarian sect; and second, because it shows the toleration, verging on indifference, of the Whig cabinet. Then there are accounts of important controversies: the growth of teetotalism among the Methodists, the argument about the itinerant American preacher James Coughey, the dispute about acepting 'ministers' money' from the government. And third, there is the story of Methodism or of Presbyterianism itself, a narrative in which the protagonist is not an individual but a 'first-order historical entity'. As we move up this scale, individual acts are subordinated to larger movements, and it becomes more and more necessary to attribute motives, wishes and even actions to these entities, to say that Methodism grew more suspicious of Old Dissent, or Evangelicalism treated Christmas with severity. Those examples are from Chadwick, but there are even more striking instances in Halévy, who explores the collective mind of 'the Methodist preachers' for several paragraphs ('Why should they resign themselves to accept a position of humiliating inferiority to the Anglican clergymen who ignored or insulted them? Why should they. . . ?').[2]

This is still narrative, but it has taken us to the overlap with analysis, since the postulating of these entities as protagonists in a story clearly depends on an initial placing of various people, actions and doctrines under the same heading.

What are historians studying when they tell the story of a dispute within Methodism or the Church of England, either a single explicit dispute (were Methodist ministers to wear gowns and bands? Ought the slave trade to be abolished?) or an ongoing dispute that issued in various forms (just what authority was the Methodist Conference to exercise over individual congregations? How far should Christians take part in secular politics? – or is any politics secular?). What question or questions determine their choice of material, and the search for evidence? Few historiographers, as we have seen, are still naïve enough to claim that the facts simply speak for themselves.

What historians normally study is power. They relate conflicts in such a way that we perceive what forces support each side, and the outcome of the conflict is important because it strengthens one side and weakens another. Whether ministers wore gowns and bands was important because it would make them more or less like Anglican parsons, and thus make Methodism more like part of the Church or more like Dissent. Those who approved gowns and bands also approved the laying on of hands in ordination, which would weaken the element that saw the minister as deciding on his own calling, or as totally dependent on the congregation (the individualizing element, the Independent element): though the issue was complicated by the fact that the extreme 'high' Methodist party (pulling towards the Church, away from Dissent) could also object to an ordination ceremony, as unauthorized by the Church, and therefore schismatic. In any such conflict, it is essential to identify the parties that are contending for victory; without this, we cannot tell the story.

But how far do the roots of power extend? As we ask what forces supported and opposed the Methodist New Connection, the first important Wesleyan secession, we soon find that we cannot confine ourselves to Methodism, or even to religion, since orthodox members of Conference, denouncing the secessionists as 'turbulent', called them a 'destestable knot of scorpions' who set up Jacobin chapels of their own. The leader of this gorup, the Reverend Alexander Kilham, published a pamphlet in 1795 called *The Progress of Liberty*, filled with the revolutionary doctrines that came from France, and pleading for a more democratic structure within Methodism, as well as in society as a whole.[3] To identify just who the Kilhamites were must lead us to ask who the democrats were – what sort of people in the 1790s adopted revolutionary doctrines; and thus forces us to step outside the history of Evangelicalism strictly speaking, and explore its connections with other forms of social behaviour, political, economic, intellectual. And many historians do not wait until they are forced: Halévy, Thompson and Quinlan all, in different ways, examine the relationships between religion and the rest of society.

The most ambitious attempt to do this is probably Halévy's. His first volume, on the English people in 1815, has two general theses, which are stated quite explicitly: that England was a free country, and that Methodism saved England from revolution. The first thesis applies to politics ('the executive was systematically weakened in every direction'), to economics (the rapid development of capitalism) and to religion (the sects enjoyed some liberty of organization in law and more in practice). It is not easy to be sure how far this thesis is merely a convenient taxonomic device, used to range three more or less self-contained discussions under a common heading, and how far it is ideological (a defence of capitalism, of a weak executive, of religious pluralism); if the first is the case, it is possible for us to ignore it in reading any of the three parts. The second thesis, which has become very famous, arises out of the question, Why was England, of all the countries of Europe, 'the one most free from revolutions, violent crises and sudden changes'? The political institutions were not strong enough to contain 'a bourgeoisie animated by the spirit of revolution', the economic institutions were too disorganized to contain working-class discontent had it 'found in the middle class leaders to provide it with a definite ideal, a creed, a practical programme'. But the potential leaders were tamed by Methodism: their enthusiasm was diverted from changing society to questions of salvation, and they had been taught not to shake the authority of Caesar. The ruling classes 'watched the growth of this new power', and

feared Methodism almost equally with Jacobinism. Had they understood the situation better, they would have realised that Methodism was the

antidote to Jacobinism, and that the free organisation of the sects was the
foundation of social order in England.[4]

E.P. Thompson is as committed as Halévy to dealing with
interrelations between different areas of human activity. His *Making
of the English Working Class* explores radical politics, industrial
relations, class consciousness – and Methodism – between 1790 and
1830. Thompson is very conscious of Halévy's thesis that
Methodism prevented revolution, as he is of the attack on that
thesis by Eric Hobsbawm, who criticizes it by means of a regional
analysis which aims to show that Methodism was often strong in
the same areas as Chartism, and at the same times, and concludes
that the movement was neither strong enough numerically, nor
successful enough in controlling the social views of its members,
for Halévy's thesis to hold.[5]

Thompson sees the political effects of Methodism as deeply
ambivalent: on the one hand, the strict discipline imposed from the
centre by the Methodist Conference, and the extreme conservatism
of Wesley and Jabez Bunting (who declared 'Methodism hates
democracy as much as it hates sin') made Methodism an ally of the
political status quo; but on the other, the simple fact of combining
in association to run their own affairs meant that the effects of
Methodism, as of all Dissent, were democratic. Southey considered
'the manner in which Methodism has familiarised the lower classes
to the work of combining in associations' to be among the
'incidental evils' resulting from it;[6] and there were Methodists
prominent in all the popular movements from Peterloo to the
Labour Party. The break-away sects, Primitive Methodists and
Kilhamite New Connection (the 'Tom Paine Methodists') drew off
the more radical elements from orthodox Wesleyanism.
Thompson's exploration of the political tension in Methodism
means that he is not advancing a thesis but rather asking a question:
what was the political dimension of Dissent? But when he
comments on religious experience itself, we can find something
more like a thesis: an underlying materialism, to which his
explanations are constantly drawn. He tends to see personal
salvation as an evasion of social meaning, and thus his account of
the conversion of one Joshua Marsden, culminating in his
translation 'from the power of Satan to the kingdom and image of
God's dear son' is interpreted as follows:

We may see here in its lurid figurative expression the psychic ordeal in which the character structure of the rebellious pre-industrial labourer or artisan was violently recast into that of the submissive industrial worker.[7]

Edward Quinland, my fourth example, is a less distinguished historian than the other three, but deserves a place because of the special focus of his study. *Victorian Prelude* describes the change in manners that took place in England in the half century around 1800 that can be summed up as the growth of respectability. Evangelicalism was the main influence on this. The book shows no interest in church organization, quantitative measurements, or administrative practice. More than Thompson, and far more than Halévy and Chadwick, it passes on what contemporaries said about the changes that were taking place, displaying the arguments about popular education or the suppression of obscenity in the words used at the time. The prominent figures are not those who exercised power, but those who expressed opinions – Adam Smith, Hannah More, Arthur Young. When activists like Wilberforce and Place appear, it is more for what they wrote than for what they did. Looking for connections between different kinds of social activity is not necessarily the mark of the ambitious historian. Quinlan is the least ambitious of the four, and advances no general thesis, but he is rich in suggested connections – for instance, that the sentimentalism so popular in the later eighteenth century can be connected both with reform of manners and with political reaction, or that increased social mobility goes with increased orderliness. He deals with changes in language (the growth of euphemisms, for example) not by anything like a word count, but by quoting contemporary comments. One can see why a certain kind of historian would say there is no real research in Quinlan's book, but also why it gives the feel of the period better than any of the others.

One more distinction can be applied to our historians: how far do they see the past as it saw itself? Do they, for instance, name the movements they are studying with concepts used by the participants? Every good historian is pulled both ways on this issue. If he simply applies to the early nineteenth century the categories and ideas with which we operate in the late twentieth century, then he is refusing the liberation from one's own universe which the study of the past can provide. If, however, he attempts to think nothing about Evangelicalism except what the Evangelicals thought, he refuses the other liberation of studying history, that of inserting the consciousness of one age into that of another, and so achieving an awareness in depth of the nature of change.

Methodism, Evangelicalism, Dissent were familiar terms to the participants, as were Chartism and Radicalism, England and France. This is less true of capitalism, because people do not (or did not) usually have such a coherent picture of their economic life, and even less true of capitalism as an all-embracing concept (capitalist family relations, capitalist art). The distinction between studying an institution in isolation and studying interconnections is relevant here, for the more a historian moves outside a single area of human activity and attempts to study society as a whole, the more he will find himself moving beyond the terminology of contemporaries.

In the case of religion, more is at stake than terminology: for to relate religious activity to other social processes could be seen as a refusal to accept it on its own terms. Religion as a subject of study is available to believer and unbeliever alike: will they offer different histories of it, and is either of them better fitted than the other to understand it?

The Reverend Owen Chadwick is the only one of our four historians who professes himself a Christian. This is not apparent from his book, unless we want to attribute to it his reluctance to explain religion in social or economic terms; but this could just as well be due to scholarly caution. And he is also the one who denies strongly that a Christian will write the history of religion differently from a non-Christian, as we can see by turning to his *Secularisation of the European Mind in the Nineteenth Century.* 'There is no history which is not secular,' he writes. 'No statement that a fact of the past is "sacred" can exempt it from the ordinary process of historical enquiry.'[8] This principle lay behind the Higher Criticism of the nineteenth century, with its claim that the Bible should be studied like any other book, that its sacred nature should not exempt it from the scrutiny of historical scholarship. And it is not only texts which can be regarded as sacred: so can experience. At a given moment on a Sunday in, say, 1800, thousands of Englishmen were praying. The historian can estimate how many, and he can study the language in which they themselves, or their enemies, would describe the activity: that they were members of the elect on whom God had bestowed the gift of grace, that they were earning grace by the sincerity of their repentance, that they were foolishly imagining that their own righteousness would bring salvation. He can study too a different kind of language, whether of contemporaries ('God is an hypothesis, and as such stands in need of proof')[9] or of later analysts ('the lurid figurative expression of the psychic ordeal in which the character structure of the rebellious pre-industrial labourer was violently recast').[10] But suppose he chooses between these languages, declaring that one is true, or at least truer than the others: has he then (as Chadwick would claim) ceased to write history? I will not (yet) try to answer this, but will add the parallel question: does the novelist who writes about religious experience equally cease to be a novelist when he pronounced on its authenticity?

Evangelicalism and Fiction

Novels take place not in Lilliput or Wonderland or the Forest of Arden, but in a society of men and women who lead material lives in interest groups, families and social classes. 'There is no private life,' wrote Geroge Eliot, 'which has not been determined by a wider public life',[11] and that public life is always present in the novel, exerting its pressure on the unfolding story. Novelists differ greatly in the extent to which they explicitly tell us about this public world, and the historical novelist, taking us into a world we are unfamiliar with, is the one most likely to describe it at length. It is even arguable that it was the historical novel, through the enormous influence of Scott, that was responsible for the idea that fiction deals with social forces, and that George Eliot's remark (which could, of course, have been made by any historian) is a generalization from the historical novel to the novel as such.

Felix Holt, like so many Victorian novels, takes place a generation before the time it was written – at a time when the author and most of the original readers were children, a time that will be reconstructed from a mixture of written sources and the reminiscences of elders, varnished with a patina of nostalgia from childhood memory. George Eliot takes more trouble than any other novelist to reconstruct the setting by describing the then state of England (in *Felix Holt* by taking us on a coach journey in the opening chapter, in *Adam Bede* by causing a stranger to visit Hayslope and ask a number of convenient questions), but every novelist has to develop some way of telling us about the period and the subculture in which his story takes place, though the sophisticated modern will be less explicit about it. This creation of background is historian's work.

Halévy saw the eighteenth-century Church of England as an institution well integrated into secular life which failed to play any true religious role. Young men choosing between the church and the army as a career were governed by 'circumstances, parental caprice, often chance', and 'the clergy of the national Church of England were intellectually inferior to the clergy of the Established Churches of Protestant Germany'. The Anglican parsons were 'apathetic indeed, and worldly, but little disposed to play the tyrant'.[12] This view of the Church of England is exactly that of George Eliot. She does not, as he does, offer facts and figures to show the huge discrepancies of wealth among the clergy, demonstrating both the way the Church encapsulated the class structure of the whole society, and its comparative indifference to spiritual matters. What she does is to condense his view into a vivid sentence he would surely have been grateful for: the villagers 'were kept in the *via media* of indifference, and could have registered themselves in the census by a big black mark as members of the Church of England'.[13] This is the situation that produces an Evangelical revival and the growth of Dissent, but the upsurge that produces such revivals dies away into a new conformity, which in turn gives place to a new upsurge. The torpor into which Dissent can sink, when the enthusiasm fades, is vividly described by Mark Rutherford: the tiny independent congregation to which Thomas Broad preaches 'listened as oxen might listen, wandered home along the lanes heavy-footed like oxen, with heads towards the ground, and went heavily to bed'.[14] They might as well have been attending the Established Church. Halévy describes how the torpor of eighteenth-century religion was revivified by Methodism, with its livelier and more populist style of preaching, its centralized organization and its shift to political conservatism. The social basis of such a movement in the new towns and new industries is explored at great length by Thompson, and is vividly summed up in *Felix Holt*:

But when stone-pits and coal-pits made new hamlets that threatened to spread up to the very town, when the tape-weavers came with their news-reading inspectors and book-keepers, the Independent chapel began to be filled with eager men and women, to whom the exceptional possession of religious truth was the condition which reconciled them to a meagre existence and made them feel in secure alliance with the unseen but supreme rule of a world in which their own visible part was small.[15]

Here we have the simplest, most satisfying relation betwen historian and novelist. They agree about what was going on, the historian offers evidence, including facts and figures, and the novelist puts it more vividly, succinctly and wittily. She has not subscribed to the historian's contract, to tell the truth, but she has carried it out.

But things are not often so simple. Even in this situation there are epistemological problems lurking, and there are other, more complicated situations. These now stand before us like a jungle, full of lush and fascinating growths, but intertwined to a degree that makes methodology despair. As an essay in hacking a path, I now offer three discussions of issues (representative figures, power, quality of experience), and one of subject matter.

Representative Figures

If the overlap between fiction and history is confined to the explicit filling in of background by the novel, it will clearly be peripheral. The wider public life operates not only behind but also within the private life, most obviously by the novelist choosing characters who are representative – as does the historian.

Let me for instance compare Dan Taylor and Ben Rushton with Zachariah Coleman. Taylor was a Yorkshire collier who was converted by the Methodists, and in 1770 formed the Baptist New Connection, and as an itinerant preacher travelled 25,000 miles and preached 20,000 sermons. He is important to E.P. Thompson as showing the kind of Dissent that was not for but of the people, not part of official Methodism nor even official Baptism: 'spiritually perhaps he came from Bunyan's inheritance, but literally he just came out of the ground.' Ben Rushton was a handloom weaver, a local preacher with the Methodist New Connection, and an active radical – imprisoned after Peterloo, a speaker at one of the first Chartist camp meetings in 1839. He is important as showing the link between Dissent and Radical politics that was never completely destroyed by Methodist Toryism. He declared to the Chartist meeting that 'he had given nothing to the parsons since 1821', and another local preacher, Hanson, added further denunciations of the clergy:

They preached Christ and a crust, passive obedience and non-resistance. Let the people keep from those churches and chapels ('We will!') Let them go to those men who preached Christ and a full belly, Christ and a well-clothed back – Christ and a good house to live in – Christ and Universal Suffrage.[16]

Zachariah Coleman, printer, and member of the Independent Congregation of the Reverend Thomas Bradshaw, was a moderate

Calvinist in theology, and a fierce radical in politics. The rigidity of
Zachariah's Calvinism would have sat uneasily in a man of such
human feeling, were it not that 'when it came to the push he
modified it'. He is important to Mark Rutherford both as an
example of the subordination of theology to feeling – the fact that,
whatever their professed beliefs, Calvinists did not, in their dealings
with fellow men, 'accept blindly the authority of St Paul or anyone
else' – and also as an example of the alliance of Dissent and
Radicalism. Zachariah's politics bring him into contact with some
fierce anti-clericals, and he finds that the two cultures he belongs to
both do and do not sit together in his mind. He 'made the cause of
the people a religion', bringing the same enthusiasm to each cause,
but he also became painfully aware of tensions between them,
especially at times of leisured reflection. He has to decide to attend
political meetings on a Sunday evening, he is disconcerted by
reading a book on astronomy, and he finds it difficult to reconcile
the world of his pious wife, uninterested in politics, and his friends
the Caillauds, uninterested in religion.[17]

Let us put aside as trivial the question how far Coleman is based
on an actual original (he probably isn't), and accept him as
belonging to fiction. It is clear that he illustrates many of
Thompson's points, and better than Dan Taylor and Ben Rushton,
for two reasons. One is the great convenience of being able to
attribute all the points being made to the same character, without
having to look round for a fresh example each time. The second is
the fact that the tension between two elements in the subculture can
be enacted as a conflict in Coleman's consciousness: in a naïvely
omniscient author like Mark Rutherford this is done explicitly, but
in a novel in which access to the protagonist's thought was carefully
restricted, such a conflict could still be indirectly shown.

The historian offers generalizations, which he illustrates from real
people. The novelist invents his people, and if they are representative, they can imply generalizations. We now see that the fictitious
individual is more useful than the real, more able to contain the
generalization. If only he had really lived! The historian is not
allowed to invent people, but he is allowed to speak of ideal types,
as Macaulay describes the Cavalier and the Roundhead, or as
Halévy writes (with such confidence) of the Anglican clergy or the
Dissenters (who 'were ashamed of the extravagance and savage
features of the Calvinistic creed'). But compared to the novelist he
is under great disadvantages. It is not only that these bloodless
types resemble allegorical figures more than realistic portraits: they

cannot even take on the verbal liveliness of allegory, since the statements about them will remain conscious of their status as generalizations. He cannot even tell us, as Mark Rutherford does about Zachariah,

What God's purposes were he did not know. He took a sort of sullen pride in not knowing, and he marched along, footsore and wounded, in obedience to the orders of his great chief.[18]

Even in this gentle probing, the implied generalization has begun to yield to exploration of the value of the experience.

The novelist soon grows impatient with representativeness. Only the minor characters in a novel (and not always those) will remain locked up in the typical. What makes a character interesting is likely to be what makes him untypical. This generates the story, and in most novels that means a love story. So Waverley, who belongs to the Establishment, falls in love with a Highlander; Basil Ransom, the conservative, with a feminist; and Julien Sorel, *le petit paysan*, first with a bourgeoise, and then with an aristocrat. By falling in love outside their culture, even into a conflicting group, hero or heroine subjects herself, and her own culture, to an unexpected strain, and thus teaches us more about it than we could otherwise learn. But simply because this is the usual method, it can easily turn into a stereotype. Of course Zachariah Coleman, married to a pious, unsympathetic Dissenter, must fall in love with the fascinating daughter of a radical French atheist; of course Felix Holt, the earnest radical, must be attracted to the elegant, frivolous Esther, must turn out to be fond of children and sexually susceptible. The unrepresentative element historically, if it is simply a literary cliché, will have too predictable an effect on the representative figure to teach us much.

More interesting than Zachariah falling in love with Pauline Caillaud is his seeing her dance. He walks home 'with many unusual thoughts'. First is the simple fact that 'it was the first time he had ever been in the company of a woman of any liveliness of temperament, and with an intellect which was on equal terms with that of a man'; second is the fascination of the free movement of Pauline's dancing, which seems to have been idiosyncratic, even quaint, which is not only quite unlike anything Zachariah has ever seen before, but which his previous self 'would have considered as the work of the devil'.[19] The seasoned novel-reader no doubt knows what's coming, but Mark Rutherford's comparative clumsiness here turns out a positive advantage: the book seems as puzzled as Zachariah about what is happening, and instead of moving towards a conventional love story, it lingers on the disconcerting glimpse of Zachariah, his efforts to come to terms with the undermining of the faith that he still holds. Clumsiness can be a literary virtue when it suggests integrity and resistance to literary sterotypes; and as here when it springs from the attempt to explore a representative character in an unusual situation.

The one group of readers to which representativeness will be especially important will naturally be the members of the group depicted, in this case the Evangelicals. We know that they were furiously resentful of their portrayal in the Victorian novel, where they seemed to figure only as hypocrites and butts. Valentine Cunningham's study not only reports this reaction but acts as their spokesman, since he shares their indignation. Cunningham points out that Dissent 'was considered a second-class religion, and Dissenters made to be second-class citizens', and he documents meticulously the 'general failure in compassion, sympathy and tolerance shown by the novelists'.[20]

The Dissenting reader, feeling that all he stands for is being attacked, will not pause to think about the nature of literary representation, and the ways in which distortion of social reality could be considered inevitable and unimportant, even (in some genres) admirable; and Cunningham is so completely sympathetic to these readers that he too measures novelists by the same criterion as historians, rejecting (indeed, ignoring) all arguments that would assign fiction to an autonomous realm of art. He finds that only George Eliot and Mark Rutherford handled Dissent with anything like justice, and even they are not wholly exempt from the widespread charges of 'fictional antagonism and distortion, manipulating their material to make their cases'.[21] To most literary critics, this is reductive: asking no more from literature than the fulfilling of the historian's contract. (Though it does make a pleasant change in literary criticism, where the opposite form of reductivism is more common: assuming that if the novel is powerful enough, then it must (whatever the historians say) convey the 'essential truth' about a historical movement.)

To apply Cunningham's position I choose two examples: Trollope's Mr Slope (whom he does not discuss), and Dickens's Mr Chadband (whom he does). Mr Slope is an ambitious low-church clergyman who is determined to use his position as chaplain to the Bishop of Barchester for his own advancement. Like any good Evangelical, he is opposed to ritualistic high-church practices during divine service, and to Sabbath-breaking. Here are his comments on the latter.

I fear there is a good deal of Sabbath travelling here. On looking at the 'Bradshaw' I see that there are three trains in and out every Sabbath. Surely we should do all that we can to control so grievous a sin. This breach of the Sabbath alarms me much more than to hear that fifty or a hundred thousand French were landed or that our Grand Fleet was totally destroyed. I consider it as a decided token that God has given us up.[22]

What is wrong with this opinion? What is wrong is the pedantry and fanaticism that interferes with the pleasure and business of others, in the conviction that such interference makes one God's instrument. Such, I presume, is likely to be the response of the modern reader, but whether it gives the Evangelical cause for complaint will depend on what such a reader is reacting to – a travesty by Trollope, or Sabbatarianism itself. To test this, I have broken the promise I made in the last section, and used (really for the last time!) a composite quotation. With a few editorial adjustments of tenses, the above comes from Mr Slope, Mrs Proudie and the Reverend John Newton, friend of Cowper and Wilberforce, and celebrated Evangelical preacher, who contributed the last two sentences. Mr Slope's opinions are only as unreasonable as Evangelicalism itself, and the 'serious' reader, protesting at Trollope's prejudice, can console himself with the fact that the opinions, though mocked at, are given a fair hearing.

But, our reader may continue, why make Mr Slope a hypocrite? The implications of this point are trickier than might at first seem. Hypocrisy does not in itself constitute a case against the opinion professed: if anything, the opposite is true, since no opinion is worth feigning unless it is admired. Hypocrisy is the tribute paid by vice to virtue. If the novelists show almost every Evangelical as a hypocrite that is indeed offensive, but only because of the repetition. If there is nothing to say against Evangelical views except the accusation that those who profess them cannot be sincere, this may be regarded as the inadvertent compliment paid to the victim by the author's poverty of imagination.

Mr Chadband, independent preacher, spiritual adviser to Mrs Snagsby, sanctimonious, oratorial and greedy, if not exactly a hypocrite, is more self-indulgent than his puritan oratory might suggest (unless you believe that such oratory is always an excuse for greed). Here he is holding forth to the orphaned waif, Jo:

'No, my young friend,' says Chadband smoothly, 'I will not let you alone. And why? Because I am a harvest-labourer, because I am a toiler and a moiler, because you are delivered over untoe me, and are become as a precious instrument in my hands. My friends, may I so employ this instrument as to use it toe your advantage, toe your profit, toe your gain, toe your welfare, toe your enrichment! My young friend, sit upon this stool.'[23]

How does Chadband differ from Mr Slope? He is much funnier; and he is not accompanied by moral indignation from the author, though we must admit that Dickens is quite as capable of such indignation as Trollope. Here it would only weaken the effect, which is highly Dickensian. Simply turning 'to' into 'toe' is a touch of genius beyond anything in Trollope, to say nothing of the brilliant blending of awareness and unawareness of what he is doing in Chadband's boasting. The difference from Trollope is easily stated: Dickens is writing satire. That is, he has turned the object of his scorn into a lively grotesque, and our moral contempt is blended with aesthetic delight. Now if we are to apply Cunningham's criterion, and judge the portrait by how fairly it represents the reality of Evangelicalism, then we have to say that Chadband is a worse libel than Slope: for it shows Dickens's complete inability to grasp the way Evangelical language can convey genuine spiritual experience. But the literary signpost that announces 'satire' announces, at the same time, that there is no pretence of being fair. It announces that there is no overlap, here, with history, and we now see that the omission of authorial comment is not incidental but essential. The Dissenter who protests that his own clergyman is not like Chadband is a spoilsport: he needs a lesson in reading. We cannot be quite so sure this is the case with Trollope.

Power

I claimed that the historian, when he tells his story, is interested in power, and will show who is contending with whom in order to show what forces lie behind each, and explain why one side did or didn't win. Any novelist worth his salt is also interested in power, though since his canvas is smaller, what he is likely to show is not the struggle for power in the Church or the Methodist Conference, but that within the individual congregation or (in the case of Trollope) the cathedral close. The struggle between Dr Grantly's party and the Bishop's, in *Barchester Towers*, has an ideological component, but basically Trollope considers this a pretext. Travelling down to Barchester, Mr Slope 'began to form in his own mind a plan of his future life':

He . . . would in effect be bishop of Barchester. Such was his resolve; and to give Mr Slope his due, he had both courage and spirit to bear him out in his resolution. He knew that he should have a hard battle to fight, for the power and patronage of the see would be equally coveted by another great mind – Mrs Proudie would also choose to be bishop of Barchester. Mr Slope, however, flattered himself that he could out-maneouvre the lady.[24]

In the case of Dr Grantly it is wholly plausible that he should value power for its own sake, since he belongs to the old-fashioned High and Dry school so firmly categorized by Halévy, believing that the wealth and influence of the Church need no justification, that innovation in church and state is in itself an evil: there is therefore no need to make him a hypocrite, and Trollope shows unnecessary embarrassment when he gives chapter 6 the slightly facetious title 'War' and drops into the mock-heroic ('And now had I the pen of a mighty poet would I sing in epic verse the noble wrath of the archdeacon'). Indeed, his cynical disclosure of the power struggle underlying much of social life is one of Trollope's greatest virtues as a writer: he considered politics a pure matter of ins and outs, and the causes to which politicians devote themselves are trivial in the case of the Establishment, and a rationalization of envy in the case of the radicals:

On this occasion men were to be regarded, and not measures. No doubt such is the case, and ever has been the case, with the majority of active politicians. The double pleasure of pulling down an opponent, and of raising oneself, is the charm of a politician's life. And by practice this becomes extended to so many branches, that the delights – and also the disappointments – are very widespread.[25]

In the Dissenting congregation there can be a power struggle as fierce as in any cathedral close, and one that can be analysed with great explicitness. Foucault's deeply conservative theory of power

as 'a dense web that passes through apparatuses and institutions
without being exactly localised in them', his assertion that 'power is
everywhere; not because it embraces everything but because it
comes from everywhere' is a view that makes the analysis of power
almost impossibly elusive, and any ideology an oversimplification.[26] The more the individual subject is dispersed, filling a variety
of roles in the various institutions he (or she) belongs to, the truer
the Foucaultian theory will be; but the member of a sect lives a life
that is not dispersed but concentrated. Our best theoretical guide
here will be Troelstch, whose concept of the sect emphasises the
contrast between the universal applicability of its theology, and the
intensely inward-looking life-style which dominates every aspect of
the members' lives;[27] and this makes possible the study of power as
a visible element that, in the case of more dispersed subjects, would
be overlaid and distorted by other power relationships.

Power in the sect focuses on the position of the minister. On the
one hand, he is their leader and moral counsellor, who exercises
authority, above all perhaps through his sermons; on the other
hand, they chose him, they pay him, they can get rid of him. Of
course denominations differed here: Methodist ministers derived
much of their authority from the centre, Unitarians enjoyed
considerable freedom when the congregation was small and the
office endowed; the extreme of control by the congregation was
found in Independency. Conflict can arise not only between
minister and flock, but also among its members, who may split
between his supporters and his opponents. Just as every detail of the
life of members of a sect is subject to the scrutiny of the group, and
especially of the minister, so nothing that the minister does is
entirely private. Every novelist of Dissent portrays such a struggle;
and it might be revealing to begin with the crudest I know,
Mrs Oliphant's *Salem Chapel*.

Arthur Vincent, minister of the only Dissenting place of worship
in Carlingford, is in danger of being forced into resignation by his
congregation. His preaching is a success, but he takes no trouble to
be polite to the members, and the melodramatic affairs of his sister,
along with own infatuation with the local wealthy lady, leads him
into ever worse trouble. The plot is too lurid to be taken seriously,
but what is of interest is the contest within the congregation
between Mr Vincent's main supporter, Tozer, and those who want
to drive him out. It is presented as a pure struggle for power,
including a struggle for capturing the minister as prize for one's
daughter. Thus Tozer had been rather critical of Mr Vincent at

first, but once he decides to support him against his critics he voices his criticisms only in the form of warnings not to play into the hands of his enemies, the exhilaration of the fight having totally replaced any actual moral judgements.[28]

There is a parallel example in Mark Rutherford. Mr Broad, minister of the Independent congregation of Tanner's Lane, has announced that he will not vote in the forthcoming election: this displeases the radicals, and pleases Brother Bushel, staunch Tory (it is clearly assumed that no Dissenting minister, if he voted, would vote Tory). Mr Broad and his wife ponder the decision he has taken:

There was no fear of any secession on the part of the Allens, connected as they were with them through Priscilla. On the other hand, Brother Bushel, although he gave out hymns, had already had a quarrel with the singing pew. . . Mr Bushel, too, contributed ten pounds a year to the cause, and Paddingfold Green Chapel was but a mile farther off from him than Cowfold. There were allies of the Allens in Tanner's Lane, no doubt; but none of them would be likely to desert so long as the Allens themselves remained. Therefore Providence seemed to point out to Mr and Mrs Broad that their course was clear.[29]

Writing like this is disappointing, for the same reason that the attack on Mr Slope's Evangelicalism is disappointing. Attacking hypocrisy is too easy: the tension beween self-interest and principle in the minister is never explored, we are simply shown the self-interest, without Trollope's exhilarating bluntness, without even any ironic amusement at the discrepancy. Without, even, this:

'As to Reform, sir, put it in a family light,' he said, rattling the small silver in his pocket, and smiling affably. 'Will it support Mrs Mawmsey, and enable her to bring up six children when I am no more? . . . I ask you what, as a husband and father, I am to do when gentlemen come to me and say, "Do as you like, Mawmsey, but if you vote against us, I shall get my groceries elsewhere. . ." '

'No, no, no – that's too narrow you know. Until my butler complains to me of your goods, Mr Mawmsey,' said Mr Brooke soothingly, 'until I hear that you send bad sugars, spices – that sort of thing – I shall never order him to go elsewhere.'

'Sir, I am your humble servant, and greatly obliged,' said Mr Mawmsey, feeling that politics were clearing up a little.[30]

Mr Mawmsey is a kind of hypocrite, too, but he is his own kind: pompous, and stupid enough to conceal from himself (and so from others) the fact that he does not care in the slightest who wins the election. It is his very stupidity that defeats Mr Brooke, for when Mr Mawmsey 'went up and boasted to his wife that he had been rather too many for Brooke of Tipton', he is on one level completely right: Mr Brooke, fastening on an opportunity to explain his own integrity, has preferred not to notice that it has lost him a vote. George Eliot is as cynical as Mark Rutherford here, telling us that principle counts for nothing and interest for everything, but she explores the functioning of hypocrisy in exactly the way he does not.

Placing these fictional analyses of power next to those of historians, what do we see? First, that the novelists are often strikingly crude, reducing the complex interactions of self-interest and principle to a matter of simple hypocrisy. Sometimes this can be a strength, as in Trollope, whose more conventional admirers do not always notice how blunt he can be. Even family life can be seen by Trollope as a power struggle, and sometimes with breathtaking cyncism. Young Dolly Longestaffe's main occupation is annoying his father; when he receives (as he often does) notes from his mother, asking him to come and dine, to take them to the theatre, to go to the ball, 'he would open them, thrust them into some pocket, and forget them. Consequently his mother worshipped him.' Power belongs to those not weakened by affection.

Exhilarating but crude: this can be seen as the equivalent of vulgar Marxism in the historian, reducing all conflict to class struggle. Such blunt cynicism has a rather different effect when applied to individuals and to social forces: the former is both more and less offensive. George Eliot does not believe that elections are merely an occasion for taking bribes and not losing customers, and her reminder of Mr Mawmsey's true motives corresponds to a more subtle Marxism, indicating the contribution that material interests make to the outcome of conflicts.

Historians show power as a social force; novelists show it operating through the clash of individuals. The historian, if he believes power can be analysed and its outcome explained, cannot be a Foucaultian; the novelist can only be one if she ignores the wider social context of the struggle she depicts. George Eliot, for whom there is no private life which has not been determined by a wider public life, never ignores this, and is always concerned to make us aware of the dense web that passes through institutions. Indeed, it is her own image.[31]

This contrast applies not only to the depiction of power, but to the whole boundary between history and fiction. Historical narrative tells the story not of individuals but of 'the first-order entities of history', institutions and group activities that possess enough autonomy to be considered as quasi-characters in a narrative. I take the phrase from Paul Ricoeur, who uses this concept to attribute narrative even to those historians (the Annales school in particular) who have apparently replaced it by analysis. I have at least entertained the view that we can go further, and claim that all history has such entities as its protagonists: the rest is merely biography.

But in that case, a very clear divide opens up between history and fiction. For the characters of fiction are without question individuals. They occupy the centre of the picture, and primary historical entities operate either as background (the 'wider public life' that determines the private) or as forces internalized in the individual characters. In both cases, they must appear as static. The individual story will not push the larger entities out of the picture, but it will push away their narrative. The culture of Evangelicalism can live in fiction, but not the story of Evangelicalism.

Authenticity of Experience

Halévy may be right, that the eighteenth century Church lacked any true intellectual or spiritual quality, but we can at least ask how he knows. This will unleash the discussion already conducted in section II, about knowing the inside of events and the inside of people, compounded by the fact that Halévy's assertion is not about an individual but a whole movement. If we repeated the discussion it would lead to the same conclusion, that assessing the true spiritual quality of a clergyman or of the clergy as a whole will use a criterion of truth that is more like coherence than correspondence, and so will not obviously differ from exploring the inside of a fictitious character.

We ought to distinguish between the authenticity of religious experience and its quality. Authenticity certainly (was God's grace really at work here?) must be the prerogative of faith, and no secular knowledge (no knowledge, to the sceptic) can treat of it. But quality: the nature and power of the experience itself? This question really needs to wait for the next two chapters. Chapter 2 is

concerned with the communication of experience, Chapter 3
specifically with religious experience. But for the moment we are
not concerned with poetry, only with prose narrative, and there it
is clear that if the question of quality in the experience is to be
raised, the narrative and the social analysis must pause.

As example, I shall take George Eliot's historical novel. Although
Romola is set in fifteenth-century Florence, it is about many of the
same issues as her novels of Dissent. Savanarola's authority over the
Florentines has many resemblances to that of a Methodist minister:
true, he is a priest, but a priest at odds with the Pope, and he rules
by charismatic influence among those who actually hear him, using
this influence to impose puritan austerity and emotional conversion.
His authority is brought to public test when the Franciscans
challenge him to ordeal by fire, a challenge he finds it hard either to
accept or decline. The novel, like a historical work, is concerned
with the social impact of his crusade in Florence, and the alignment
of forces for and against him. In order to study this, how much is it
necessary to know about his own spiritual life? 'I used to think him
a narrow-minded bigot,' said Tito, 'but now I think him a shrewd
ambitious man.' George Eliot does not leave this question open: she
has no hesitation in taking us inside his consciousness,

a consciousness inconceivable to the average monk, and perhaps hard to be
conceived by any man who has not arrived at self-knowledge through a
tumultuous inner life: a consciousness in which irrevocable errors and
lapses from veracity were entwined with noble purposes and sincere
beliefs, in which self-justifying expediency was inwoven with the tissue of
a great work which the whole being seemed unable to abandon. . .[32]

This is not a clear endorsement or rejection of Tito's judgement:
she finds an ambivalence at the heart of Savanarola's own
experience. That individual ambivalence corresponds to the balance
of forces inside his 'congregation' of Florence. We are back again
with the cleavage – if cleavage it is – between history and
biography. The historian of Florence, as of the Roman Catholic
church, can leave Tito's question unanswered, as the historian of
Methodism can rest in uncertainties, mysteries and doubts about
Wesley. But Savanarola like Addison can step from the history of
Florence into a biography or a historical novel.

Sermons

That really concludes the argument of this chapter. But since all the discussion so far has been based on questions imposed by me on the writers, none of it has emerged direct from the experience of reading the novels, or of studying Evangelicalism. I therefore add a final section, constructed on rather different lines.

The central cultural experience of the Dissenting sect was the sermon: how, we may ask, does that find its way into history or fiction? The first answer is that it does not find its way into history, and will not do so as long as history is narrative and analysis: how can the story pause to include – or compose – a whole sermon? This is not just a matter of space. For the historian to treat of sermons would require what Rorty calls 'reconstruction': historical interpretation of the works making up a canon. As far as I know, Evangelical sermons in the eighteenth and nineteenth centuries have never received the kind of attention that leads to the formation of a canon ('the great sermons') which the historian can then proceed to interpret.

Chadwick and Halévy hardly ever quote sermons, and even Thompson and Quinlan, much more likely to quote original sources, are so interested in the spilling of Evangelicalism into politics or secular morality that they are more likely to quote pamphlets or private letters. The novelist, however, who enjoys the advantage of being able to make up his sermons, and who perceives the centrality of the preaching itself, is unlikely to resist having at least one. All the novelists of Evangelicalism, George Eliot, Elizabeth Gaskell, Trollope, Dickens, Mark Rutherford, Mrs Oliphant, give us a sermon or its equivalent. Or rather, they give us its equivalent. There is no more place in a novel for a whole, real sermon, than there is in a history, and once again this is not only because of length. Nothing in a novel is there simply for its own sake. Balzac's fascination with how paper is manufactured, Melville's with whaling, enrich *Illusions Perdues* and *Moby Dick*, but they require to justify their presence by their interaction with power, survival and human relationships. A sermon in fiction is not there simply for the reader who wants some theology, it will be treated as resulting from certain experiences of the preacher, or causing certain experiences in the audience. The sermon in a novel must therefore be defamiliarized: wrested from the context in which all it contains is predictable. It must be an unusual sermon, or (better) a normal sermon seen in an unusual light.

The nearest to a real sermon is that of Dinah Morris in chapter 2 of *Adam Bede*: it is the longest, and its language is genuinely Methodist. Dinah is a representative figure of Methodism, not for the trivial reason that she was based on the author's aunt, Mrs Samuel Evans, but because her piety imbues everything she says and does. Yet in one crucial respect she is not representative: 'Nothing could be less like the ordinary type of the Ranter than Dinah. She was not preaching as she heard others preach, but speaking directly from her own emotions.' We know a good deal about Methodist preaching, enough to know that the term 'Ranter' is not unjustified. According to Lecky, for whom 'a more appalling system of religious terrorrism has seldom existed', the Methodist 'preached especially to the nerves', dwelling upon judgement, hell and the lost condition of mankind.[33] Dinah is at the other extreme from this: even when she grows agitated she is moved by love, appealing to her hearers with tears to turn to God. She addresses them as 'Dear Friends', she reminiscences about her childhood, she tells them she is as poor as they are, she concludes by urging them to think 'what it is – not to hate anything but sin; to be full of love to every creature'.[34] Dinah is speaking directly from her own emotions, and the emotions are all benevolent. If Lecky is right, this is not Methodism.

This is not really defamiliarization: it is better described as a slanted version of a Methodist sermon. And it is not hard to see why it has been slanted. 'The tale of the Divine Pity was never yet believed from lips that were not felt to be moved by human pity', wrote George Eliot in *Janet's Repentance*,[35] telling the story of how Mr Tryan, the Evangelical clergyman, touches the heart of Janet through his humanity, as Dinah touches Bess Cranage because she so obviously cares.

Man in religion contemplates himself as the object of the Divine Being, as the end of the divine activity; thus in religion he has relation only to his own nature, only to himself. The clearest, most irrefragable proof of this is the love of God to man, the basis and central point of religion.[36]

That is the view of religion both Dinah and Mr Tryan illustrate, here stated in a sentence penned by George Eliot herself, in her translation of Feuerbach's *Essence of Christianity*. 'In religion man contemplates his own latent nature': so to understand Dinah's Methodism, we must understand Dinah herself. The sermon makes its selection from Methodist vocabulary and Methodist ideas to fit a humanist view of what religion can mean.

There are three sermons in Mark Rutherford's fiction: two in the 'Autobiography' and one in *The Revolution in Tanner's Lane*. The last has the most interesting strategy for leading us to see it as a human document. Mr Bradshaw preaches on the text 'the Spirit of the Lord came upon Jephthah', and tells the story of the Hebrew general who vowed that if he was granted victory he would sacrifice the first creature (the first person, Mr Bradshaw claims) he met as he went home, and who met, and had to sacrifice his only daughter. Mr Bradshaw finds the story terrible and inspiring, and denounces the 'comfortable' dismissal of 'Jephthath's rash vow'. God showed that he had elected Jephthah by the burden he laid upon him: 'Be sure if God elects you he elects you to suffering.' Mr Bradshaw's conclusion is that we cannot choose how great our sacrifice shall be: 'Take your own heart, your own blood, your very self, to the altar.'[37]

We have been told that Mr Bradshaw is a widower whose wife had died giving birth to a daughter who also died; we are then told of the effect of the sermon on Major Maitland, the good-natured gentlemanly radical who has come to chapel because of his friendship with Zachariah. Zachariah is disappointed that the sermon is not founded on 'some passage in the New Testament which would have given him the opportunity of simply expounding the gospel of Christ', but the Major has been deeply impressed, and determines to read the Bible again.

One can imagine that sermon being preached in an Independent chapel in 1816, though it is hardly typical: it makes no mention of salvation or, for that matter, of damnation (so it would hardly do as a Methodist sermon), it is entirely concerned with the price God exacts in this world for election. It has a special meaning for the preacher, but since he is a minor character this is never explored. It makes a special impact on the Major presumably because it contrasts so vividly with his easygoing nature (and it may even be intended as a premonition of his eventual death); but this too is never explored. Whatever resonance it may have in the novel as a whole must be felt within the sermon itself; in this it is characteristic of the unsystematic, fitfully powerful fiction of Mark Rutherford. Like Dinah's sermon, it is plausible, and uses orthodox vocabulary, but it, too, hovers on the edge of the secular.

Hearing a sermon is an unusual experience for the Major; preaching on that text suggests an unusual experience in the minister. This adds up to the required effect on the reader, the

feeling that the experience is unexpected. The same can be said, in a
very different way, of Rufus Lyon's preaching in *Felix Holt*. He
chooses an unpromising-looking text, 'And all the people said,
Amen', but from this 'mustard-seed of a text' grows a 'many-
branched discourse', of which we are given one paragraph, in
which he urges that the great shout in Israel, like any great shout
for the right, was not achieved by every one peeping round to see
what his neighbours in good coats are doing.

> But this is what you do: when the servant of God stands up to deliver his
> message, do you lay your souls beneath the Word. . . ? No; one of you
> sends his eyes to all corners, he smothers his soul with small questions,
> 'What does Brother Y. think', 'Will the church members be pleased?'[38]

The mental agility of the preacher, his imposing his authority on
the congregation, the tension between zeal and anxious respectability in the audience, the application of Biblical text to everyday
behaviour: all these are part of the culture of Independence, and the
paragraph is very representative indeed. But it does not strike us as
straightforward historical illustration. In the first place, the single
paragraph, the slice through the middle of the sermon, defamiliarizes it, giving it a fragmentary and somehow sharper effect. And
second, Mr Lyon is not actually preaching, he is preparing his
sermon, dropping into his habit of thinking aloud as he paces
among the piles of books in his study. We do not know therefore if
he would actually have been quite as blunt when in the pulpit. This
defamiliarizes even more, to the point of making the scene almost
comic, especially since Lyddy, the minister's servant, opens the
door at that point to announce a visitor, and Mr Lyon, though he
falls 'at once into a quiet conversational tone', continues to invoke
scripture in urging her not to groan.

If this is comic, the humour is mild. But Mr Slope, who preaches
in Barchester cathedral on the text 'Study to show thyself approved
unto God, a workman that needeth not to be ashamed, rightly
dividing the words of truth', is much more broadly handled. His
sermon is given mostly in paraphrase, interlarded with frequent and
lengthy comments on preaching, and on Mr Slope – authorial
intervention at its most Trollopian and self-indulgent: I shall ignore
them, though as we shall see there is a good deal of authorial
judgement in the sermon itself. Mr Slope preaches in order to goad,
insisting on exactly those points most distasteful to the clergy of the
diocese. 'His object was to express his abomination of all

ceremonious modes of utterance, to cry down any religious feeling which might be excited, not by the sense, but by the sound of words, and in fact to insult cathedral practices.' Mr Slope delivers his low-church case against chanting in carefully chosen words, full of apologies and awareness that 'the practices of our ancestors could not be abandoned at a moment's notice', but with a firm conviction that outward ceremonies merely distract 'at a time when inward conviction is everything'. The response both of Dr Grantly, in the audience, and of Trollope, holding his authorial pen, is to explode in wrath:

Here was a sermon to be preached before Mr Archdeacon, Mr Precentor Harding, and the rest of them! before a whole dean and chapter assembled in their own cathedral!

Why does Trollope consider the sermon so outrageous? We do not need Cunningham to point out the distressingly obvious answer, that he disliked Evangelicals. In all his novels we can see what kind of clergyman he favoured, tolerant, kind-hearted, mild and often worldly men; the obverse of that is the prejudice against men like Mr Slope. 'The words of our morning service,' he declared from the pulpit in Barchester,

how beautiful, how apposite, how intelligible they were, when read with simple and distinct decorum! But how much of the meaning of the words was lost when they were produced with all the meretricious charms of melody, etc, etc.[39]

Why 'etc, etc'? Not just, we may be sure, as a reminder that there is no room in a novel for a whole sermon. It is a sign of dismissal: Mr Slope went on and on with this sort of thing. But that sort of thing is what Evangelicals believed, and Mr Slope is simply stating the case against ritual. On ritual as on Sabbatarianism, Trollope is prejudiced.

Now Trollope's dislike of Evangelicalism can hardly have been greater than E.P. Thompson's. Thompson's hatred surfaces every now and then in remarks like 'it is difficult to conceive of a more essential disorganisation of human life, a pollution of the sources of spontaneity bound to reflect itself in every aspect of personality'.[40] The grounds for dislike are not quite the same, for Thompson hates it for its conservatism as well as for its sourness, but we can still see him as following in the line of Dickens and Trollope. What does such prejudice issue in? In broad comedy, which in Trollope seems rather unfair, in Dickens seems gloriously, creatively unfair. And, if one is a responsible historian, it need not appear at all, except in passing remarks. Though Thompson is much more open about his personal preferences than Halévy or Chadwick, his intense dislike of Methodism does not seem to have influenced his scrupulous arranging of the evidence about whether Methodism was authoritarian or democratic. We might say of him what we more usually say of novelists, Never trust the artist, trust the tale.

Conclusion

So wide-ranging a discussion demands a conclusion, but it cannot be very tidy or coherent. I have tried to show that both history and literature are interested in representative figures, and that both, for different reasons, soon leave them behind: the historian because he cannot do much with lifeless allegory and needs real people, the novelist because the unrepresentative figure is more interesting, and is even the better way to breathe life into what is representative. I have tried to show that both history and literature are interested in power: the novelist in how it is sought and exercised by individuals, the historian by groups. Only by the historian can a group be seen as an entity that acts and changes. And I have tried to return to the question of showing the inside of events, the task in which the historian most closely resembles the novelist. In showing all this, I hope I have also shown how much common ground there is between history and fiction, yet without denying the reality of a territory on each side of the broad and populated frontier.

2

Crying

'When I hear you feel not well,' wrote Anne Sexton to Tillie Olsen, 'I say (simply) Oh shit! But that's not very poetic.'[1]

'Whatever portion of the faculty of expressing what he thinks and feels we may suppose even the greatest Poet to possess,' wrote Wordsworth in the Preface to *Lyrical Ballads*, 'there cannot be a doubt but that the language which it will suggest to him must in liveliness and truth fall far short of that which is uttered by men in real life under the actual pressure of those passions, certain shadows of which the poet thus produces or feels to be produced in himself.'[2] So the fallacy of confessional poetry (if fallacy it is) is committed by Wordsworth rather than by the confessional poet herself. Both of them held the view that the true important origin of poetry lies in the emotional life of the poet, who is a man speaking to men – or as we would prefer to put it in these post-Plath, post-Sexton days – a human being speaking to people. Here is the origin of the demand that poetry should be sincere. Both realize that there are plenty of people with a profound emotional life who are not poets – including the poet when not writing; and that if poets are to be measured by their sincerity they must be compared with what the non-poets say when 'under the actual pressure' of their passions. Wordsworth – who was never tempted to say 'Oh shit' – seems (astonishingly) to believe they will be more eloquent than the poets. Sexton admits very bluntly that when not writing she is inarticulate. To believe that 'Oh shit' is less sincere, less indicative of being truly moved than 'All my Pretty Ones' or 'Tintern Abbey' would be a form of snobbery so extreme as to be repulsive. But not to believe it? Is that not to abolish poetry?

Here we have the central problem of the view of literature that regards it as the true voice of feeling, the expression of the poet's emotion, whose necessary (even if not sufficient) condition is sincerity. Clearly there is a demarcation dispute here. What is the territory on the other side of the frontier: that is, to what form of discourse are we comparing literature if we regard it as the expression of emotion? The most immediate, most extreme form is likely to be non-verbal – bodily gestures and contortions, gasps, sighs, laughter and weeping. I shall take 'cry' as the verb that most conveniently designates these, since 'crying' is conveniently ambiguous. It can refer to any emotional exclamation (one can cry out in pain or joy, fear or distress, triumph or anger), or to the particular emotion which we most associate with lyric poetry, sorrow or grief. This chapter is therefore about the overlap and differences between literature and crying.

Expression

First, for the origin of the theory. This is easy, surely, for it is the child of Romanticism. There are, to be sure, anticipations right back to Plato, Aristotle and Longinus, but they are unsystematic and even doubtful. Is the traditional doctrine of inspiration, for instance, the same as the doctrine of literature as the expression of emotion? When Socrates informs Ion that a poet cannot compose as long as he has his reason, is he suggesting that when inspired he is able to draw on his emotions instead? This might seem an obvious corollary to us, since we have internalized inspiration – what once came from being breathed on by the Muse now comes from gaining access to deeper levels of the self – just as we have internalized the gods who direct the action of Greek tragedy, so that Aphrodite becomes (what on one level she always was) a symbol for sexual passion. Would the *Ion* itself lead us to make this translation? Socrates asserts that the poem is given to the poet from outside, that the words are uttered by a god 'who speaks and expresses himself to us through the poet'. There is a suggestion, in the previous section, that this is a way of talking about emotion: Socrates describes how the rhapsode (the performer) 'breaks into tears at a sacrifice and festival', and Ion adds that the same happens to the audience: 'I can see them from up on the platform, weeping and looking fierce and marvelling at the tale'.[3] Plato explains this with the image of the chain: the Muse inspires (excites emotion in) the poet, who passes it to the rhapsode, and he to the audience.

Here we are dealing with emotion both as cause and as consequence of the work.

The image of the chain blurs this distinction, but if we are looking for expression theory it must be drawn. Before Wordsworth, Senancour or Whitman, there is plenty of emphasis on emotion, but it is always the emotion of the reader or the listener. When the emotive quality of literature is mentioned in eighteenth-century criticism, the poet is exhorted: 'Touche-moi, étonne-moi, déchire-moi; fais-moi tressaillir, pleurer, frémir, m'indigner d'abord.'[4] Before the Romantics, too, there is plenty of emphasis on the figure of the poet, but it is moral, not emotional: the true poet must, like the true orator, be a good man ('vir bonus dicendi peritus')[5] When Milton claims that the poet must himself 'be a true poem', he is thinking not in aesthetic but in moral terms: 'a composition and pattern of the best and honourablest things; not presuming to sing high praises of heroic men, or famous cities, unless he have in himself the experience and the practice of all that is praiseworthy.'[6]

For a straighforward account of the qualities needed to form the poet in traditional Renaissance theory, we can turn to Ben Jonson's *Timber*, whose list contains four items: a goodness of natural wit, or *ingenium*; the exercise of those parts, or *exercitatio*; imitation (*imitatio*), to be able to convert the substance or riches of another poet to his own use; and exactness of study and multiplicity of reading, *lectio*.[7] There is no suggestion, or even hint, that the poet's own emotional life, and his access to it, is relevant. No Romantic critic could have read this list without thinking it was a recipe for a competent versifier rather than a poet, that these admirable qualities would never lead to real poetry unless they found room for the true voice of feeling.

That phrase comes from Keats, who asked his friend Reynolds to 'pick out some lines from Hyperion, and put a mark + to the false beauty proceeding from art, and one / to the true voice of feeling'.[8] The usual opposite to true feeling, in poetry, would be 'artificiality'; by using the term 'art', which has no prejorative associations, Keats is, I take it, deliberately overstating his view that all that matters is feeling.

Let us start from some passages that are very obviously expressions of emotion.

O, Mother, Mother!
What have you done? Behold, the Heavens do ope,

The Gods looks down, and this unnatural scene
They laugh at. Oh my Mother, Mother: Oh!
You have won a happy victory to Rome.
But for your son, believe it: Oh believe it,
Most dangerously you have with him prevailed,
If not most mortal to him. But let it come.[9]

O cursed, cursed slave! Whip me, ye devils,
From the possession of this heavenly sight!
Blow me about in winds! Roast me in sulphur!
Wash me in steep-down gulfs of liquid fire!
O Desdemon! Dead Desdemon; dead. O!O![10]

I don't want to think – I needn't think. I don't care for anything but you, and that's enough for the present. It will last a little yet. Here on my knees, with you dying in my arms, I'm happier than I have been for a long time. And I want you to be happy – not to think of anything sad; only to feel that I'm near you and I love you. Why should there be pain? In such hours as this what have we to do with pain? That's not the deepest thing; there's something deeper.[11]

The moving speech in which Coriolanus breaks down and calls off the attack on Rome has no figurative language, yet no one could mistake it for prose. It works almost entirely through repetition and rhythm, the linguistic devices that most obviously convey emotion. Not only does Coriolanus make his own overmastering emotion clear, he appeals to Aufidius, who has heard his mother's plea, and who confirms him, for 'I was moved withal' clearly means 'And you must have been even more moved'.

The language of Othello's speech, in contrast, is rich, even extravagant, in its images, all of them for Hell. This need not in itself convey emotion, but along with the carefully placed imperatives, which control the rhythm, this shows that he is suffering the torments of the damned.

In the third passage, Isabel Archer, as her cousin Ralph Touchett lies dying, discovers – and confesses – the love she has always felt for him. It is not clear (it often isn't, with James) whether there is a sexual element in the love: probably not in Isabel's case, but one cannot be sure in Ralph's. Because there have always been reticences between them, and even moments when Isabel almost seemed to dislike him, the emotional release, when it comes, is profound and intense. Although it is in prose, it has as much repetition, and almost as marked a rhythm, as the verse passages.

It is hard to imagine writing that more completely gives itself to expressing emotion than these passages, yet there is an obvious problem. All three are spoken by fictitious characters, who are not poets. I have begun with these slanted examples in order to raise, from the outset, the question of genre. The theory of expression concerns the writer's emotion, but what do we know of Shakespeare's feelings towards his mother or towards his wife, of James's unconfessed love? Taken on their own, these passages seemed obviously expressive; placed in context, how can they be?

There are two solutions. One is to say that *Coriolanus*, *Othello* and *The Portrait of a Lady*, taken as wholes, are expressions of the emotion of Shakespeare and James. 'Great works of objective literature,' claims Middleton Murry, 'must, no less surely than the personal expression of the lyric poet or the confidential essayist, be referred back to a peculiar originating emotion.'[12] This must then mean that everything in the work is part of that expression – the riot of the citizens, Menenius' speech on the belly, Volumnia's conversations with Virgilia, the scheming of the tribunes. If Shakespeare was expressing emotion in writing *Coriolanus*, that emotion will not be easy to name. Middleton Murry admits that it will be 'infinitely complex, . . . infinitely difficult to define or to describe', and clearly there must in the writing of *Othello* or *Coriolanus* have been a thousand detailed decisions taken with little or no reference to this originating emotion. This will be even more true of a novel, with its complicated action, its comic, passionate or analytic parts, its ficelles and its main characters. In the end, it seems necessary to ask if we are saying anything useful by calling *The Portrait of a Lady* the expression of James's emotion.

The other solution is to say that plays and novels, at their most intense moments, tend to turn into lyric poems: that Shakespeare is writing a poem about his mother, James is pouring out a powerful feeling of suppressed love. This can be claimed on various levels of biographical indirectness. The simplest form will look for the woman (or man?) whom James loved, for whom he cherished a long and secret passion, or will postulate a deep Oedipal feeling and perhaps a hidden resentment of Shakespeare towards his mother, and in treating these passages as expressions of that will more or less ignore their place in the whole work. But the mechanisms of displacement could be very elaborate, and all we really need is to claim that some strong emotion is here being tapped.

It is clear that the expression theory has two levels of usefulness.

In the case of lyric poetry, in which the poem is offered as spoken by the poet himself in his own person, in which the obvious function is to present an emotion, the idea of expression can be directly applied. In the case of more elaborate literary forms, in which we hear the author's own voice obliquely if at all, the claim that what we are given is the expression of his emotion can only be true in a much more indirect sense, and its direct application will only be to certain very intensely emotional passages; and even on these, it will tell us nothing about their function in the work as a whole. What it can do is offer a reason for the intense power of such passages.

Confession and Poetry

That the lyric should press its emotional function to the point when it seems to turn into a cry became an orthodoxy for one school of poets in the 1950s. These are the 'confessional poets', Robert Lowell, Anne Sexton, Sylvia Plath (probably the three central figures), along with a few others: W.D. Snodgrass (who can actually claim to have been the first), Adrienne Rich (whose political commitment goes along with a strong confessional element), and that putter-on and taker-off of masks, John Berryman. Is confession, then, a kind of emotional outburst? If so, we must clearly rule out a closely related meaning of the term: the Roman Catholic practice of confession, which forms part of the sacrament of penance. This practice has a number of rigid depersonalizing conventions: the kneeling posture, the unseen priest, the setting in church, the imposing of penance, the granting of absolution. How this differs from the more immediately personal sense of confession is vividly illustrated by an episode in Hawthorne's novel *The Marble Faun*. When Hilda, living alone in Rome, is unable to bear any longer her burden of solitude and secret knowledge, she strays into St Peter's, and, earnest Protestant as she is, finds herself irresistibly drawn by the obvious emotional attractions of Popery. What attracts her most is confession, and finding that one of the confessionals is marked *Pro Anglice Lingua*, she cannot resist the temptation to kneel there and 'sob out all her troubles':

She did not think; she only felt. Within her heart was a great need. Close at hand, within the veil of the confessional, was the relief. She flung herself down in the penitent's place; and, tremulously, passionately, with sobs, tears, and the turbulent overflow of emotion too long repressed, she poured out the dark story which had infused its poison into her innocent life. . .

And, ah, what a relief! When the hysteric gasp, the strife between words and sobs, had subsided, what a torture had passed away from her soul![1]

The ensuing dialogue with the priest has its comic dimension, as he points out to her that she has completely mistaken the nature of confession, and that as a heretic she is not entitled to make use of it, or to receive absolution – not even to have her utterance treated as confidential. What she learns is that confession as ritual is quite different from confession as release; and in discussing the confessional poets I shall use the term only in Hilda's sense.

Since they are a clearly identified group, who knew one another, often well, and influenced one another's work, there is no difficulty in knowing who was and who was not a confessional poet. We can say that David Wright and Jenny Joseph, say, are not confessional poets, let alone D.H. Lawrence, Hopkins or Christina Rossetti, to say nothing of Donne, Herbert or Shakespeare. As a matter of literary history, confessional poetry was a particular movement, locateable in space and time with some precision. But is this simply a matter of terminology? Did this movement simply bring into explicit focus a tendency inherent in all lyric poetry, or did it attempt something beyond the range of earlier poets, something that derives from living in the latter twentieth century, perhaps even from being American?

A. Alvarez, who has been one of the leading apologists for the school, believes that this is so. For him, confessional poetry is essentially a response to our time:

If [McLuhan] is right, the old formal arts are no longer wholly meaningful and the artists are in imminent danger of being made redundant. For the impact of the 'electronic culture' threatens to shatter all the traditional disciplines which are worked so hard for, and acquired only slowly and with much difficulty. Suddenly, unexpectedly, they no longer seem of much use. To survive and communciate the artist may have to abandon his inheritance, his training, even his habits of mind, and start again from the beginning . . . in the face of this threatening transformation the Extremist style is the most courageous response.[2]

'Extremist' is Alvarez' preferred term, for, he explains, speaking of Lowell, 'though the subject-matter was largely the kind of material that is dug up in psycho-analysis, the poems were in no vulgar sense confessional.' Alvarez sees this group of poets as essentially modern, as extending the territory of poetry in a way that is only possible for the alienated consciousness of those who live in the age of conurbations, psychoanalysis and concentration camps. It is no accident that one of Alvarez' favourite terms of commendation, writing of modern poets, is 'breakthrough': for him, the extremist poets are valuable because they strive to find ways of colonizing new experience for poetry. The term derives from Sylvia Plath, who said in a BBC interview: 'I've been very excited by what I feel is the new breakthrough that came with say Robert Lowell's *Life Studies.* . . .This intense breakthrough into very serious very personal emotional experience, which I feel has been partly taboo.'[3] And Alvarez praises Sylvia Plath herself for breaking even further through:

Just as Lowell's poetry is an extension of the Romantic agony into modern, analytic terms, so Sylvia Plath's is a logical extension of Lowell's explorations: she simply went further in the direction he had already taken.[4]

This clearly assumes that literature progresses, or at least has to keep up with the times, that as society changes poets learn to do new things. 'Progress' is a misleading term, of course, since it is the horrors of our century that have demanded – and rendered possible – the breakthrough: this results in an ambivalent evaluation of a poetry that is on the one hand a symptom of our spiritual malaise but on the other creates something worthwhile by its ability to express it with such perfection – a *fleur du mal*.

In contrast to Alvarez' view we can set that of Donald Davie. In 'Sincerity and Poetry', Davie confesses (the word seems ironically apt) that he now wishes to abandon 'what seemed until a few years ago, the solidly achieved consensus of opinion about poetry and the criticism of poetry'; this is the rule (sic) 'that the "I" in a poem is *never* immediately and directly the poet; that the poet-in-his-poem is always distinct from . . . the poet as historically recorded.' This rule meant that the question 'is the poet sincere?' was always impertinent and illegitimate. It was a good rule, says Davie, for poetry in English written between 1550 and about 1790; 'but it illuminates little of the poetry in English written since 1780.' And in linking the reinstatement of 'sincerity' as a criterion with confessional poetry, with Lowell's *Life Studies* and Ginsberg's *Howl*, Davie is placing these poets, far more firmly than Alvarez, in the Romantic tradition. Confessional poetry, for Davie, is not linked with specifically twentieth-century horrors (he even wants to detach it from any necessary connection with horrors, claiming – with a slight affront to idiomatic usage – that one can confess to virtues as well as to vices); it is linked with the idea of poetry as a highly personal statement, not altogether detachable from the poet as biographical individual, an idea that has been with us ever since *Lyrical Ballads*.[5]

Now once we take the step from Alvarez' view to Davie's – from confessional poetry as a product of our own age, the age of war, psychoanalysis and urban distress, to confessional poetry as a product of Romantic emphasis on the individuality of the poet, an emphasis that was already with us in the utterly different Victorian world of peace, retrenchment and reform – we can at least consider taking the further step back to 1550 (I presume Davie chose that date because we don't read much poetry before Wyatt and Surrey). In principle, I don't see why we shouldn't go back to the beginnings of English poetry, or indeed to Sappho and Catullus. If therefore we ask how confessional poetry differs from other lyric poetry, and answer by means of comparisons spread over the whole history of poetry, we shall automatically address the question historically. After looking at the confessional poets themselves, we can look back at the nineteenth century, and ask if we have confessional poetry there; finally back to the Renaissance and ask if we had it there. If the answer to the last question is no, then Davie is right. If the answer to both questions is no, then Alvarez is right.

Mere Confession

Poetry readers who are old enough grew up with Thomas Hood's 'I remember' as a favourite anthology piece:

I remember, I remember
   The house where I was born,
The little window where the sun
   Came peeping in at morn;
He never came a wink too soon,
   Nor brought too long a day,
But now, I often wish the night

Had borne my breath away. . . .

I remember, I remember
  The fir-trees dark and high;
I use to think their slender tops
  Were close against the sky
It was a childish ignorance,
  But now 'tis little joy
To know I'm farther off from heaven
  Than when I was a boy.[6]

It is not dificult to indicate why poems like this are out of favour
today. The childhood reminiscence is patently in the service of a
sentimental religiosity and a naïve view of childhood innocence,
and such religiosity commands little respect among poetry readers.
What singled out Hood's poem from innumerable other children-
are-close-to-Heaven poems was its apparent autobiographical
content, its claim to authenticity; and it is precisely this which
might make the modern reader dislike it most, as he observes that
there is hardly any real remembering in this poem of reminiscence:
the 'violets and the lily-cups' are stereotypical, not remembered,
flowers; the sun comes 'peeping' because to it has been transferred
some of the coyness of the poem itself. It comes as no surprise to
turn up a scholarly edition of Hood's poems and learn that Hood
was born in the heart of London, and that the idyllic landscape
'should   be   considered   a   poetic   not   an   autobiographical'
reminiscence.

  How is the modern poet to react against this tradition if he wants
to write about his childhood? Larkin's method is to parody it.
Calling attention to the tradition by naming his poem 'I remember,
I remember', he describes how he accidentally revisits his birthplace
('where my childhood was unspent') and recalls a series of non-
memories:

By now I've got the whole place clearly charted.
Our garden first, where I did not invent
Blinding theologies of flowers and fruits,
And wasn't spoken to by an old hat. . .
  . . . I'll show you, come to that,
The bracken where I never trembling sat,
Determined to go through with it; where she
Lay back, and 'all became a burning mist'.[7]

The content here mocked is not Victorian sentimentality but Lawrentian intensity; but the form of mockery relates the poem to all previous childhood reminiscences in much the same way that Shakespeare's 130th sonnet ('My mistress' eyes are nothing like the sun') is related to the Petrarchan catalogue of beauties. And just as Shakespeare's poem tells us nothing about what his mistress is actually like, so Larkin tells us nothing about his own childhood. By making fun first of locking the act of reminiscence into a stereotype, and then of a stereotype posterior to and quite different from Hood's, it extends its parody forward in time, so that it is not too much to claim that it is parodying poems (by Lowell and Sexton) that had not yet been written.

What then would a genuine (modern, sordid) childhood reminiscence be like?

St Marks 1933

The fourth form dining-table
Was twenty feet by four,
six boys to a side;
at one end, Mr Prendie the Woodchuck,
dead to the world, off picking daisies;
at the other end, another boy.
Mid-meal, they began
to pull me apart
'Why is he always grubbing in his nose?'
'Because his nose is always snotty.'
'He likes to wipe his thumb in it.'
'Cal's a creep of the first water.'
'He had a hard-on for his first shower.'
'He only presses his trousers once a term.'
'Every other term.' 'No term.'

Over the years I've lost
the surprise and sparkle of that slang
our abuse made perfect.
'Dimbulb.' 'Fogbound.' 'Droopydrawers.'
'The man from the Middle West.'
'Cal is a slurp.'
'A slurp farts in the bathtub.'
'So he can bite the bubbles.'
How did they say my face

was pearl-grey like toe-jam –
that I was foul
as the gymsocks I wore a week?
A boy next to me breathed my shoes,
and lay choking on the bench.
'Cal doesn't like everyone.'
'Everyone doesn't like Cal.'
'Cal,
who is your best friend at this table?'
'Lowell, Low-ell'
(*to the tune of Noel, Noel*).

This was it, though I bowdlerize . . .
All term I had singled out classmates,
and made them listen to and remember
the imperfections of their friends.
I broke one on the other –
but who could break them,
they were so many,
rich, smooth and loved?

I was fifteen;
they made me cry in public.
Chicken?

Perhaps they had reason . . .
even now
my callous unconscious drives me
to torture my closest friend.

Huic ergo parce, Deus.[8]

There is no explicit parody or literary reference here: it is too busy
remembering. And there is no form either: it is too busy
remembering. The only thing that can be called form is the echoing
off each other of the boys' remarks ('once a term. Every other
term. No term.'), and that form comes from the boys, not from the
poem, which sounds, and probably is, mimetic at this point. To
that extent he has not lost all the 'surprise and sparkle of that slang',
but elsewhere in the poem he has either lost it totally, or is
revealing how drearily predictable it was ('dead to the world, off
picking daisies'). That a poem so undistinguished in its diction

should mention that the slang was surprising and sparkling is an almost suicidal device, since it invites us to think that the writing is not even as good as fifteen-year-old schoolboy slang.

Carefully, ploddingly factual ('twenty feet by four, six boys to a side' takes us straight back to Wordsworth's notorious 'I've measured it from side to side, 'Tis six feet long and four feet wide'), the poem is clearly trying to sound like an actual memory, matching the mimesis of the remembered rhythm with further accuracy of remembering (he still knows what the tune was). Then, when the memory is over, the poet confesses to his own complicity in the humiliating experience (so making it more humiliating still) and concludes by confessing that the complicity continues still:

even now
my callous unconscious drives me
to torture my closest friend.

This is the psychological lingua franca of modern self-observation: there is nothing distinctive about the sentence, which could conclude a thousand different self analyses, all of which could speak of 'torturing', of a 'callous unconscious', and (most unthinking, most revealing of clichés) 'drives'.

Here, surely, we have all the characteristics of confession: factual accuracy of remembering, self-centredness, self-abasement expressed in clichés. And – arguably – none of the characteristics of poetry. This poem treats poetry as Hilda treated the practice of confession in St Peter's. It goes without saying that the choice of this poem does not do justice to Lowell: I have chosen, as one of the limit cases for the argument, an instance where confessional poetry becomes, quite simply, confession.

Anne Sexton and the Practice of Confession

Confessional poetry being a practice, not just the subject of individual poems, we ought to turn now to a body of work, and the choice of poet almost makes itself. No poet was more consistently and uniformly confessional than Anne Sexton, and her name has almost become identified with the genre.

Take, for instance, 'The Double Image'. This poem in seven parts is addressed to her daughter Joyce, who was taken from her and brought up by her mother-in-law, because of her mental illness

and her inability to look after the child herself. The title refers to
the portrait of Anne which was painted 'instead' and the portrait of
her mother, angry and unforgiving ('On the first of September she
looked at me / and said I gave her cancer'), which hung opposite
each other at the top of the stairs ('She eyes me from that face, /
that stony head of death'). The poem is filled with facts about the
poet's life and mental history: her age and her daughter's, specific
locations ('I came to my mother's house in Gloucester,
Massachusetts'), specific incidents ('once I mailed you a picture of a
rabbi / and a post card of Motif number one, / as if it were normal /
to be a mother and be gone'), facts about her illness, often tersely
stated (I . . . tried a second suicide' . . . 'I checked out for the last
time / on the first of May'); it is also filled with images for her
mental distress:

– Ugly angels spoke to me. The blame
  I heard them say, was mine. They tattled
  Like green witches in my head, letting doom
  leak like a broken faucet –

and with images for her love for her daughter and the joy of
reunion; and along with that, analyses of her own motives in
wanting the child back:

I, who was never quite sure
about being a girl, needed another
life, another image to remind me.
And this was my worst guilt; you could not cure
nor soothe it. I made you to find me.[9]

The poem was modelled on W.D. Snodgrass's 'Heart's Needle'[10]
about his separation from his daughter because of divorce, which
Anne Sexton was deeply influenced by, and which, she claimed,
made her write this poem about her own similar experience, and
even led her to demand her daughter back (so poetry does influence
life, after all! But perhaps only the life of poets). 'The Double
Image' is certainly representative of her first three volumes, which
contain her best and her most clearly confessional work. The world
which these volumes establish is easily described: it is a world of
mental illness, with details of admission into hospital, suicide
attempts, medical treatment, and also images for the terrifying
experiences themselves:

This August I began to dream of drowning. The dying
went on and on in water as white and clear
as the gin I drank each day at half-past five.
Going down for the last time, the last breath lying,
I grapple with eels like ropes – it's ether, it's queer
and then, at last, it's done. Now the scavengers arrive
the hard crawlers who come to clean up the ocean floor.
And death, that old butcher, will bother me no more.[11]

It is a world of family love and conflict, describing her childhood,
her often hostile feelings towards her mother (and her insistence on
her mother's hostility to her), and her love for her own daughters,
her re-enactment of their pain. When her trip to Europe is
described, her crossing of the Atlantic reminds her of her mother's
similar voyage, her time in Paris reminds her of 'Nana' (a beloved
great-aunt):

I read your Paris letters of 1890.
Each night I take them to my thin bed
and learn them as an actress learns her lines.[12]

Also prominent in this world is an intermittent religious concern,
which leads her to compare herself with Jesus Christ (this became
much more prominent in her later work), not as a way of finding
redemption and consolation, but as a way of suggesting that Jesus
too was crazy and suffered ('I sat in a tunnel when I was five. . .
Maybe Jesus knew my tunnel / and crawled right through to the
river / so he could wash all the blood off'),[13] even of seeing herself
as exceptional ('I'm no more a woman / than Christ was a man').[14]
And, finally, there is a concern (also intermittent, also intense) with
the physiology of being a woman: she writes about sex,
menstruation, childbirth with total openness.

It is not difficult to see why this material is called 'confessional',
but when we try to say why we can notice that there are two,
possibly three, reasons not necessarily connected with each other.
First, there is the factual element: she provides plenty of
biographical detail, identifies the members of her family, states the
time and place of many of the episodes, not attempting to disguise
the fact that all these things happened to the poet-outside-the-
poems. That is one meaning of 'confessional'. Second, there is the
sordid, often degrading nature of the experiences: she confesses to
pain as well as joy and (more difficult) to experiences that deprive

her of dignity in her suffering – precisely what one is normally most ashamed to own up to. That is another meaning of 'confessional'. And then there is a peculiar and disturbing intensity in the language, an attempt to render raw and disturbing experience through ugly and disturbing images that do not always seem to be under control ('grapple with eels like ropes'); and along with this, a deliberate jokiness, a shrugging off of her own suffering as something melodramatic:

Sleepmonger,
deathmonger,
with capsules in my palm each night,
eight at a time from sweet pharmaceutical bottles
I make arrangements for a pint-sized journey.[15]

This is the quality that makes Sexton most like Plath, and it too could be called confessional (or even, because of the self-dramatizing, 'confessional').

Anne Sexton's poetry aroused intense responses. Reviewers disliked the thrusting upon them of such intimate details: 'These are not poems at all,' writes Charles Gullans, 'and I feel that I have, without right or desire, been made a third party to her conversations with her psychiatrist. It is painful, embarrassing and irritating.'[16] 'Art requires more than emotional indulgence,' writes Patricia Meyer Spacks.[17] At the same time audiences (supported by some enthusiastic reviewers) gave her standing ovations at readings, judges showered literary prizes on her and psychiatrists (though some might hold that this confirms Spacks's point) used her poems as therapeutic material with their own patients. Clearly all this brouhaha was set off by the confessional element.

But on the other hand, Sexton herself sometimes insisted that confession is not art, and that a poem needs to depart from factual truth and raw emotion. 'I'll often confess to things that never happened,' she writes, and she did on occasion alter the facts when writing. Thus 'The Double Image' makes no mention of her elder daughter 'because the dramatic point was I had one child and was writing to her', and also takes liberties with the facts of how often she went into hospital. More striking is the fact that there are a few fictitious poems in the volumes that do not sound very different from the confessions. 'Two Sons', for instance, is a bitter resentful poem spoken by a woman to the two sons who have married without telling her beforehand, sending home 'silly postcards' to announce the fact,

one of them written in grease
as you undid her dress
in Mexico, the other airmailed to Boston from Rome.[18]

Almost every reader of Anne Sexton knows that she had daughters not sons, but if we can postulate a reader who was ignorant of the biography, he would not, surely, perceive this poem as any different from the others.

Fiction is only the most obvious, and not necessarily the most complete way of detatching oneself from one's own experience. Anne Sexton's ambivalence on the need for such detachment is clear. On the one hand, she claims 'if you could just document the imagination, experiences, everything, even some wit, whatever, of one life, one life, however long it may last, it might be of some value', and says of her work, 'It was not a planned thing. . . I was just writing, and what I was writing was what I was feeling, and that's what I needed to write.' On the other hand, when she sent Snodgrass the as yet unpublished 'Double Image', she asked anxiously 'if you think this works, if it has a reason for its violence, a reason for being written (or rather read) aside from my own need to make form from chaos.'[19]

Forms of Courage

The content of John Berryman's *Dream Songs* is not very different from Sexton's poetry: mental illness, depression and exhilaration, emotional intimacy (with friends, in his case, not family), self-doubt and self-abasement; but they are not written in the first person. His speaker is Henry, whom he described as 'an imaginary character, not the poet, not me, . . . who has suffered an irreversible loss and talks about himself, sometimes in the first person, sometimes in the third, sometimes even in the second'.[20] Many of Berryman's critics have smiled sceptically at this, insisting that Henry clearly 'is' Berryman, finding the protest charming but claiming they are not deceived. But was Berryman intending to deceive? Is his statement a denial of the biographical source and factual correctness of Henry's confessions, or is it an account of a poetic strategy, one that may indeed have in itself a mimetic element, for one of the oldest of all confessional devices is to begin 'a friend of mine' or 'I've got this friend', and it is not at all certain that the usefulness of the device depends on its being believed. Clearly it requires a kind of courage to begin 'I' instead of 'my friend', but it is not quite the same kind of courage as that required to tell what happened: we can call them pronoun courage and narrative courage, and the absence of the first may enable the second.

To some confessional poets pronoun courage is important, to others not. Adrienne Rich, who clearly feels she has moved into being a confessional poet, says of her early sequence, 'Snap-shots of a Daughter-in-Law', 'I hadn't yet found the courage to do without authorities, or even to use the pronoun "I" – the woman in the poems is always "she".'[21] Yet Berryman's disturbing creation of Henry, the persona who occasionally when mocked turns into Mr Bones, and holds dialogues with himself, certainly doesn't sound like cowardice: the poems would not be better if the speaker were always a simple 'I', they would be less challenging, less exploratory. It is not certain that Berryman's disclaimer disguises or is meant to disguise the biographical origin of much of the material in the poems.

Here we have the beginnings of a terminology. Let us accept that the writing of a confessional poem is an act of courage. The kinds of courage required will then resemble the kinds of material that we have already surveyed as constituting the subject matter of Sexton's poetic world. Narrative courage will allow the retelling of particular incidents in all their specificness, and will include the mentioning of those factual details that make an episode sound real: whether these details are factually true or invented is exactly the same kind of decision as whether the first or third person is used, and the courage required could be called either factual courage or pronoun courage – I choose the latter phrase because of the way it draws attention to poetic strategy. Finding the imagery to confess to the feelings of disgust, self-hatred and despair that makes these poems so challenging is also an act of courage, but of a different kind, and I shall call it emotional courage. Turn back for a moment to Anne Sexton's lines already quoted: 'This August I began to dream of drowning. . .' Which requires more courage, to talk about the gin you drink each day at half-pat five, or to say that you grapple with eels like ropes? That may be a matter of temperament: what is certain is that only the latter could be said to require any talent.

Armed with this terminology, let us now move back in time. We

can find a similar contrast between Lawrence and Yeats. After a
quarrel with Frieda, Lawrence walked out into the night to nurse
his anger and fear:

Tonight I have left her alone,
They would have it I have left her for ever.

O my God, how it aches
Where she is cut off from me!

Perhaps she will go back to England.
Perhaps she will go back,
Perhaps we are parted for ever. . . .

The image of her being cut off from him is repeated frequently, and
provides the poem's title ('Mutilation'). It concludes:

A cripple!
Oh God, to be mutilated!
To be a cripple!

And if I never see her again?

I think, if they told me so
I could convulse the heavens with my horror.
I think I could alter the frame of things in my agony.
I think I could break the system with my heart.
I think, in my convulsion, the skies would break.

She too suffers
But who could compel her, if she chose me against them all?
She has not chosen me finally, she suspends her choice.
Night folk, Tuatha De Danaan, dark Gods, govern her sleep,
Magnificent ghosts of the darkness, carry off her
    decision in sleep,
Leave her no choice, make her lapse meward, make her,
Oh Gods of the living Darkness, powers of Night.[22]

On a very different road, Crazy Jane met the Bishop:

I met the Bishop on the road
And much said he and I

'Those breasts are flat and fallen now,
Those veins must soon be dry;
Live in a heavenly mansion,
Not in some foul sty.'[23]

Lawrence has pronoun courage: it is (in both senses) painfully
obvious that he is telling us the truth. He also has narrative courage:
he wants us to know that there was a quarrel, that he is filled with
anger, self-pity and helplessness. The self presented to us is not as
physically repulsive as Lowell's schoolboy self; whether it is
spiritually as unattractive will depend on which we dislike more,
malice or self-pity. Whereas Lowell grovels by looking back and
telling us how despicable he was (and still is), Lawrence writes – or
feigns to write – while still in the grip of the emotion. Both poems
are totally formless. Both poems when it comes to finding a
language for the emotional intensity, offer only cliché: 'convulse the
heavens', 'alter the frame of things', 'break the system' (Lowell, it
will be recalled, told us of his 'callous unconscious').

Yeats, like Berryman, writes crisply and economically, the
persona of Crazy Jane serving much the same function as that of
Henry: it both diguises and reveals. Our knowledge that the poet is
not an old woman with flat breasts makes it easier for him to defy
respectability and assert his acceptance of filth: 'Love has pitched his
mansion in / The place of excrement'. And in both poets, the
tighter writing does not involve any loss of the colloquial: each of
these poets can create a rhythmic pattern without any loss of speech
rhythm.

I will drop all pretence of neutrality at this point, and say that we
have been looking at the difference between mere confession, and
confessional poetry.

The Case for Self-Pity

Now let us move back further in time, to the nineteenth century:

Twice

I took my heart in my hand
  (O my love, O my love),
I said: Let me fall or stand,
  Let me live or die,
But this once hear me speak ·

(O my love, O my love) –
Yet a woman's words are weak;
  You should speak, not I.

You took my heart in your hand
  With a friendly smile,
With a critical eye you scanned,
  Then set it down,
And said: It is still unripe,
  Better wait awhile;
Wait while the skylarks pipe,
  Till the corn grows brown.

As you set it down it broke –
  Broke, but I did not wince;
I smiled at the speech you spoke,
  At your judgement that I heard:
But I have not often smiled
  Since then, nor questioned since,
Nor cared for corn-flowers wild,
  Nor sung with the singing bird.

I take my heart in my hand,
  O my God, O my God,
My broken heart in my hand:
  Thou hast seen, judge Thou.
My hope was written on sand,
  O my God, O my God:
Now let Thy judgement stand –
  Yea, judge me now.

This contemned of a man,
  This marred one heedless day,
This heart take Thou to scan
  Both within and without:
Refine with fire its gold,
  Purge thou its dross away –
Yea, hold it in Thy hold,
  Whence none can pluck it out.

I take my heart in my hand –
  I shall not die, but live –

Before thy face I stand;
    I, for Thou callest such:
All that I have I bring,
    All that I am I give,
Smile Thou and I shall sing,
    But shall not question much.[24]

There is a case to be put up that this is not a confessional poem. Pronoun courage it has, and the fact that the poet omitted it from *The Prince's Progress* in 1866, and indeed did not publish it in her lifteime, suggests that she thought of it as too intimate. Yet there is no reason to think that Christina Rossetti ever made a declaration of love to a man that was refused, so it could be said to lack narrative courage. What of emotional courage, the most important of the three? Here the answer is difficult. The poem surely is deeply true to the poet's emotional development: it shows the parallelism and interconnections between the sexual love she was clearly capable of and the love of God, whether we take the former as an incarnation of the latter, or the latter as a sublimation of the former. What it also shows is her stoicism, her refusal to indulge in self-pity, and the willingness of her final submission. The stoicism is presented with a visible tightening of the lip ('But shall not question much') which clearly implies the intensity of the feeling being suppressed, and it is arguable that the poem gains its power not from the explicit stoicism but from the implicit grief and despair. To have surrendered to these would have meant self-pity; but so explicitly not to surrender to them leads to the clichés of renunciation, ('Refine with fire its gold, / Purge thou its dross away'), and arguably weakens the poetic force.

   To say this is to come close to suggesting that self-pity can be a poetic virtue; yet the most serious critics of Anne Sexton tended to say just the opposite. Here is Patricia Meyer Spacks:

The verse implicitly argues that anguish is self-justifying, neither permitting nor demanding the further pain of balanced self-knowledge or the illuminations of controlled imagination and poetic technique. In life we forgive sufferers the necessities of their obsessions. In literature we must ask more: acknowledging the pain that produces such work as Anne Sexton's later poems, yet remembering that art reqires more than emotional indulgence, requires a saving respect for disciplines and realities beyond the crying needs, the unrelenting appetites, of the self.[25]

The critic appeals to a criterion that is an intimate blend of the aesthetic and the moral – indeed, earlier in the review she actually remarks that the poems display 'an apparent incapacity for self-criticism either moral or aesthetic', and the balancing (as if they were equivalents) of 'balanced self-knowledge' with the purely aesthetic, even technical requirement of 'the illuminating of . . . poetic technique' clearly implies an equivalence between moral and aesthetic control. Spacks is actually reviewing the posthumous *45 Mercy Street*, and I am sure she is right in preferring the earlier poetry, and finding it more controlled. To many critics (to Leavis and his followers, for instance) it is self-evident that artistic success is a moral achievement. Though I respect this position, my uneasiness at the way it is formulated can be indicated by saying that it would clearly lead us to prefer Christina Rossetti's poem to anything by Anne Sexton, even to this:

Music Swims Back to Me

Wait Mister. Which way is home?
They turned the light out
and the dark is moving in the corner.
There are no sign posts in this room,
four ladies, over eighty,
in diapers every one of them.
La la la, Oh music swims back to me
and I can feel the tune they played
the night they left me
in this private institution on a hill.

Imagine it. A radio playing
and everyone here was crazy.
I liked it and danced in a circle.
Music pours over the sense
and in a funny way
music sees more than I.
I mean it remembers better;
remembers the first night here.
It was the strangled cold of November;
even the stars were strapped in the sky
and that moon too bright
forking through the bars to stick me
with a singing in the head.
I have forgotten all the rest.

They lock me in this chair at eight a.m.
and there are no signs to tell the way,
just the radio beating to itself
and the song that remembers
more than I. Oh, la la la,
this music swims back to me.
The night I came I danced a circle
and was not afraid.
Mister?[26]

This may be Anne Sexton's finest poem. It was also her first
confessional poem ('her first breakaway from adolescent lyrics in
rhyming iambic pentameter,' says Maxine Kumin),[27] and the fact
that her first confessional poem was never later surpassed no doubt
tells us something about the confessional mode. Though the
situation in this poem is hinted at, not stated, the essential details
are not difficult to supply: the speaker is in a mental hospital,
probably for the second time, remembering an earlier occasion
when, left alone, she danced in a circle by herself. The emotion is
clear too: she is very frightened, as is most brilliantly conveyed by
the choked-off movement of the first line and the last. The asylum
is mentioned in nervous euphemisms ('ladies', 'this private
institution on a hill') that try to cope with the fear by putting it
aside. And counterpointed against the choked movement of fear is
the rhythm of the music that swims back to her.
    Surely we can contrast this with 'Twice' by saying that the earlier
poem balances grief and despair against acceptance in what is clearly
a moral act; and 'Music Swims Back to Me' balances fear against
frenetic excitement in what is more like a surrender to the tensions
of experience. The result, for me, is that though I can admire
'Twice' more, I can be more moved and disturbed by Sexton's
poem. To say this is (surely) to question the equivalence of
'balanced self-knowledge' and 'the illuminations of controlled
imagination and poetic technqiue'; 'Music Swims Back to Me' is
just as much about 'the crying needs, the unrelenting appetites of
the self' as is Sexton's worst poem. I conclude from this
comparison that Christina Rossetti is, in one important sense, not
yet a confessional poet, and (more controversially) that this is a
limitation in her art. She might write more disturbingly for a touch
more self-pity.

Shame

Now I move back another twenty years to Elizabeth Browning's *Sonnets from the Portuguese*, privately printed in 1847, and included in her works three years later. They are a series of forty-four love poems written to her husband, and since her letters to Robert were all scrupulously preserved and posthumously published, we have the opportunity of comparing two renderings, in prose and verse, of the same situation.

Nearly a year ago! how the time passes! If I had 'done my duty' like the enchanted fish leaping on the gridiron, and seen you never again after that first visit, you would have forgotten all about me by this day. Or at least 'that prude' I should be! Somewhere under your feet, I should be put down by this day! . . .

Well, I do think of it sometimes as you see. Which proves that I love you better than myself by the whole width of the Heavens: the sevenfold Heavens. Yet I think again how He of the heavens and earth brought us together so wonderfully, holding two souls in His hand. If my fault was in it, my will at least was not. Believe it of me, dear dearest, that I who am as clear-sighted as other women, . . . and not more humble (as to the approaches of common men), was quite resolutely blind when *you* came – I could not understand the possibility of *that*. . .

How one writes and writes over and over the same thing! But day by day the same sun rises, . . . over, and over, and nobody is tired. May God bless you, dearest of all, and justify what has been by what shall be, . . . and let me be free of spoiling any sun of yours! Shall you ever tell me in your thoughts, I wonder, to get out of your sun? No – no – Love keeps love too safe! and I have faith, you see, as a grain of mustard-seed![28]

Beloved, my Beloved, when I think
That thou wast in the world a year ago,
What time I sat alone here in the snow
And saw no footprint, heard the silence sink
No moment at thy voice, but, link by link,
Went counting all my chains as if that so
They never could fall off at any blow
Struck by thy possible hand, – why thus I drink
Of life's great cup of wonder! Wonderful
Never to feel thee thrill the day or night
With personal act or speech, – nor ever cull
Some prescience of thee with the blossoms white

Thou sawest growing! Antheists are as dull
Who cannot guess God's presence out of sight.[29]

It is clear that these two texts are not related as source to poem: the
letter is so complex and variegated that it is as much a *text* as the
poem, as much, that is, of a rendering of experience that in itself is
inaccesible to us. This makes the comparison richer, not poorer,
as we can easily see if we compare Elizabeth Barrett's letters with
Anne Sexton's, which command a far thinner range of verbal
resources and come closer to providing us simply with factual
statements of where the poems start, that is, are more like sources
– and for that reason offer a less fruitful comparison with the
poems.

How do letter and poem differ? First, there is the much greater
range of tone in the letter, whose linguistic register moves from
'the sevenfold Heavens' – inserted as an exclamatory pause to
convey awe – to 'enchanted fish', a playful touch of folktale, pulled
in as a reminder of the everyday, mischievous mood of the woman.
In comparison with this, the poem maintains a uniform high style:
to convey awe it uses a complex period ('Wonderful / Never to feel
thee. . .') rather than a pause, a change of rhythm and an
exclamation. Then there is the matter of self-presentation. Humble
towards Robert, she is jauntily self-confident about herself *per se*, in
a way that the poem cannot encompass. As far as explicit
statements of love and its analogy with religious faith is concerned,
both texts are very explicit, but the hint conveyed in the last line
and a half of the poem would be too much for the letter: to
compare Robert Browning to God would be outrageous in a letter
beginning 'Dear Robert' and signed with her name: only in the
relative impersonality of the love poem can it be ventured on. The
'Beloved' of the poem is not quite as definitely Robert Browning as
is the 'dear dearest' of the letter.

That Elizabeth Browning felt the poems to be quite as intimate as
the letters is made clear by the charmingly dated anecdote of how
she gave them to Browning:

One day, early in 1847, their breakfast being over, Mrs Browning went
upstairs, while her husband stood at the window watching the street till
the table should be cleared. He was presently aware of some one behind
him, although the servant was gone. It was Mrs Browning, who held him
by the shoulder to prevent his turning to look at her, and at the same time

pushed a packet of papers into the pocket of his coat. She told him to read that, and to tear it up if he did not like it: and then she fled again to her own room.[30]

If her shame was so intense, how did she come to publish the poems? We know that it required some persuasion by Robert, but she yielded. She adopted the strategy of claiming that they were translations: a thin diguise that like Berryman's persona 'deceived no one', yet is important as a poetic strategy, suggesting that the speaker of the poems must be seen as part of the tradition of romantic love and the idealization of the beloved. The fiction is immediately destroyed by the presence of the poet's (female) name on the title page – destroyed biographically, that is. That leaves us with two ways of reading the poems, the Petrarchan (which assumes the speaker to be a man) and the biographical (the speaker as a submissive wife), and the strongest achievement of the poems is the joining of these two. Portuguese is just the right choice of language – remote enough for almost every reader to be unable to verify if they *are* translations, yet the sort of language in which such poems might well have been written – a much better choice than her original suggestion of 'from the Bosnian', though that, given the unlikeliness of even so learned an author knowing a remote Slav tongue, would surely have been an even more transparent fiction. To the question, how did she bring herself to publish poems of which she was so ashamed that she could only give them to her husband when his back was turned, the answer is clear: she regarded them as confessional poems, and believed (or could be persuaded to believe) that love poetry *is* confessional, and therefore she had no right to conceal it.

But the poems do not after all open the door into the bedroom – ·or the bathroom. There is nothing like Anne Sexton's poem 'Menstruation at Forty' (which for some critics was the last straw: 'she dwells insistently on the pathetic or disgusting aspects of bodily experience,' complained James Dickey). Would this subject have seemed less or more intimate to Elizabeth Browning than the intense submissiveness of wifely love? The question is obviously absurd, since it could never have occurred to her to write on such a subject – though there are moments in Anne Sexton's poems that would certainly have seemed acceptable to her, and could easily be turned into the poetic idiom of the 1840s – indeed, are perhaps already in it:

In two days it will be my birthday
and as always the earth is done with its harvest. . .

or

I would have possessed you before all women
calling your name,
calling you mine.[31]

(The modern poet, writing in free verse, is able to stick more
closely here to the biblical rhythms; and poetically this is surely not
an advantage.)

There is no element of confession involved in admitting to bodily
processes: the embarrassment or repulsion this poem would have
aroused in Elizabeth Browning (and, no doubt, still arouses in
many modern readers) is quite different from the shame of speaking
of married love. It is the shame of disgust, not of intimacy. Indeed,
'Menstruation at Forty' becomes a poem precisely in so far as it
moves from the physiology to questions of motherhood and
emotional involvement.

Confession is something that causes us shame. Real confession
will cause shame because we have done wrong, confessional poetry
deals with experience that it is deeply painful to bring into public,
not because it is disgusting, nor because it is sinful, but because it is
intensely private. Which experiences cause this shame changes as
the culture changes, but shame itself is a universal experience. It
was at least as hard for Elizabeth Browning to own to her passion
as for Anne Sexton to own to the mysteries of her body. In that
sense, she is quite as much of a confessional poet.

The Rhetoric of Confession

Finally, and perforce briefly, a glimpse behind the Romantics:

Alas 'tis true, I have gone here and there,
And made myself a motley to the view,
Gored mine own thoughts, sold cheap what is most dear,
Made old offences of affections new.
Most true it is that I have looked on truth
Askance and strangely. But by all above,
These blenches gave my heart another youth,
And worse essays proved thee my best of love.

Now all is done, have what shall have no end –
Mine appetite I never more will grind
On newer proof, to try an older friend,
A god in love, to whom I am confined.
　　Then give me welcome, next my heav'n the best,
　　Ev'n to thy pure and most most loving breast.[32]

Can a Renaissance sonnet, written within so fixed and familiar a set
of conventions, ever be seen as a personal confession? The usual
answer of the literary historians is no: the poet must be seen as
having dropped into the role of sonneteer and lover, and even the
claim that he has brushed aside the conventions ('look in thy heart
and write') became in its turn a convention.

But this is as much of an oversimplification as the romantic view
which ignores convention altogether. The subsuming of biographical author into conventionalized speaker is a double-edged
argument: if the former cannot be detached from the latter, the
latter too cannot be detached from the former. Take for instance the
first two lines: are they to be attributed to a conventionalized
persona? The question is astonishingly complicated, the first
complication being whether 'made myself a motley to the view'
refers to the profession of acting or simply means 'made a fool of
myself in public' (Stephen Booth insists that the latter is the
primary meaning, but concedes that the former is possible – and
virtually every reader of this sonnet has known that the author was
an actor). In both cases, surely, the reference is biographical:
Shakespeare's profession is certainly a fact about the man, not
normally suggested by the persona of the doting lover – and nor is
the detailed account of shame so bitingly spelt out by the next two
lines. The degradation here is not unlike that which Lowell and
Sexton confess to ('I am only a coward / Crying me me me'). Yet
even this painful admission is made as part of a rhetorical strategy:
the balanced placing of the words shows the poet in perfect control
(there would be names in Puttenham for most of the verbal
devices). Yet the subject is unable to control his behaviour. The
union of the two, inextricable but distinct, makes up the persona.

Then, in the sixth line, comes 'But by all above'. That must
mean 'I really mean this': offering the gesture of breaking out of the
persona, though the breaking out does not (as it might in Lowell)
require a breaking of the surface texture of the poem, an
abandonment of rhyme or metre or rhetorical strategies. Of course
the poem cannot escape from the persona, but it is important to

notice that it tries. Shakespeare's sonnets are not like the sonnets of Daniel (or even Ronsard), a series of beautiful variations on conventional themes, addressed to a Delia or a Rosemarie who may well not have existed. Shakespeare gives no idealizing name to either the young man or the mistress, and behind the sequence we get fragmentary glimpses of a situation that is never explained. If that were an invented fiction, we should be astonished at how incompetent the invention was, especially from a poet of such obvious competence; what it sounds like is a real-life situation that some readers know about, and others will have to put up with not knowing, and this fits with the circumstances of 'publication' ('his sugared sonnets among his private friends'). This is very like Lowell writing *For Lizzie and Harriet* without bothering to tell us who Lizzie and Harriet are, and indicates the sense in which both Shakespeare and Lowell are coterie poets (clearly confession is more likely among coterie poets than others). But the work of a coterie poet is always available to those beyond the coterie, and the way in which they guess at the esoteric facts (or disdain to guess at them, and universalize the poem), will be determined both by the reader's predilections, by the strategies of the poems themselves, and by the assumptions of the age. In the 1590s, you would have to ask someone who knew someone who knew the poet. Today the higher journalism does this for you, and anyone can join the coterie.

I am claiming that there is confession in the sonnet as certainly as there is in Sexton or Lowell, but that it cannot be separated from the rhetoric. The fact that there is very little detail of his behaviour (what did he actually say to his friends that made him such a motley to the view?) means that the poem lacks what I called narrative courage, but does not make it less intimate. The lack of specificity was a defect in the case of 'I remember, I remember', because vagueness led so easily to cliché, but it could not possibly be seen as a defect in the iron control of this technique, where everything builds up to revealing the shame of the first part and the irony of the second. Because the confessional element is inextricable from the poetic devices, the agonized question of Anne Sexton – 'if it has a reason for its violence, a reason for being written (or rather read) aside from my own need to make form from chaos' – would have seemed odd to Shakespeare, or to anyone in the sixteenth century. He would have understood the question, but realized it was not one he had ever had occasion to ask. Everyone knew that if it was a poem it would have to have a reason – an aesthetic reason – for being written and read, and making form out of the poet's own inner chaos would be a byproduct. If that were your primary aim, you would go to the confessional.

Both Alvarez and Davie offer valuable insights into this kind of poetry, but both seem to me to overstate its newness. Of course we can all recognize a poem of the 'extremist' school, as we can all recognize a post-Romantic poem, but the clearest signs of recognition may be comparatively superficial (the Elizabethans didn't have diapers or (that kind of) institution on a hill). However great the adjustments as we move back in time, however much people have changed about what causes them shame, however close the relations between rhetoric and confession in earlier times, I suggest that lyric poetry was never wholly detachable from confession, just as, if it is to have any claim to be poetry, it can never be wholly identified with it.

Expressing and Betraying

This history of confessional poetry has shown, I hope, that it always raises the question of expression; and expression, in turn, raises the need for a distinction which I must now proceed to draw. There are two opposites to expression. I begin by comparing two attempts to express the same emotion:

– Be near me when my light is low,
   When the blood creeps, and the nerves prick
   And tingle; and the heart is sick,
   And all the wheels of Being slow.[1]

– Oh weary life! oh weary death!
   Oh spirit and heart made desolate!
   Oh damned vacillating state![2]

I hope I will command assent if I judge that the first of these, with its careful, pained rhythms, its clogged monosyllables, is poetry, and the second is merely exclamation. But does this mean that Tennyson, who wrote both, was in greater distress when writing the first? I don't believe there is conclusive evidence for this, since we know little of the origin of the second. We must surely leave open the possibility that as much emotion lies behind the second, that is, that expression may fail not for lack of emotion, but for lack of articulateness.

The distinction we need is drawn by Collingwood:

When it is said that the artist in the proper sense of that word is a person who expresses his emotions, this does not mean that if he is afraid he turns pale and stammers; if he is angry he turns red and bellows; and so forth. . . The characteristic mark of expression proper is lucidity or intelligibility; a person who expresses something thereby becomes conscious of what it is that he is expressing, and enables others to become conscious of it in himself and in them.[3]

Collingwood's term for going pale and stammering is betraying emotion. Every expression theory needs this distinction. Croce makes it by distinguishing aesthetic and naturalistic expression; Dewey by distinguishing the expression of emotion from its naturalistic discharge.

Now we can approach the frontier. Beyond it lie the crying and the laughing, the gestures and the postures, the clichés and worn-out phrases in which deeply sincere emotion is betrayed. To accuse all these sincere inarticulate people of insincerity because they are not poets would be absurd. Wordsworth was so anxious not to denigrate the emotional life of ordinary men and women that he felt it necessary to attribute to them an articulateness, an expressive power, that they clearly do not have. To distinguish between the discharge and the expression of their emotions would have removed his problem.

We can construct a scale of increasing articulateness in the expression of emotion. I will omit the pre-verbal, though in terms of naturalistic discharge these are the most powerful cases of all. Then comes 'Oh', which is on the edge of being a word: it finds its way freely into some very complex dramatic verse, as both *Coriolanus* and *Othello* have shown. Then comes (from Anne Sexton or anyone else) 'Oh shit!' and a hundred other expletives. Then come the formulae used by all the world in perfectly genuine situations: 'You've broken my heart', 'It's a lovely day', 'I've missed you so', 'How could you do such a thing?' We could still call these inarticulate, though they are formulae perfectly adequate for their purpose if that purpose is to assimilate that emotion to a norm. Expression, however, individualizes:

The anger which I feel here and now, with a certain person, for a certain cause, is no doubt an instance of anger, and in describing it as anger [or, I will insert, in discharging it in such phrases as 'How could you do such a thing!'] one is telling truth about it: but it is more than mere anger, it is a peculiar anger, not quite like any anger I shall ever feel again. To become fully conscious of it means becoming conscious of it not merely as an instance of anger, but as this quite peculiar anger. Expressing it, as we saw, has something to do with becoming fully conscious of it; therefore, if being fully conscious of it means being conscious of all its peculiarities, fully expressing it means expressing all its peculiarities.[4]

Hence the two opposites to expression. One is mere inarticulateness: turning pale and stammering, turning red and bellowing. The other is the use of formulae, which will range from naming the emotion ('I'm furious!') to the most elaborate rhetorical clichés. This requires us to realize that the fluency of a poem which follows stereotypes is a kind of inarticulateness.

Barbara

On the Sabbath-day,
Through the churchyard old and grey,
Over the crisp and yellow leaves, I held my rustling way;
And amid the words of mercy, falling on my soul like balms;
'Mid the gorgeous storms of music – in the mellow organ-calms,
'Mid the upward streaming prayers, and the rich and solemn
    psalms,
    I stood careless, Barbara.

My heart was otherwhere
While the organ shook the air,
And the priest, with outspread hands, blessed the people with a
    prayer;
But, when rising to go homeward, with a mild and saint-like shine
Gleamed a face of airy beauty with its heavenly eyes on mine –
Gleamed and vanished in a moment – O that face was surely thine
    Out of heaven, Barbara! . . .

I searched in my despair,
Sunny noon and midnight air;
I could not drive away the thought that you were lingering there.
O many and many a winter night I sat when you were gone,

My worn face buried in my hands, beside the fire alone.
Within the dripping churchyard, the rain plashing on your stone,
  You were sleeping, Barbara.

From the great number of poetasters who might have contended
for the place of illustrating this point, I have chosen Alexander
Smith, whose poem 'Barbara' is discussed by F.R. Leavis in an
eassy that raises many of the issues we now need to address.[5]

Leavis does not linger to point out what is wrong with the
language of the poem ('there would be no point in proceeding to
detailed analysis'): and certainly it is easy to point to the clichés, not
merely the worn linguistic counters of everyday speech, but poetic
cliché, that is, phrases which are striving to achieve distinction, but
in a too-familiar way. Virtually every adjective is predictable, and
once we have caught the swing of the rhythm it is very easy to
continue:

In vain, in vain, in vain,
You will never come again,
As I watch the dark clouds weeping, and taste the bitter rain.
Wherever you are lingering, I know you think of me.
I hear you in the moaning of the dark and lonely sea,
As I carry in my heart the thought that you too long for me,
  Barbara!

(Readers are invited to divide parody from original in this stanza.)[6]

The quality of the poem may not be in question; but what of the
conclusions that Leavis draws?

It doesn't merely surrender to temptation; it goes straight for a sentimental
debauch, an emotional wallowing, the alleged situation being only the
show of an excuse for the indulgence. . . If one wants a justification for
invoking the term 'insincerity', one can point to the fact that the poem
clearly enjoys its pang; to put it more strictly, the poem offers a luxurious
enjoyment that, to be enjoyed, must be taken for the suffering of an
unbearable sorrow.[7]

To his straightforward condemnation of the poem's artistic
value, Leavis has added two other points, moral and biographical.
The moral judgement is very emphatic, as this quotation shows;
and since morally culpable acts are committed by people, one
naturally asks who is being so sharply castigated here. Since Leavis

is careful to say that 'the poem' enjoys its pang, it looks as if he is blaming the readers who wallow in what they mistakenly believe to be unbearable sorrow; but I am by no means sure that Alexander Smith himself is being let off. Not only does Leavis use the term 'insincerity', from which it is difficult to remove all biographical meaning, but having gone on to maintain the enormous superiority of Hardy's 'After a Journey', he concludes: 'It is a case in which we know from the art what the man was like; we can be sure, that is, what personal qualities we should have found to admire in Hardy if we had known him.'

In the hands of a moralist, expression theory is a terrible weapon. If you believe that the quality of a poem depends on the emotion of the author, it is essential to introduce the distinction between expressing and betraying, otherwise we shall be led, as Leavis was, to the cruel *non sequitur*: bad poem, therefore no genuine grief. And if we then add the moral judgement: bad poem, therefore no grief, therefore self-indulgence pretending to be grief, poor Alexander Smith (about whose life I suspect Leavis knew no more than the rest of us) ends up as a corrupter of his evidently equally culpable sentimental readers. And since Leavis, along with the chuckling readers of *Scrutiny*, has not written any poems at all, the indictment of Smith is for failing a test to which the judges have not submitted themselves.

And now, returning to our scale, and asking where and how genuine expression begins to appear, I remark that it often appears in moments, even in fleeting glimpses:

– When I go into a room, it moves
   with embarrassment, and joins another room.[8]

– Wait mister. Which way is home?
   They turned the light out
   and the dark is moving in the corner.[9]

– O sister mother, wife,
   Sweet Lethe is my life.
   I am never, never, never coming home.[10]

Moments like this in the confessional poets (Lowell, Sexton, Plath) do not, at their first impact, need a context. An image, a rhythm (or, in the middle quotation, both together) catches us with sudden authenticity, and an emotion is conveyed. For the full effect we no

doubt need the context of the whole poem, but it is remarkable
how powerful, and how self-contained, such moments can be.
Images like these emerge from their poems as Coriolanus' surrender
to his mother emerges from the play.

But we must of course look at whole poems. In the next chapter
I shall discuss Donne's Holy Sonnets as expressive, in the course of
setting expression against another function. Here is a purer
example:

Surprised by joy – impatient as the Wind
I turned to share the transport – Oh! with whom
But thee, deep buried in the silent tomb,
That spot which no vicissitude can find?
Love, faithful love, recalled thee to my mind –
But how could I forget thee? Through what power,
Even for the least division of an hour,
Have I been so beguiled as to be blind
To my most grievous loss! – That thought's return
Was the worst pang that sorrow ever bore,
Save one, one only, when I stood forlorn,
Knowing my heart's best treasure was no more;
That neither present time, nor years unborn
Could to my sight that heavenly face restore.[11]

It would be easy to dismiss this sonnet as ordinary, no different
from the hundreds of others Wordsworth so conscientiously turned
out over his long career. The diction is at times commonplace ('my
heart's best treasure'), the adjectives conventional ('most grievous
loss'), and the last line labours with inversion. Yet it is not a
conventional poem, because of its exclusive concentration on
capturing a moment, or rather two moments, of emotion. There
are none of the conventional topoi of the sonnet sequence, and there
is no explanation of the situation. Most readers would assume it to
be addressed to a woman he had loved; yet when we learn that it's
about his daughter we do not find this odd: it is so exclusively
about the shape of the emotion that the person addressed can easily
change. The argument is simply summarized: a moment of joy led
me, as I turned to share it with you, to realize that I'd forgotten you
were dead, and that was 'the worst pang that sorrow ever bore',
except for the moment of first fully realizing you dead. Two
moments of intense emotion are compared, and no attention is
wasted on filling in the situations – what the joy was, whether that

earlier moment was at the deathbed or the graveside. The sole concern of the poem is, largely through syntax, to become fully conscious of all the peculiarities of that particular grief. This poem has to be called an expression of emotion, because there is nothing else it sets out to do.

By treating it in this way, we learn to read it. The same could be said of another Wordsworth sonnet:

Composed upon Westminster Bridge

Earth has not anything to show more fair:
Dull would he be of soul who could pass by
A sight so touching in its majesty:
This City now doth like a garment wear
The beauty of the morning; silent, bare,
Ships, towers, domes, theatres and temples lie
Open unto the fields, and to the sky;
All bright and glittering in the smokeless air.
Never did sun more beautifully steep
In his first splendour valley, rock, or hill;
Ne'er saw I, never felt, a calm so deep!
The river glideth at his own sweet will:
Dear God! the very houses seem asleep;
And all that mighty heart is lying still![12]

If one were giving an account of this poem, it would clearly be possible to say that its subject is London seen in the early morning, that its theme is the apparently lifeless quiet of a town that has not yet woken up, that its diction is plain and its syntax inclines to the exclamatory. All true, but these statements, even if expanded, seem to leave out what is most important. Suppose we begin, instead, by asking what emotion the poem expresses. As it happens, I have often done this, to see what answer students will give: awe, they say, or reverence, or feeling for beauty, or solemnity – words that describe the scene itself, and the feelings you would expect it to arouse, but do not quite describe the poem. If however we see it as the expression of surprise, every detail in it begins to matter. The first line, instead of being a neutral, perhaps rather solemn, announcement of the subject, begins to throb with excitement. The fourth line is read with an extra stress on the first two words ('This city', of all places!). The list of nouns in line 6 is heard with mounting excitement: that rocks, trees, lakes, waterfalls and valleys should lie open unto the fields is expected enough, but the list of objects in the poem announces with mounting firmness how urban they are, how astonishing that they should take on this numinous quality. In the sestet the emphasis is even more marked: 'Never did sun. . .', 'Ne'er saw I . .' are explicit in their surprise, and the last two lines, in their quiet animism, note the fact that in the centre of the city is a natural presence untroubled by the impending smoke and bustle.

Coleridge attacked mechanistic ideas of association by using the organic analogy that is so often present in expression theories.

I almost think that Ideas *never* recall Ideas, as far they are Ideas – any more than Leaves in a forest create each other's motion – the Breeze it is that runs thro' them – it is the Soul, the state of Feeling.[13]

If we assimilate the sonnet on Westminster Bridge to the conventional Wordsworth, if we read it as a solemn tribute to beauty, we miss nothing and everything: we can perceive every leaf, but we will miss the breeze.

A Theoretical Problem: Expressing the Dispersed Subject

To assert that a poem expresses emotion clearly assumes that the emotion had a previous and independent existence, just as it assumes someone who is feeling the emotion, the speaking subject of the poem. The claim therefore that the subject is dispersed, that there is no independent substantive self which lies behind the poem as its cause, must destroy – surely – any possible theory of literature as expression. And this is of course the now widespread structuralist claim. As its primary theorist we can take Foucault, whose most notorious statement of this view is that 'man is only a recent invention, a figure not yet two centuries old, a new wrinkle in our knowledge, that he will disappear again as soon as that knowledge has discovered a new form'. Foucault's project, clearly intended as a contribution to that new knowledge, is 'to get rid of the subject itself', that is to say, to arrive at an analysis which can account for the constitution of the subject within a historical framework'. The 'so-called literature of the self', therefore, cannot be understood unless it is put into the framework of 'practices of the self', which is constituted immediately by a symbolic system, and behind that by 'real practices – historically analysable practices'. The archaeology of knowledge, by disinterring the underlyng episteme at any period, contributes to the understanding of these practices.[1]

Now to see how this dispersal of the self will undermine the theory of expression, we need to look at its application to poetry, and for that purpose I choose Antony Easthope. Here is a strong and clear attack on the idea of the autonomous subject in poetry:

The unnecessary and impossible search for a transcendental subject – the 'real man' 'behind' the text – is familiar in literary criticism. . . Serious literary analysis has recently made advances on the basis that the subject is constituted as an effect of discourse; there is no space, no 'John Milton' behind the discourse in which the sonnets take place.[2]

And so in his book *Poetry as Discourse* Easthope attacks the expression theory, choosing the Wordsworth of the Preface to *Lyrical Ballads* as his main target. Romantic poetic theory, he claims, is founded on a misrecognition:

It affirms that experience is represented in language but denies any activity of means of representation in producing this represented. . . Wordsworth's 'Preface' consistently asumes that language is all but transparent to experience, that the enounced is virtually untramelled by enunciation. A poet has greater 'power in expressing what he thinks and feels', and transparency inheres in the concept of expression.[3]

The thrust of Easthope's book is to emphasize the 'productive energies' of the reader and to attack what he calls the bourgeois tradition in poetry, which 'treats the poem as a manifestation of "presence" even when it really knows it's only a poem'. Most of English poetry from the Renaissance, with the only partial exception of modernism, is found guilty of this error, and in its conclusion the book announces with a sigh of relief that this canonical tradition has 'had its day'.

I hope this is a fair summary of how the denial of the autonomous subject leads to a rejection of the theory of expression. Now in commenting on this, I am faced with an immediate choice: whether to discuss the underlying doctrine or its application to the theory of expression. The attempt to get rid of the subject affects most forms of serious discourse today, and it would not be difficult to set against each other statements by Foucault, Althusser or

Derrida on the one hand, Ricoeur, Searle or Nuttall on the other, in order to map out the dispute. That would be the task of a theoretical prolegomena to literary criticism, and one can be certain of one thing, that such a project would not get around to engaging with specific works of literature. One can be reasonably certain too that as the humanists and the post-structuralists lay out their positions, perhaps abusing one another in the process, the question whether man is just a wrinkle in our knowledge will not be settled by rational discussion, by one side convincing the other.

I therefore propose to ask whether the subversion of the autonomous subject need deprive us of the doctrine of expression. Suspending the philosophical question (a good post-structuralist strategy, after all) I shall engage some poetry and some prose in order to see what we need to say about it, and whether any philosophic position can deprive us of that need.

'But,' sayest thou – (and I marvel, I repeat,
To find thee trip on such a mere word) what
Thou writest, paintest, stays; that does not die:
Sappho survives because we sing her songs. . .'
    Thou diest while I survive?
Say rather that my fate is deadlier still. . .
When all my works wherein I prove my worth. . .
Alive still in the praise of such as thou,
I, I the feeling, thinking, active man. . .
Sleep in my urn. It is so horrible. . .[4]

Cleon, the eponymous speaker of Browning's dramatic mono-logue, is a distinguished elderly Greek poet writing to his patron Protus, voicing the dissatisfactions of an old man who can only live vicariously (he does not envy the lovers on the Grecian urn). These lines are the most passionate rejection of post-structuralism I know. Do not pass off the metaphors as if they were literally true, they say. Instead of asserting the metaphorical nature of all language, the poem insists on the importance of the literal. 'Thy fair slave's an ode' it says, not in order to assert that everything is text, but in order to tell us that odes made of words are mere text, as worthless in the end as the metaphoric immortality that awaits Cleon when he will no longer have any consciousness of it.

My other example is very different in subject and in genre. An article by Irving Howe on 'Writing and the Holocaust' discusses the experience of the concentration camps. 'We became aware,' writes Primo Levi, 'that our language lacks words to express this offence, the demolition of man'. Every serious writer approaching the Holocaust sooner or later says much the same. If there is a way of coping with this difficulty, it lies in a muted tactfulness recognising that there are some things that can be said and some that cannot.[5] Howe then goes on to quote Eliot on 'the triumph of feeling and thought' over 'the natural sin of language', and relates it to what has become a 'virtual cliché', that 'language cannot deal with the Holocaust'.

I do not apologize for choosing two extreme examples: the individual pain of an old man who cannot accept mortality, the social pain of the greatest crime of our century, each leading to the agonized discovery that language is inadequate. What will the Easthopian interpretation of these two texts tell us? 'A poem can only create "presence", reveal "the persona of a poet", as the effect of poetic techniques.' So the Cleon who speaks of age, the Primo Levi who speaks of concentration camps, are 'constituted as an effect of discourse'.

It is not easy to see what this position is attacking. Who has ever denied that what we know about Wordsworth is derived from reading what he wrote? There may be mystically inclined believers in communication who like to close their eyes and just think about Wordsworth, thus entering into direct communication with the author independently of the medium of language, but they will seem as eccentric to the humanist as to the structuralist. To believe in the poem as an act of communication from author to reader has never involved a denial of the productive energies of the reader. Romantic criticism placed great emphasis on the personal experience of the reader, on the need to grow gradually into a full awareness of what a poem can imply. It is only in middle age, Quiller-Couch asserted, that we will learn to appreciate fully the ripeness of Chaucer's Prologue, written in his middle age. There is, admittedly, not much empahsis on the ideological position of the reader, but concern with the difference between callow youthful reading and later, fuller appreciation raises the same issues of the need for active reader involvement as do matters of ideological difference.

Though he does not draw the distinction explicitly, Easthope sets two factors against the doctrine of direct communication. One is the activity of the reader; the other is the precedence of signifier over signified, the fact that 'all discourse must be understood as determined linguistically, according to the laws of its own materiality': the author then is not a free agent, and the text he writes comes not from him but from the constraints imposed by the language itself. Here we have a close parallel to the discussion of realism earlier. Easthope's attack on Romantic theory is very like the Romantic attack on Augustan conventions, just as Barthes' attack on realism is very like the realists' attack on earlier conventions, the difference being that the Romantics and the realists are trying to free themselves from the artificialities imposed by those conventions, the structuralist critics wish to claim that to free oneself is impossible, and one should therefore admit that one is imprisoned. Once again, we are up against either/or thinking. Either the author communicates his emotion to a passive reader through a transparent medium, or the author is dead, language is not transparent, the reader produces the meaning. All the complex possibilities, the interaction of language, author and reader, the variations in the relative importance of each, have been waved aside by an act of theoretical dogma.

Let us perform an exercise: let us restate what we get from Cleon or from Levi in terms of the abolition of the subject. As we read 'Cleon', we might say, we construct a speaker: his language addresses itself to the relation between experience and the verbalization of experience, and tries to break out of the paradox that, being language, it can only verbalize. Protus, we are told, confused literal and figurative; Cleon, distinguishing them, asserts his belief in the reality of extra-textual presence.

As we read Howe's article, we might also say, we are told that language cannot convey the experience of the Holocaust. Of course not: language can never move outside itself, and what Howe (and before him Levi) discovered is the impossibility of stepping outside the text to an originary, extra-textual trace. *That* is the natural sin of language.

Both these accounts correctly identify the issue raised by our two texts, but as they do so they come up against a danger. In the first case, is our critic to say that Protus was right – that the deconstruction of what Cleon says is tantamount to confusing (or denying the difference between) literal and figurative? In the second case, is he to assert that since we have no direct access to the experience itself, we must accept our imprisonment within the text as inevitable? In both cases, this would be the exact opposite of what the text says. The critic has therefore to take one further step, and here he is faced with a choice. He can simply deny what the texts assert. Of 'Cleon' he can say that the confidence which his rhythms express is ironically undermined by the self-refuting nature of his position. Of Howe, he can point out that by choosing so extreme a case he has brought us sharply against the impossibility of logocentrism. Reading against the grain in this way demonstrates that the value of a text may lie in its internal contradictions.

My reason for choosing these extreme examples will now surface. To read in this way would be outrageous: it would reveal a callousness so distasteful that few critics will find the insensitivity (or the courage) to admit to it. Are we to tell the survivor of the concentration camps that his suffering has no reality outside a text, that the impossibility of finding the language to convey it is a conveniently sharp example of the impossibility of any communication of experience? Comfortably far from old age and Auschwitz, the critic reduces the pain of experience to a philosophic nicety. The fact that there are survivors of the camps still alive is rhetorically effective for my point, but strictly speaking irrelevant: it is enough to say that these experiences took place, and were endured. And logically, it is not even necessary to invoke such extreme experiences: the fact that any experience took place and was endured is, in a correspondingly minor degree, insulted by the denial of the subject.

If on the other hand the critic does not wish to deny what the texts assert, he must perform a finesse. He can say that the text gives us a simulation of an extra-textual experience, that though we cannot make direct contact with Cleon's despair or Levi's frustration, we can be given the words that enable us to imagine that such contact is possible. The author is a deduction by us, and that deduced author performs a verbal action that we describe as expressing emotion.

Now we must pause on a distinction I have so far glossed over. I have referred to the authors as Levi and Howe (indiscriminately) and as Cleon, but the three have different status. Howe, the actual author, had no direct experience of the Holocaust; nor did Eliot, whom he quotes; but Levi did, and wrote an account of his own imprisonment. If we deny a clear ontological status to these experiences, it is Levi whom we are insulting: Howe might protest, but it would not be on his own behalf. This is oddly similar to the situation in Browning's poem. Many readers will have noticed (perhaps protested at) the fact that I have persistently called the author 'Cleon', and attributed the experience to him: I wanted to postpone the point that Cleon is a fictitious character, and the poem is by Browning (to whom the experience must, ultimately, be attributed). To remind the reader of this is in one way to weaken my argument: there was no transcendental subject to his dramatic monologue, 'Cleon' is entirely the creature of the text. But it is also to strengthen it; for if we find it helpful to regard the lines as expressing the speaker's emotion when the speaker did not exist, how much stronger will be the case for the theory of expression when Browning or Christina Rossetti write in their own person about their actual feelings.

For the last time I revert to Easthope's argument. One of his main charges against what he refers to as the 'canonical' or 'bourgeois' tradition of English poetry is that it 'disavows enunciation', encouraging the reader to identify himself with the subject of the utterance, and so creating 'the effect of an individual voice "really" speaking by concealing the way it is produced as an effect'. By an ingenious argument, this is attributed to iambic pentameter, which 'diasvows its own metricality', removes emphasis from the signifier, and 'would disclaim the voice speaking the poem in favour of the voice represented in the poem, speaking what it says'. That last sentence should make it clear that what we have here is a question of genre. The poem in which the author claims to speak, direct, in his own voice, is the lyric, and we have already seen how hard the lyric strives to offer us the speaking voice. There is plenty of non-lyrical 'canonical' poetry, which uses a rich variety of devices (metre is only one) to 'force attention to the words as words', and to 'foreground the enunciation' as well as the utterance. One such device – perhaps the most prominent of all – is to postulate a fictitious speaker. The dramatic monologue is quite clearly not a poem in which 'Browning speaks', and that is why I insisted on referring to the subject as 'Cleon'. But taken out of context, the lines I quoted could easily have come from a lyric, and could be read as direct expression of emotion in the same way as the speech of Coriolanus. Emphasizing enunciation as well as utterance (approved by Easthope) and direct communication of the subject's emotion (disapproved by Easthope) turn out not to be opposite poles of a continuum, but quite compatible with each other.

In rephrasing my account of the two passages I said that the text gives us a simulation of extra-textual experiences; and we can say the same of any passage quoted in this chapter, whether a letter by Elizabeth Browning or a poem by Anne Sexton. We now see that, depending on our theoretical position, there are several ways we can say this. We can say that the extra-textual emotional experience really took place, in what the Derridian would call the transcendental subject; or that it was simulated by the poet (a fictitious character's experiences cannot take place); or that it is postulated by the reader as a result of his reading experience; or various combinations of these. If we consider it theoretically inadmissible to say that the speaker of a poem is Anne Sexton, and that it expresses her emotion, we shall have to find a different way to make the point. We might say that the speaker is 'Anne Sexton' or 'Primo Levi', and that the text 'expresses' the motion of the 'author'. Or that the speaker is ~~Anne Sexton~~, and that it ~~expresses~~ the emotion of the ~~author~~. This would be to use the terms *'sous rature'* (under erasure). This locution is introduced by Derrida in *Of Grammatology*, where he allows the use of – indeed, insists on using – certain Marxist and structuralist concepts under erasure. They are concepts that are both essential and untenable, and must therefore be used in a way that admits of their ultimate impossibility:

Now, we cannot consider Marx's, Engels' or Lenin's texts as completely finished elaborations that are simply to be 'applied' to the current situation. In saying this, I am not advocating anything contrary to Marxism.[6]

Now is there any reason why only certain favoured concepts should be treated in this way? The critic who does not wish to advocate anything contrary to Christianity or humanism (or for that matter psychoanalysis, freemasonry or astrology) might want to extend this epistemological scepticism to other concepts. That would grant to any system of thought the provisional existence needed to enable it to function. There seems, in short, no valid objection to retaining *any* concept under erasure. Which ones are so retained will be a matter of which system of thought we give our allegiance (or ~~allegiance~~) to. In saying this, I am not advocating anything contrary to Romantic theory.

Indeed, it can be argued that a total paradigm shift is less radical in its implications than a partial one.

Moving of th'earth brings harms and fears,
  Men reckon what it did and meant;

But trepidation of the spheres,
Though greater far, is innocent.[7]

Abolishing the subject is trepidation of the spheres. It cannot abolish the need to say certain things about a poem, and may have to license us to go on using concepts like expression even while their validity is being theoretically undermined by a philosophic school which, like all philosophic schools, will succeed in convincing some and not convincing others.

3

Persuading

Literature as Didactic

The view that literature should improve the world was a commonplace for centuries. It is hard to dispute the claim that the world needs improving, and every good act beyond the purely individual and spontaneous will involve the use of language. The study of how language can be used to persuade others to act in the right way is traditionally known as rhetoric, and the separation of rhetoric from literary criticism is a recent affair: it was in a treatise on the Art of Rhetoric that Thomas Wilson claimed that all the poets' tales pertain 'to the amendment of manners, to the knowledge of truth, to the setting forth of Nature's work, or else to the understanding of some notable things done'. Milton's concern was to justify the ways of God to men, Wordsworth hoped that if his projected revolution in our idea of poetry took hold, 'our moral feelings influencing and influenced by these judgements will, I believe, be corrected and purified'.[1]

If the purpose of literature is didactic, it overlaps with writing which sets out to persuade us, writing whose purpose lies outside itself, in causing us to forgive our enemies, vote conservative, fight for the revolution, be stern with our children, go to church regularly, or buy a Volvo. What name shall we give to language with such a transitive, pragmatic goal? The obvious terms are rhetoric, propaganda, advocacy. 'Rhetoric' is certainly the traditional term, and its meaning could be stretched to include all the above goals, but it usually refers not to the writing itself that advocates goals, but to the study of how most effectively to produce such writing, not the product but the skill. 'Propaganda' has a wider meaning than just a kind of writing: from the Roman Catholic congregation for the Propaganda, for the spreading of the faith, it has widened to mean an association or concerted scheme for the propagation of any cause, and in popular speech has narrowed to the writings that promote such a goal, usually with a pejorative overtone. Either of these would have done as a chapter heading, but it seemed to me more accurate to take a term without ready-made connotations, a term like 'advocacy' or, to show the parallel with the previous chapter, 'persuading'.

What was once held by everyone is now held by no one: modern aesthetic theory no longer takes didacticism seriously, and for good reason. If literature is advocacy, then its success can be measured in terms of results, and to know how good a work is, we would not need to read it ourselves, but would simply need to know what it had caused to happen. Dickens is still sometimes praised for his contribution to improving the treatment of the poor, the law's delays, or slum conditions, but there is no evidence that his work had any such effect: to find out whether it did would require some carefully pinpointed research, and this would almost certainly show that Thomas Hood's tear-jerker 'The Song of the Shirt' had more effect than *Bleak House*. Indeed, if results are a yardstick of excellence, then there is little doubt what would be the best novel and the best poem of the nineteenth century. *Uncle Tom's Cabin* may well have made an important contribution to the abolition of slavery, a far more indisputable contribution than that of *Oliver Twist* or *Bleak House* to the already widely denounced evils they exposed. And the one poem that we can say with confidence changed the course of history is a music hall song of 1878. The Russian army had invaded Turkey and encamped in front of Constantinople, but Russia was forced to negotiate away some of its gains at the Congress of Berlin because of the willingness of Britain to go to war. There was no real reason, in terms of realpolitik, for the British intransigeance: it was imposed on the government by popular jingoistic feeling, which was whipped up by a popular song sung everywhere in the streets of London:

We don't want to fight, but by jingo if we do,
We've got the ships, we've got the men, we've got the money too.

As well as giving a new word to the language, this song undoubtedly produced political results.[2] We might of course hesitate to call it didactic: that will depend on what we think of jingoism. To the propagandist himself, what is advocated will be virtue, but there are obviously two questions involved: whether propaganda produces results, and whether they are results we approve of. We might well have to face the uncomfortable thought that the right results are less successfully advocated than the wrong – that, for instance, the jingo song was effective, though we deplore jingoism, whereas 'We shall overcome' has not succeeded in its (admirable) goal of abolishing nuclear weapons.

Why has the didactic function of literature been so massively rejected? Or (it is the same question, asked in reverse) why were the apologists for literature so misled as to judge it, all down the centuries, by its ability to promote virtue? One answer could be precisely that they were apologists, defending literature against its moralistic opponents, persuading themselves that what they loved was also good for them. Another and more complex answer is that didacticism has not really been rejected, it has simply grown more subtle. Let us take what was the most influential school of criticism in the mid-century, that associated with F.R. Leavis and *Scrutiny*. In the previous chapter I more or less assumed (but also, I hope, showed) that Leavis's criticism is moral in its concern; now is the moment to offer more support for this claim. The charge that his concerns were moral rather than aesthetic is one to which Leavis would probably have had a mixed reaction: he would have objected to the dichotomy as offering a trivialized conception of the aesthetic, and indeed since the term 'aesthetic' itself is one of those that seems most to have annoyed him, he might well have regarded the accusation as a compliment. Here is a typical paragraph from Leavis's criticism:

If depth, range and subtlety in the presentment of human experience are the criteria, then in the work of the great novelists from Jane Austen to Lawrence – I think of Hawthorne, Dickens, George Eliot, Henry James, Melville, Mark Twain, Conrad – we have a creative achievement that is unsurpassed by any of the famous phases or chapters of literary history. In these great novelists . . . we have the successors of Shakespeare; for in the nineteenth century and later the strength – the poetic and creative strength – of the English language goes into prose fiction. In comparison the formal poetry is a marginal affair.[3]

What is striking about this is, first of all, its lack of interest in technical and generic matters. There is no hesitation in judging fiction and poetry – and Shakespeare – by the same criterion, for they are all trying to do the same thing: to 'present' human experience with 'depth, range and subtlety'. We seem to be present at a kind of Judgement Day, at which everyone will have to submit to the same examination – however different your life, your opportunities, your problems, from that of a foreigner from another century, one of you will be saved, the other damned. However different the technical means, the kind of story, the literary effects aimed at, still the epic poet and the satirist, the realistic novelist and the writer of love lyrics, are all judged by the very general criterion of depth, range and subtlety. That these qualities might tug against each other, that the superficial might range wider, that the less subtle might be the more profound, is not considerd. 'Heart of Darkness', writes Leavis, 'is by common consent one of Conrad's best things',[4] and the deliberately casual language springs not only from the wish to put the reader at ease, it also implies that any less general term than 'things' might fail to submit all literary works to the bar of a common judgement. All this, I suggest, is the mark of the moralist; and when we turn to the criteria Leavis uses when he praises – life, maturity, intelligence, self-knowledge – it is not surprising to find that there is nothing literary about them: they are the criteria by which we praise or blame our fellow human beings. However subtle the language may sound, we are not far from *vir bonus dicendi peritus*, the doctrine that the good orator (poet, novelist, dramatist – and, one wonders, painter and musician?) must be a good man.

The reply of Leavisites to all this is that I am operating with a very crude notion of morality: that literature is a moral activity because it sharpens our attitudes, our moral awareness, our sensitivity to others, not because it does anything so vulgar as produce results. But moral philosophy, indeed all moral termin-ology, is not about attitudes but about actions: to take what has become the most celebrated example of our time, the fact that some concentration camp commanders read Rilke does not seem to have been incompatible with some of the most immoral acts one can think of.[5] We do not know how sensitive they were as readers, but we cannot make the convenient assumption that they weren't. We would then have to say that the activity of reading poetry, though it may have many virtues and rewards, cannot be considered moral.

The answer which this book will canvass is that of course there is an overlap between literature and persuading, as there is between literature and most forms of writing. The aim of this chapter will therefore be neither to accept nor to reject didacticism, but to discriminate: to map out the area they have in common, and then to see how differences can emerge even within that common territory.

I cannot treat of every cause that gets advocated in writing, and must select. If literature sets out to make us good Christians, it overlaps with the sermon; if to behave better to our mother-in-law, it overlaps with moral advice or family quarrels; if to shop at Sainsburys or drive a Volkswagen, with advertising; if to vote labour, report terrorists to the police and demonstrate against apartheid, with political propaganda. I shall choose for discussion the first and the last. I think it is very questionable if moral advice, offered in general terms, ever has a significant effect on behaviour; and though some of the parallels with advertising are fascinating, advertisements have never been taken seriously as literature. Religion and politics, however, are always with us, and no one has expected the poets and storytellers to leave them alone.

Both sections of this chapter concentrate at length on a single example, chosen with care because of the way it raises the issues: but the strategy in each is different. In comparing literature with sermons, I take the idea of overlap very literally, looking at actual sermons, and thus, inevitably, stressing resemblance as much as difference. But this would have been too easy a method for politics, since most political propaganda is so obviously unliterary, and there I have concentrated much more closely on the political novels themselves, asking what they do which is like and unlike a political speech or pamphlet. Inevitably, this leads to greater emphasis on differences, so I will say at the beginning that in both fields there is resemblance, and there is difference.

Sermon and Poem

And, first, religion. I take it as self-evident that the purpose of a sermon is didactic, that is, it aims to produce effects that can be specified in advance, and once that effect has taken place there is no further need for the text to exist. St Paul saw preaching as 'the power of God unto salvation',[1] and no orthodox Christian preacher would ever have rejected this aim. For Hooker, sermons are 'the keys of the kingdom of Heaven, as wings to the Soul, as spurs to the good affections of man', and he concludes by comparing them to food and to physic – clearly examples of what matters only for its effects, not for its continued existence.[2] That a sermon, however, can serve not only to awaken hearers to repentance but also to show off the talents of the preacher was widely recognized, and as widely condemned. Such an extra purpose would be an abuse, and therefore, we might think, need not be fed into our concept of the genre; but it does not differ much from purposes that (with rather different wording) would seem natural and proper in a poem.

It will be most convenient, in comparing sermon and poem, to control other variables as tightly as possible, and the best way to do this is to have them both by the same author. That makes the choice of example virtually inevitable, since our greatest religious poet was also one of our most celebrated preachers.

Donne's Sermons and Donne's Poems

The central theme of Donne's religious writings was unquestionably sin, so let us begin with a sermon on sin, preached on the text 'For mine iniquities are gone over my head, as a heavy burden, they are too heavy for me' (Psalm 38:3). After a short introduction the sermon announces its division into parts, which is based on a separation of the words of the verse, one by one:

First, they were *peccata*, sins, iniquities; and then *peccata sua*, his sins, his iniquities, which intimates actual sins; . . . the sins are his own sins; and then, which is a third circumstance, they are sins in the plural, God is not thus angry for one sin; and again, they are such sins, as have been long in going, and are now got over, *supergressae sunt*, they are gone, gone over; and then lastly, for that first part, *supergressae caput*, they are gone over my head.[3]

This word-by-word division is common, even normal, in Donne's sermons, and was clearly expected by his hearers; but it does not always correspond with the substantive division of the argument. In this case, the division between *supergressae sunt* (my sins are gone over my head) and the later heading *gravatae nimis sunt* (they are too heavy for me) soon reveals itself as a distinction without a difference; and one of the most important parts of the discussion, that on original sin, occurs twice, under *sua* (our sins are our own, and responsibility cannot be fobbed off) and under *supergressae* (they have got over our heads because we have sold ourselves to them). I shall follow the substantive and not the verbal division in my brief account of the sermon. After pointing out the levels of scriptural meaning ('Historically David; morally, we; typically, Christ'), the sermon turns to the idea of sin, and dismisses 'that subtility of the School' that sin is nothing, showing that this philosophical nicety 'will not ease my soul, no more than it will ease my body, that sickness is nothing, and death is nothing'. Returning to the moral meaning, clearly the most important for a sermon, it tells us that though we are not all Davids ('lovely and beloved in that measure that David was') we are all Adams, and must accept responsibility for sin – which leads to the paradox that only if I say my sins are my own will they cease to be mine, and be made the sins of Christ. This section culminates in the assertion that 'to the guiltiness of original sin our own wills concur as well as to any actual sin'. The sermon then turns to Augustine, describing his susceptibility to (as we would now say) peer-group pressure, and how that led him to pretend to sins he had not actually committed. It then goes on to explore the idea of sin stretching over us like a roof or arch, illustrating this with 'a passage of mine own': lying at Aix, he learned that he was lodging in a house full of Anabaptists who all detested one another, and who symbolized 'how many roofs, how many floors of separation, were made between God and my prayers in that house'. Finally we are returned to the question of original sin. 'Now, how are we sold to sin? by Adam? That's true.' But though true, it is not to be used as an excuse, and the conclusion drives home insistently the doctrine that 'because we do not but consent to that first sale, in our sinful acts, and habits, we have sold ourselves too, and so sin is gone over our heads.'

Here now is a poem about sin:

If poisonous minerals, and if that tree,
Whose fruit threw death on else immortal us,
If lecherous goats, if serpents envious
Cannot be damn'd, alas why should I be?
Why should intent or reason, borne in me,
Make sins, else equal, in me more heinous?
And mercy being easy and glorious
To God; in his stern wrath why threatens he?
But who am I that dare dispute with thee
Oh God? Oh! of thine only worthy blood,
And my tears, make a heavenly Lethean flood,
And drown in it my sins' black memory;
That thou remember them, some claim as debt,
I think it mercy, if thou wilt forget.

Holy Sonnet IX[4]

Let us not be afraid to begin with the obvious: the poem is much
shorter, and is in verse. This point of course is not in dispute: what
could be disputed is how important it is. To say that a poem differs
from a sermon in having a metrical pattern and rhyme scheme, in
this case that of a sonnet, is to say nothing against the dismissive
charge that it is merely a piece of versified theology, using verbal
patterns of merely superficial interest to dress up what could as well
be said in prose. The usual answer to this is that patterning, in a
true poem, is not superficial: rhyme, metrical structure and rhythm
bite deep into meaning, and enable the poem to respond to the
quick of its argument. The use that this poem makes of the sonnet
form is not difficult to spell out. The Petrarchan division of octave
and sestet corresponds to the two halves of the argument: protest at
God's apparent unfairness, and the need for submission; then a
subdivision of the octave into two quatrains gives us two stages of
the protest, the first general, beginning with extreme analogies and
culminating in blunt self-pity, the second more technically
theological, and culminating in fear. The sestet replies to this but
also allows itself a concluding couplet, as if trying to be a
Shakespearean sonnet as well: in fact it divides into three, a line of
self-rebuke, three lines of prayer, and two lines of brilliant paradox
(there is an overlap between the self-rebuke and the prayer, since
'Oh God' could be taken either with what precedes or what
follows).

 Holy Sonnet XVII, the sonnet on his wife's death, is a more
complex case:

Since she whom I loved hath paid her last debt
To Nature, and to hers, and my good is dead,
And her soul early into heaven ravished,
Wholly on heavenly things my mind is set.
Here the admiring her my mind did whet
To seek thee God: so streams do show their head;
But though I have found thee, and thou my thirst hast fed,
A holy thirsty dropsy melts me yet.
But why should I beg more Love, when as thou
Dost woo my soul for hers, offering all thine:
And dost not only fear lest I allow
My love to saints and angels, things divine,
But in thy tender jealousy dost doubt
Lest the world, flesh, yea Devil put thee out.[5]

This poem too is a mixture – the same mixture – of Petrarchan and Shakespearean structure. The most obvious division is into octave and sestet, but the octave is divided into two quatrains, and the sestet culminates in a couplet. In sonnet IX the two quatrains concluded with brief fierce questions rhyming with each other ('Alas why should I be?' 'Why threatens he?'); in sonnet XVII they conclude with two whole lines, rhyming with each other and closely parallel. Line 4 is calmly dignified, this dignity deriving from both sound and syntax: the metrical inversion of the first foot leads to a phonetic parallelism between 'wholly' and 'heavenly', which alliterate, are both trochaic, and end similarly; and the syntax of the line (a delayed main clause after the complications of the 'since' clauses that precede) is quite straightforward (the inversion that places the subject in the middle does not delay comprehension in the way the first three lines do). Line 8 is intense, this intensity deriving from a similar syntactic directness and a similar phonetic parallelism (three trochaic dissyllables in an iambic line, all ending in the same sound, and followed by three monosyllables).

These are the two crucial lines of the octave (his aspiration to God seen first as dignity then as restlessness), and each provides the climax of its quatrain in a way that is clearly using the sonnet structure. The sestet makes a totally different assertion, based on a totally different image, that of God as a jealous lover. This reverses the argument, and turns us to its theological implications: 'Why should I beg more Love?', since grace will come not from my efforts but from God's free gift. This ought to be comforting, and on one level is; but at the same time it makes the free gift of grace seem like insane jealousy. The analogy can be read in two directions. If we move from vehicle to tenor, it says that what seems like the behaviour of a jealous lover is actually our assurance of salvation. But if we read from tenor to vehicle, it says: we all know about the wonderful doctrine of prevenient grace, but look how petty it appears when you think about it.

I have tried to show that the fact of verse is not trivial, that the obvious patterning of the sonnets is important because it involves more complex patterns that articulate the meaning of the poem. This has two implications. First, that the analysis necessarily becomes normative: if these complexities were not present then the metrical pattern would be a trivial matter, or (in traditional terminology) we'd be dealing with verse, not poetry. And second, that this extension of the idea of pattern breaks down the clear distinction between poem and sermon, for such freer and more functional patterning is found in the prose of the sermons.

Miserable man! a Toad is a bag of Poison, and a Spider is a blister of Poison, and yet a Toad and a Spider cannot poison themselves; man hath a dram of poison, original-Sin, in an invisible corner, we know not where, and he cannot choose but poison himself and all his actions with that; we are so far from being able to begin without Grace, as then where we have the first Grace, we cannot proceed to the use of that, without more.[6]

There is a good deal of skill to admire in this: the parallelism with its slight differences, so that the shift from 'bag' to 'blister' seems to say that Nature does not offer exact parallels – yet at the same time the phonetic parallel (the monosyllabic toad with its monosyllable of poison, followed by the dissyllabic spider with its blister) seems to say that under the difference there is exact equivalence, as required for the point. Or there is the careful parallelism of 'cannot/cannot but', the placing of 'poison' or of 'without'. Though we have not the backbone of regularity provided by the metre, we have some of the flesh that a true poem puts on the bones.

Besides metre, poems use figurative language: these are the two traditional markers of poetry. That sermons can be as rich in figurative speech as poems was obvious to contemporaries, and was justified from the example of the Bible. Sidney, enthusing about the language of the Psalms, praises David for his 'notable Prosopopeias' and calls it 'a heavenly poesie'.[7] Donne says the same:

There are not so eloquent books in the world, as the Scriptures. Accept those names of Tropes and Figures, which the Grammarians and Rhetoricians put upon us, and we may be bold to say, that in all their Authors, Greek and Latin, we cannot find so high, and so lively, examples, of those Tropes, and those Figures, as we may in the Scriptures.[8]

(and a few lines later he claims that a good part of the Scripture is 'in a metrical, in a measured composition, in verse', thus subverting our one clear point of difference). Since both sermon and poem would use biblical sources and model themselves on biblical language, this would serve as a justification for figurative language in either. Donne's sermons are so rich in figures that it is difficult to find any poetic device that they do not use:

And as prisoners discharg'd of actions may lie for fees, so when the womb hath discharg'd us, yet we are bound to it by cords of flesh by such a string, as that we cannot go thence, nor stay there; we celebrate our own funerals with cries, even at our birth; as though our threescore and ten years life were spent in our mother's labour, and our circle made up in the first point thereof, we beg our Baptism with another Sacrament, with tears.[9]

This opens with a formal simile and closes with another, plays on the words 'discharged' and 'bound', on the idea of the circle, and on the parallel between tears and water, and running through it is the paradox that birth is like death. It is difficult to find a much higher concentration of figurative language in even his wittiest poems.

Donne's Emotion

I have chosen an extreme example: this or any other sermon has long passages with little figurative language (though this is less true of Donne's sermons than of many others). But at least we cannot, using figurative language as the passport, keep the sermons out. Another possible strategy, however, would be to look at function, and point out that a poem stretches away to one or more of the other frontiers – to expression for instance. Of course we need to be anachronistic to maintain this: as chapter 2 made clear, the doctrine that rhetoric arouses emotion and poetry expresses it is a Romantic doctrine – though it is, at least once, anticipated by Donne:

I thought, if I could draw my pains
Through Rime's vexations, I should them allay.
Grief brought to numbers cannot be so fierce,
For he tames it, that fetters it in verse.[10]

Not merely expressive, we see, but therapeutic: so we can guess that the pains of religion (fear of damnation) can be allayed in these religious sonnets, just as the pains of love were in young Jack Donne's *Songs and Sonnets*. But the case for treating the Holy Sonnets as expressive must rest not just on such occasional anticipations of later doctrine, but on the claim that expression is not a theory of Romantic poetry, but a Romantic theory of poetry – of all poetry, including that written more or less in ignorance of the theory.

What if this present were the world's last night?
Mark in my heart, O Soul, where thou dost dwell,
The picture of Christ crucified, and tell
Whether that countenance can thee affright?
Tears in his eyes quench the amazing light,
Blood fills his frowns, which from his pierced head fell.
And can that tongue adjudge thee unto hell,
Which pray'd forgiveness for his foes fierce spite?
No, no; but as in my idolatry
I said to all my profane mistresses,
Beauty, of pity, foulness only is
A sign of rigour: so I say to thee,
To wicked spirits are horrid shapes assigned,
This beauteous form assures a piteous mind.[11]

Surely it is possible to read this poem as the expression
of emotion just as much as either of the Wordsworth sonnets
discussed in chapter 2. The emotion is clearly fear, and the
opening line, if read in a terrified whisper, is unforgettable in its
impact. After the description of the imagined picture of Christ in
his heart, the octave culminates in a question ('And can that
tongue. . .') This is not a calm, even confident inquiry about the
redemptive power of Christ, but a desperate attempt to believe that
the answer might be no. Then comes the strained argument of the
sestet: beautiful people are pitiful, ugly people are hard-hearted,
Christ was beautiful, therefore. . . It's a Platonic argument in
origin, and we might (just) imagine it being taken seriously, if it
were not for the outrageous reminder that he used to try it as a
seduction technique (with, of course, a very different meaning for
'pity'). This makes it very clear, surely, that the argument issues
from desperation, that it is strained not because the poem is over-
ingeniously written, but because the speaker is terrified. Once this
way of reading the poem has suggested itself, it seems to me
irresistible.

But not all Donne's devotional poems are like that. His other
sequence of sonnets, *La Corona*, for instance, is a formal meditation
on the life of Christ, consisting of seven linked sonnets on the
themes of the crown, annunciation, nativity, temple, crucifying,
resurrection and ascension. The last line of each sonnet is the same
as the first line of the next, and the last line of all is the first line of
the first, to give the sequence the shape of a circle – crown, or
rosary. The sonnets rehearse the doctrines of incarnation and

atonement, and the paradoxes that derive from them; though they call themselves 'a crown of prayer and praise', they are not prayers with the personal urgency of the Holy Sonnets, and the poet's own emotions are nowhere introduced.[12] By critics of a romantic tendency, they have always been regarded as verse, not poetry. To write off *La Corona* simply because it lacks the urgent presence of the poet, however, would be to use expression theory to write off a great deal of poetry (Donne's verse letters, for instance, as well as his *Litany*, besides many of the devotional poems of Vaughan and some of Herbert's). If expression is a touchstone for all poetry, even for all lyric poetry, it will have to be used more subtly, in a way that could be applied to a sermon too. Indeed, there are sermons in which Donne's emotions are very obviously present:

When upon our calamity we see the anger of God piled up and upon that, our sin, when I come to see my sin, in that glass, not in a Saviour bleeding for me, but in a Judge frowning upon me. . .[13]

When we shall have given to those words, by which hell is represented in the Scriptures, the heaviest significations . . . as fire, and brimstone, and weeping, and gnashing, and darkness, and the worm, . . . It is a pile of fire and much wood (there is the durableness of it) and the breath of the Lord to kindle it, like a stream of Brimstone (there is the vehemence of it): when all is done, the hell of hells, the torment of torments is the everlasting absence of God, and the everlasting impossibility of returning to his presence. . .[14]

Here we have fear of damnation, closely comparable to the fear expressed in sonnet XIII; what is to stop us from seeing such passages as expressive too? An interestingly indirect confirmation that this can be done is seen, I suggest, in the pained disapproval they have aroused in Donne's most celebrated modern admirer:

About Donne there hangs the shadow of the impure motive; and impure motives lend their aid to a facile success. He is a little of the religious spellbinder, . . . the flesh-creeper, the sorcerer of emotional orgy. . . Without belittling the intensity or the profundity of his experience, we can suggest that this experience was not perfectly controlled, and that he lacked spiritual discipline.[15]

This is from Eliot's essay on Lancelot Andrewes, whose sermons he prefers to Donne's precisely because 'Andrewe's emotion is purely contemplative; it is not personal, it is wholly evoked by the object of contemplation, to which it is adequate; his emotions wholly contained in and explained by its object.' And in indicating Donne's inferiority Eliot invokes, in disdainful inverted commas, the Romantic doctrine of expression that I have anachronistically employed: 'Donne is a "personality" in a sense in which Andrewes is not: his sermons, one feels, are "a means of self-expression".'

This is not disinterested criticism. Writing in 1926, only a year or two before he announced himself as classicist in literature, Anglo-Catholic in religion, royalist in politics, Eliot is surely trying to dissociate himself from Romanticism. The admiration for spiritual discipline, the disdain for 'experience that is not perfectly controlled', closely parallel to the attack on Hamlet for being 'dominated by an emotion which is inexpressible because it is in *excess* of the facts as they appear',[16] suggests a reaction against his own early poetry, perhaps against the open-endedness of modernism itself, and even against his own enthusiasm for Donne, along with a belief in traditions of spiritual discipline that will measure out the appropriate amount of emotion for each situation.

But what do we mean by emotion? If Eliot had written 'Andrewes' purpose is purely contemplative; his sermon is not personal . . . ; his language wholly contained in and explained by its object', would his meaning have lost anything? It is, that is to say, arguable that Eliot wants sermons without emotion, sermons whose content is wholly determined by a tradition of meditation that dictates what it is appropriate to think and say on each occasion, and that this eliminates anything we need to call emotion. This is the Eliot who wants no truck with enthusiasm, who is establishing his royalist, Anglo-Catholic, classicist credentials.

In this essay only Donne's sermons are mentioned; but it is difficult to see that the case would be different with the Holy Sonnets. They are just as subject to the accusation that the emotion is 'not perfectly controlled', and that the poems are 'a means of self-expression'. Or are they? Here we come up against yet another complication, that this way of reading Donne's devotional poems has been assailed by the most influential scholarly criticism of the last three or four decades, that which assimilates them to an extra-poetic tradition.[17] There has been much argument about what tradition, and the controversy between Martz, who relates them to Ignatian meditation, and Lewalski, who insists that the influences are Protestant, is of great interest for the history of religion, but of virtually no literary interest: for both critics regard poems as serving the same purpose as meditation, devotion or sermon; neither looks at the differences. This extended attempt to depersonalize Donne's poems has not, as far as I know, any of the ideological purpose I have attributed to Eliot (except perhaps for the more complex case of Helen Gardner, the most doctrinaire but also the most sensitive of the learned critics). And so although Lewalski advances the opposite view of Martz on Donne's theological allegiance, she too accepts the general principle that the way to establish the importance, even the validity, of a devotional poet is to rescue his poems from the untidness of personal experience, and fit them neatly into a tradition: 'The Protestant Pauline paradigm of salvation and the emotional states *supposed to* accompany it, influenced variously but profoundly the religious lyrics of Donne, Herbert, Vaughan, Traherne and Taylor, in regard to subject-matter, structure and range of feelings portrayed' (my italics).[18]

The best counter I know to this line of criticism is a brilliant article by John Stachniewski on 'The Despair of Donne's Holy Sonnets'. Stachniewski enters into the Catholic–Protestant controversy in order to attack the Martz–Gardner–Grant view that the Holy Sonnets derive from Ignatian meditation, and claims that they are essentially Calvinist. But more important for our purposes is his concern to treat them *as poems*, and this means to see them as the expression of emotion, as embodying 'the strain between an intense psychic state which gave rise to them, and the verbal and formal restrictions imposed on the expression of that state by verse'. (In the previous discussion I emphasized the correspondence between form and content in poetry; this is a useful reminder that the tension between them can be equally effective.) The part of Stachniewski's argument of central concern to us runs as follows:

It is not, after all, a matter of indifference at what distance from the poems Donne's personal experience lies. Responses to them will be conditioned by the assumption adopted. If Donne wrote poems about despair from a pious and assured standpoint, or if he was rehearsing a boyhood drill, he is both cleared of the theological reprehensibility of a state of mind which involved insult to God and of an autobiographical directness which embarrasses some theories of creativity.[19]

Eliot's, clearly, would be one such theory; so would those of the learned critics who locate Donne's poems in traditions of meditation, whether Catholic or Protestant, without distinguishing what makes them poems.

Why did Donne write Calvinist poetry? The obvious answer is, because he was a Calvinist; but this truism conceals the important question, can a poem be Calvinist, in the sense that what gives it its force as a poem is a matter of doctrine? When Lewalski commends the accuracy of Donne's theological terminology, is she making a point about the poetry?

This is my play's last scene, here heavens appoint
My pilgrimage's last mile. . .
Impute me righteous, thus purg'd of evil,
For thus I leave the world, the flesh, the devil.[20]

This is another poem on the fear of damnation, and a poem that fits better than most into the Ignatian scheme, for it begins with *compositio loci* (but then, as Stachniewski points out, so do most short dramatic lyrics; and the opening is more vivid here than in any meditation). As befits a meditation on the subject, it concludes with a plea for mercy; as befits a poem, the plea is urgent and intense; as we by now expect from Donne, the plea is desperate. At this point the Donne who has always loved to introduce technical terms into his poems, often in prominent positions, as if drawing attention to his own cleverness, introduces a theological term. Lewalski's commentary singles out the phrase 'impute me righteous', and congratulates Donne for getting his theology right:[21] this seems to regard it as normal to write poems in theological language. But this is not a normal thing for even a devout poet to do; and I suggest we should rather see it as bravado ('Look, I know the jargon'). Its introduction here serves the expressive purpose of showing the urgency of the plea.

Stachniewski nonetheless insists that the poems are Calvinist, and his reason for doing so is particularly interesting. He sees in Donne an emotional conviction of the truth of Calvinist doctrine, but does not use this to remove the element of outrageousness in the way they are presented. 'Donne presents himself as a victim of Calvinist tenets which he seems voluntarily to have espoused.' This is precisely the case that William Empson makes for *Paradise Lost*, which he regards as a challenge to Christian orthodoxy rather than an exemplification of it. If God appears to behave badly in the action of the poem, we need not dismiss this as modern misreading, for Milton would have considered it a disservice to Christianity to whitewash those actions which are meant to test the believer's faith. God is on trial in the poem because 'all the characters are on trial in any civilized narrative'.[22]

This argument neatly bypasses the old dispute between critic and scholar, between significance and meaning, between rational and historical reconstruction. The critic, looking for modern significance, finds the doctrine outrageous, and may try to rescue the poem from the limitations of its belief system: the poet is then said to transcend his age. The scholar, confining himself to historical reconstruction, returns him firmly to his age, and insists that it is only we who find the doctrine outrageous: good Calvinists clearly were not shocked by Calvinism. The Stachniewski-Empson position, as I understand it, avoids both these extremes by maintaining that a poem may bring to the surface precisely those shocking elements that Calvinists may well have felt more deeply than we do, though they did not find it so easy to say so. 'I am not proposing a new way to read the poem,' says Empson, 'because I claim to point out what often went on in the minds of pious readers who were deeply impressed by it.'[23] We can put this point several ways. Poems do not expound doctrines, they test them; or, poems bring out the contradictions in doctrine, since they are not declarative but interrogative. The first is New Critical language, the second structuralist. The theoretical battles that rage so hard between critical schools obscure the fact that for the purpose of providing a vocabulary to state the relationship between a poem and its theology, either will do.

Both Donne's poems, then, and on occasion his sermons, can be read as expression:

But whether the gate of my prison be opened with an oiled key (by a gentle and preparing sickness), or the gate be hewn down by a violent death, or the gate be burnt down by a raging and frantic fever, a gate into heaven I shall have, for from the Lord is the cause of my life, and with God the Lord are the issues of death.[24]

Since I am coming to that Holy room,
    Where with thy Choir of Saints for evermore,
I shall be made thy Music; as I come
    I tune the instrument here at the door,
    And what I must do then, think here before.[25]

Here is Donne (rather uncharacteristically) regarding death with
confidence. Apart from the fact of verse in the second passage, is
there any important difference between the two? Can we really say
that one is as a key to the Kingdom of Heaven, as physic unto
diseased minds, and the other an act of self-expression? Both are
powerful, even unforgettable; both employ an extended conceit;
both are in the first person. Is there any important difference in
their relation to experience? I suggest that the best way to tackle
this question is to focus on the personal pronoun: does the word 'I'
function in the same way in each? In the Hymn the 'I' is clearly
proferred as the poet himself. If we discovered that the poem had
been written when he was in perfect health this would not
necessarily undermine its poetic value (except for naïve Romantics,
looking for 'sincerity'), but we'd have to say that the fact that the
speaker is in good health forms no part of the poem's meaning. In
the sermon, 'I' is virtually the same as 'you'. The sermon is about
death, and it moves in and out of examples in which the choice of
pronoun seems indifferent:

We celebrate our own funeral with cries, even at our birth; as though our
forescore and ten years of life were spent in our mother's labour. . .

It may be the mere dust of the earth, which never did live, never shall. It
may be the dust of that man's worm, which did live, but shall no more. It
may be the dust of another man, that concerns not him of whom it is
asked.

How thou passedst all that time last night thou knowest. If thou didst
anything that needed Peter's tears, and hast not shed them, let me be thy
Cock, do it now.[26]

When the preacher introduces something as his own experience and
no one else's, it is likely to be an illustrative detail like the house of
Anabaptists where he lodged: that it happened to him is true but
unimportant. Significant experiences, in contrast, can glide from
one person to another, for in this context I = you = he = we.

The Audience

Another way of saying this is that the sermon has an audience.
'What a coronation is our taking of order,' Donne exclaims to his

hearers, '. . . and what an inthronization is the coming up into a Pulpit.' For it enables him to preach, and thus to imitate God:

That God should appear in a Cloud, upon the Mercy seat, as he promises Moses he will do, that from so poor a man as stands here, wrapped up in clouds of infirmity, and in clouds of iniquity, God should drop, rain, pour down his dew, and sweeten that dew with his honey, and crust that honeyed dew into Manna, and multiply that Manna into Gomers, and fill those Gomers every day, and give every particular Man his Gomer, give every soul in the Congregation, consolation by me.

No doubt it was a delight to Jack Donne the poet to feel he had responsive readers, but never so immediate and vivid a delight as this. For clause after clause, he rejoices in the privilege God has granted him:

That when I call to God for grace here, God should give me grace for grace, Grace in a power to derive grace upon others, and that this this Oil, this Balsamum should flow to the hem of the garment, even upon them that stand under me; that when mine eyes look up to Heaven, the eyes of all should look up upon me, and God should open my mouth, to give them meat in due season.[27]

Elsewhere he compares the preacher to an eagle, remarking that in Scripture the simile is used of God himself.[28] On his departure for Germany in 1619 he preached a farewell to his auditors that naturally suggests comparison with his poems of Valediction ('Of my Name in the Window', 'Of the Book', 'Of Weeping', 'Forbidding Mourning'). The poems are all concerned with the pain of parting, and the perfection of a relationship that can survive it. They all work by analogy: their union in separation is like gold to airy thinness beat, or like twin compasses, or like the presence of his name written on the window pane, their tears are like coins, or worlds, or the ocean. We learn about union or separation, but nothing about that woman or that parting. In the sermon on the other hand there are particulars:

Remember my labours, and endeavours, at least my desire, to make sure your salvation. And I shall remember your religious cheerfulness in hearing the word, and your christianly respect towards all them that bring that word unto you, and towards myself in particular far above my merit.[29]

This is much less dazzling than the compasses, or the tears which 'a
globe, yea world, by that impression grow', but it does show
awareness of an interaction between actual people. Donne hopes to
be remembered not through the brilliant conceit of carving on the
window 'this ragged bony name to be My ruinous Anatomy', but
because they listened to him bringing them the Word.

Since the purpose of a sermon is to teach, there must be pupils,
and awareness of this fact can permeate every moment of it.

And new Philosophy calls all in doubt,
The Element of fire is quite put out;
The Sun is lost, and th'earth, and no man's wit
Can well direct him where to look for it. . .[30]

I need not call in new Philosophy, that denies a settledness, an
acquiescence in the very body of the Earth, but makes the Earth to move
in that place, where we thought the Sun had moved; I need not that help,
that the Earth itself is in Motion, to prove this, that nothing upon Earth is
permanent; the Assertion will stand of itself, till some man assign me
some instance. . .[31]

This is a favourite idea of Donne's: everything is in flux, even our
ideas of what is flux and what is stasis. There is no difference in
content between the two passages, but the poem drops its assertion
into that void where poems have their being, waiting for someone
to come and read them. The sermon is offered to a particular
audience who are waiting to be convinced, or to resist, and who are
invited to consider and accept the reasoning. Once we have become
aware of this, we can detect it in even the slightest transitions: in
the imperatives ('consider the greatest bodies on earth. . .'), in the
habit of occasionally slipping into the second person or the plural
we, in the tone of the lecturer saying confidently 'I may be
wrong' ('till some man assign me some instance') or anxious to be
understood ('The Gentiles . . . describe the sad state of Death so,
Nox una obeunda, that it is one everlasting Night; to them, a Night;
but to a Christian, it is *Dies Mortis*, and *Dies Resurrectionis*, the Day
of Death, and the Day of Resurrection.'[32]

I hope no scholarly reader will feel tempted at this point to assert
that Donne himself, in the 'Hymn to God my God, in my
Sickness', denies the distinction I am here exploring.

So, in his purple wrapp'd receive me Lord,
　By these his thorns give me his other Crown;
And as to others' souls I preach'd thy word,
　Be this my Text, my Sermon to mine own,
　　Therefore that he may raise the Lord throws down.[33]

The claim that this poem, which may be his last, is an attempt to do for himself what he has so long done for others, that is that it is a sermon, is only worth making because poems are not normally sermons. For once, now, he is his own audience; lying helpless on a sickbed, he cannot get away, so Dr Donne tells what is left of Jack Donne that he had better listen. This triumphant figure forces us to grant that there is a difference, even a fundamental difference, between sermon and poem: unless there were, what would be the point of abolishing it at a moment of crisis?

We have found three significant differences between sermon and poem. First, a poem is in verse: this is a matter of technique, or verbal means for attaining the end. Second, a poem (at any rate a Holy Sonnet, in the first person) can be expressive rather than didactic. And third, a sermon has an audience, in a literal and pervasive sense, and a poem does not. The first two points, however, could be true of sermons as well: they are never literally in verse, but once we treat the patternings that verse uses as more than superficial, we come across elements that may be found in prose too. Similarly, sermons will not set out to be expressive (but nor, perhaps, do pre-Romantic poems: they achieve expression, or have it thrust on them). What keeps the sermon from achieving it fully will be, above all, the third element, the ever-present consciousness of audience.

There are real breaks and contrasts here, but they do not quite correspond to the generic difference we began from: the frontier has not, by traditional generic distinction, been drawn in quite the right place. As frontiers quite properly never have been.

Politics

In the field of politics, didactic views of literature will not lie down. This is inevitable, as long as people care about political questions: if improving the world (or preserving it from disaster) is important, then it is natural (and not necessarily discreditable) to ask what contribution poems and novels can make to this task. The socialist will want them to promote socialism, the feminist to transform gender relations, the Conservative to defend the free market economy. The simplest way to apply this standard would be to prefer works that espouse these goals, but most readers are sophisticated enough to avoid this: it would at once founder on the well-known fact that readers of very different political persuasion can agree on literary value. The argument is more likely to claim that any true literary experience works towards an appreciation of human equality, of the value of the feminine, of the virtues of freedom, an appreciation that, when we think about it politically, leads to the position we hold.

South Africa

To conduct this argument with the bluntness that is desirable, we need explicitly political material; and it will be most trenchant if we take an example where we are all likely to feel the same political sympathy, so that there will be no stock resistances aroused by preprogrammed arguments. I therefore choose South Africa, which in the 1980s is everyone's cause: apartheid, central to every institution in the country, has few friends outside South Africa. As a preliminary, let us look at the subject itself. In politics, apartheid keeps political power firmly in the hands of the whites, though they form only fifteen per cent of the population. Residential apartheid means that the different racial groups live in different parts of the country, or different areas of a town: this culminates in the 'separate development' of the Bantustans, which have a kind of technical independence but are in practice dependent on South Africa. Social apartheid means that white and black attend different schools, and (in part) different universities, do not mix as friends, and do not intermarry. The Nationalist government at first formalized and has recently rescinded much of this residential and social separation, but this can be seen as tinkering with the edges, since the separation has always been fairly complete. Economic apartheid means enormous discrepancies of wealth, most of which is in white hands (though there are also some wealthy Indians), while the economy is dependent for its flourishing on black labour in industry and on black domestic servants.

I hope that account will seem objective, but if we continue it we will soon run into controversy. It may seem objective to say that sixteen per cent of the population is white, ten per cent coloured (of mixed races), three per cent Indian and seventy-three per cent

African; but is this division into four groups the correct one? If the political struggle over apartheid itself is seen as central, then the basic analysis should be into two: the whites, who control the system, and the non-whites, who are its victims. On the other hand, the groups can be further divided. The government likes to divide the Africans into tribes, a division that is considered superficial by many Africans, who see it as a form of divide and rule; but the history of other African countries since independence suggests that tribalism is by no means dead. As for the whites, the division into English and Afrikaans speakers is so important that until recently it provided the subject-matter of most political conflict within the white democracy. Afrikaaners consider them-selves to have been the victims of British imperialist aggression, and the central events of their view of history (the Great Trek and the Boer war) illustrate this. Since Afrikaners form the majority, and have always provided the politicians, the party divisions have been between those who place Afrikanerdom in the centre, and those who believe in co-operation among all the whites. These two groups unite in their support of apartheid, which has in the past been opposed by hardly any whites. But now it seems to have moved much nearer to the centre of the political agenda, perhaps as a result of outside pressure, since apartheid is almost universally condemned by world opinion.

But that statement is itself controversial, since many radicals, indignant at British investment in the South African economy, will claim that much of this condemnation is hypocritical. This claim is so important in its literary implications, that we cannot either dismiss it or simply accept it. Hypocrisy is everywhere and nowhere: it is, I shall suggest, of obsessive interest to the novelist.

Not surprisingly, this complex, plural, conflict-torn society has produced a rich and controversial literature. Here are two descriptions of apartheid:

The cities, industries, mines and agriculture of the country are the result of the efforts of all its peoples. But the wealth is utilised by and for the interests of the White minority only. . . The bulk of the land is in the hands of land barons, absentee landlords, big companies and state capitalist enterprises. . . The minds of White people have been poisoned with all manner of unscientific and racialist twaddle.[1]

Harriet has been brought up to realise her life of choices and decent comfort is not shared by the people in whose blackness it is embedded: once protected by them, now threatened.[2]

The assertions of the African National Congress offer a clear and even simplistic analysis of South African society, in order to announce a political programme designed to change it. Such an analysis would be weakened by too many qualifications, by too vivid an awareness of the tensions inherent in living in that society, by asking too sharply whether a non-apartheid society would generate similar tensions. Nadine Gordimer's description is perfectly compatible with the ANC statement: it even implies that Harriet was exceptional, that most white South Africans are brought up not to realize this, or not to realize its implications. But the second passage announces itself very clearly as a different kind of writing, inviting us to enjoy the precision and suggestiveness of 'embedded', the elegant accuracy of the last, terse statement.

In order to explore the relation between these two discourses, for that is clearly our concern in this section, we must have some sort of political classification of the literature. Two classifications are possible: according to whom it depicts, and according to the political stance of the book. And by the first, we can mean which group according to official, 'objective' classification (Afrikaners, coloureds, urban Africans, and so on), or which political position. Among the whites, the main political distinction will be between the supporters and opponents of apartheid, and each of these can be subdivided. Among the supporters, there will be the traditional *Herrenvolk* view, often expressed with mere hostility and contempt ('blerry Kaffirs should know their place'), and the more relativist rhetoric that has now spread from English to Afrikaans circles ('I couldn't feel easy about sitting down with a black man, it's the way I've been brought up'). Among the opponents, the obvious division is between liberals and revolutionaries, a difference that can be seen in political, ideological or moral terms. Morally, we can define the liberal as the believer in the value of human contact across racial boundaries, the revolutionary as the one who considers it sentimental to place too much importance on individual contact. Politically, the liberal believes in gradual, the revolutionary in sudden change: it is usually assumed that sudden change is violent, gradual change peaceful, but this may be one of the unexamined clichés of our time. Ideologically, the revolutionary will be a Marxist, and will see apartheid as a consequence of capitalism; the liberal (or one kind of liberal) may claim that capitalism is the enemy of apartheid, that the development of a free labour market will cause this authoritarian, pre-capitalist system to collapse.

God's Stepchildren

This analysis could continue indefinitely, growing more complicated, opening up more and more possibilities of regroupings and rearrangements. It is time to relate these complexities to the problems of literary representation, by turning to actual novels. I think it will be helpful to begin with one that seems to support apartheid, and I have chosen *God's Stepchildren* (1924), by the once popular novelist Sarah Gertrude Millin.

The Reverend Andrew Flood is an earnest young missionary who comes to South Africa in 1821, fails pathetically to make any real converts in his isolated settlement, goes native and marries a Hottentot woman. The novel then tells the story of four generations of the resulting mixed race, and the problems that face them. Some live like Hottentots, and some, who look white, pass themselves off as Europeans, but are always found out in the end. To depict the sufferings of coloured folk is not in itself ideological, but we can apply a few touchstones in order to discover the judgement implied by the book itself. Barry, who looks white and is rich, is sent to school in Cape Town, and looked after by his wholly white and much older half-sister Edith. He lives in perpetual fear of discovery (discovery, that is, of his mixed blood and his dark-skinned relatives). Now we can ask whether this fear is caused by the prejudices of the society that will punish the innocent Barry for his origin, or whether there is some kind of corruption within Barry himself.

Yet as far as Barry himself was concerned, it was not only the fear of discovery and contumely that burdened his heart, it was, with advancing years, the fear that, being what he was, he could not maintain accepted white standards. He sometimes wondered whether he had the same instincts and feelings as the other boys. It was true, of course, that he did better at schoolwork than many of his fellows, but that, he fancied dimly, might not be the most important mental aspect.[3]

The omniscient author seems to have little doubt here that the prejudice of a racist society is based on – even justified by – something in Barry himself. I do not want to be unfair to Sarah Gertrude Millin: there are moments in the book when we are reminded that coloured blood would not matter in England, that any child may have 'evils' in its blood, but this passage seems decisive. Furthermore, the fact that the story is about those of mixed race is itself given a central importance. In South African society, a black African is likely to be poorer and more discriminated against than a coloured man, and he will not of course have the opportunity of passing for white. If Millin chose coloured protagonists because this opportunity produces a problematic situation, she is like any novelist in search of a good plot, but that does not seem the only reason: there are constant suggestions that the Coloureds are especially unfortunate because they stand between two pure-bred races, and are worse off than either:

In other parts of South Africa, among the Zulus, the Pondos, the Swazis . . . the people were big, black and vigorous . . . ; but here . . . they were nothing but an untidiness of God's earth – a mixture of degenerate brown peoples, rotten with sickness, an affront against Nature.[4]

Heredity tends to be the belief of the conservative, environmentalism of the liberal and the radical. It is what we would expect: environment can be changed, heredity cannot, and a belief that social evils can be cured will naturally look to the possibility of cure. A detail of vocabulary is worth noticing. Today we speak of genes, our forebears spoke of blood; and 'blood' seems to belong more deeply to the individual, it seems a way of both asserting that the taint is inescapable and also claiming that it is all-pervasive, even that it is his fault. Not only is Millin a strong hereditarian, it leads her into a very interesting inconsistency. She frequently reproaches her characters (or their community) for their obsession with colour. 'What mattered was simply pigmentation. . . All that Mrs Lindsell noticed was the olive skin. . .' But it could be argued that all that Millin notices is the olive skin. When she describes or discusses the character or situation of any of her personages, she seems to think about one thing only: writing a story about miscegenation, that is what she concentrates on. She reproaches her characters for doing what she does.

God's Stepchildren is a novel of narrow focus: the emotional lives of its characters emerge from nothing but colour. If they laugh, fall in love, make money or respond to the landscape, these are described cursorily, but we linger on colour. This make it a novel about racial purity, since that theme keeps rising to the surface, elbowing away the rich complexities of the lives of the characters. This also means that it is a novel of limited interest, for much the same reason: we know where the author stands, precisely because she damps down the complexities which we expect to find in a realistic novel.

The Grass is Singing

Turning now to more recent fiction, I begin with the Afrikaners. The staunchest supporters of apartheid have always been the rural whites, most of all those who are poor. That group forms the subject of *The Grass is Singing*, Doris Lessing's first and (many would claim) finest novel. (There is incidentally some uncertainty whether the novel takes place in South Africa or Rhodesia, but for our purposes this difference is unimportant.) It is the story of the murder of a white farmer's wife by her black houseboy: we are told of the crime in the first chapter, and the rest of the book narrates the events that led up to it. We discover that the Turners were a pathetically inadequate couple, neither competent at farming, nor capable of any warm human feeling towards each other, their neighbours or their employees. They quarrel about how to handle 'their' Africans, and it is not easy to say which of them is more prejudiced.

'Why shouldn't I ask him?' she demanded. 'He's lying, isn't he?'
'Of course he's lying,' said Dick irritably. 'Of course. That is not the point. You can't keep him against his will.'
'Why should I accept a lie?' said Mary. 'Why should I? Why can't he say straight out that he doesn't like working for me, instead of lying about his kraal?'
Dick shrugged, looking at her with impatience; he could not understand her unreasonable insistence: he knew how to get on with natives; dealing with them was a sometimes amusing, sometimes annoying game in which both sides followed certain unwritten rules.[5]

Dick is used to handling Africans, Mary isn't. Dick is cynical, Mary vindictive. Dick is easygoing, Mary fiercely moral (about others). There are several ways of describing this difference, but there is no way in which either can be described as a well-wisher. As we read on, we discover that Mary's inadequacy is so deep as to constitute neurosis. She cannot endure her African houseboys, flies out at them in unreasonable rages, and in her aggressive phase she lashes one of the farm labourers with a sjambok. He is the one who later becomes the houseboy, and the strangest and most powerful part of the book records the imperceptible shifts by which her frenetic hostility to him changes into dependence, until in the end, when she is capable of no effort, he does everything for her, including putting on her clothes. When the neighbouring whites begin to realize what has happened, they close ranks in accordance with what the author calls 'the first law of white South Africa':

Thou shalt not let your fellow whites sink lower than a certain point; because if you do, the nigger will see he is as good as you are.[6]

As a study of racial attitudes, this book has an enormous strength, which is at the same time a limitation: it shows that white South Africans are neurotic about colour. In fact, it says so:

Whenever two or three farmers are gathered together, it is decreed that they should discuss nothing but the shortcomings and deficiencies of their natives. They talk about their labourers with a persistent irritation sounding in their voices: individual natives they might like, but as a genus, they loathe them. They loathe them to the point of neurosis.[7]

Those sentences could have been part of a political pamphlet: but no pamphlet would then go on to show, as *The Grass is Singing* so astonishingly does, that it really meant what it was saying, by showing how profound are the links between Mary's neurosis and her hatred of blacks, and how the neurotic mechanisms we are watching can lead her from hating Moses to needing him. It is a masterpiece of insight and re-creation. But the question it poses is inescapable: is Dick, are the other whites, also neurotic, or was the author just mouthing a phrase when she wrote of the men 'they loathe them to the point of neurosis'? Can a society be sick? The answer to this, surely, has to be, yes and no. If we cannot say that Nazi Germany was sick because of its pathological hatred of Jews (and everyone will add further examples according to her own views), then we cannot make precisely those political judgements that it is most important to make: Mary Turner is a wonderful figure to show the ordinary white woman's pathology. But societies that we may feel sure are sick or depraved do go on functioning, and to call someone neurotic is to say that she is ceasing to function. Unless we can show what is normal about white South Africa or Nazi Germany, unless we can remember that the Turners' neighbours, the Slatters, are also racists, but will never collapse like Mary (and later Dick), then we have not really begun to understand how it functions. Mary therefore has to be shown both as failing to function by the standards of her society, and as providing insights into its norms. That this is impossible is not to the book's discredit.

There is one thing in this story which remains unsaid: why did Moses kill Mary Turner? The best known theory of the unsaid in literature is probably that of Pierre Macherey, whose theory of latency derives from Nietzsche's remark that in everything that a man allows to be seen, we can ask what he is concealing, what he wants to prevent us seeing. That which is not said in a book is not, according to Macherey, a lack we can supply, an inadequacy which it might be our task to see to: it has a necessary status in the work. The concept is a useful one, though I have to say that Macherey does not do anything with it. His strategy of argument is exactly the opposite to that which I am trying to use in this book: he asserts and modifies a position by moving abstract nouns around, by hesitating between, say, 'pacte' and 'contrat' without explaining what he understands the difference to consist in, by moving about among the words 'pourquoi', 'fin', 'signification', 'sens', at a distance from any attempt to apply them. But the idea of the unsaid can still help us in this argument. Why, for instance, do we learn nothing about Moses' motivation? All through the story, we are never fully taken into his consciousness, but this is part of its strength: it keeps him at a distance from us, the (probably white) readers, in a way that enacts the situation we are being shown. It is not difficult to deduce a good deal about Moses from what we see, until we come to the climax. Did he kill Mary out of revenge for the blow with the sjambok much earlier? Out of shame at her shame? Out of revulsion from the intimacy imposed on him? Out of his realization that he was now certain to get into trouble, and because of her? Out of none of these? The novel gives us no clear hint? Moses is its area of necessary silence. That is, surely, its strategy for dealing with apartheid: whether Doris Lessing is unable to understand Moses, or deliberately does not try to, we can still feel the presence of the unsaid as a way of representing a cleavage in the society. Some readers will regret this omission, others will feel that it gives the book a mysterious power.

Liberals and Revolutionaries

The Grass is Singing is not a typical South African novel. Most of them depict not the supporters of apartheid but its liberal opponents. There are two reasons for this. One is that both the novelists and their readers usually belong to this group: it is natural, is it not, for the novelist to depict what she knows, and perhaps it is natural – at any rate for one kind of novelist – to depict those she agrees with. The other and more interesting reason is that white liberals neither fit into nor reject the society they live in. The liberal questions and complicates what his society takes for granted; but he cannot live out his own values. Almost all his actions, while he lives in South Africa, imply an acceptance of the apartheid that he rejects. This contrasts him with the conservative (English or Afrikaans) who accepts the society, or the revolutionary who lives out his rejection of it: both these have their problems, but they do not live in the state of contradiction that makes the liberal such rich material for the novelist. Nadine Gordimer states the dilemma succinctly: 'I have always refused to join any exclusively white clubs, yet how absurd when I make regular use of other white facilities: trains, taxis, theatres.' This is the contradiction perceived by those radicals who accuse the respectable critics of apartheid (from Johannesburg liberals to Western governments) of hypocrisy. Mere hypocrisy – the clear-cut opposition between what you profess and what you do – is as I suggested earlier, of very limited interest. But the hypocrisy that is forced on one by the circumstances of one's own life is of enormous interest. The neatest example of how this can issue in the action of a novel comes from Nadine Gordimer herself. In *The Lying Days*, the social worker, Paul, who is very sympathetically treated, works within official structures that he is more and more being led to question, until in the end he spends his evenings denouncing the community centre that he works so hard to build during the day. There is the liberal's dilemma, in a nutshell of contradiction.

And the radicals? Those for whom liberalism is timid and hesitant and fails to confront the need for fundamental change; those, that is, who advocate strikes, pickets, armed struggle or terrorist attacks. And the non-whites? Those who live on the receiving end of apartheid, to whom it means not a bad conscience but daily oppression: poverty, eviction, brutality. To put these two groups together is not of course to deny that there are plenty of moderate, liberal and (even more) non-political blacks, but it is justified for two reasons. One is that since the African National Congress adopted the policy of armed struggle in 1961, and even more since the Soweto riots of 1976, most revolutionaries have been black. The second is that the actual situation of the black man in South Africa is necessarily like that of the white revolutionary: he is shut out compulsorily from white society in the way the revolutionary has chosen to be shut out, by going underground or by going into exile. The tensions of benefiting from a system you condemn (the basic situation of the white liberal) are abandoned by the revolutionary, never available to the black man. So I shall look at the revolutionary and his presence in literature, as a way in to looking more generally at the non-white.

The case for revolution has been stated frequently. Ben Turok, writing in the *Socialist Register*, links violent methods to fundamental transformation of society, the replacing of Conventional Democracy ('based on a belief in the need to extend the existing parliamentary structure to embrace the Black people') by Revolutionary Democracy, which

envisages a seizure of power by the oppressed and the creation of a new state structure with a wholly new popular power base and which will give expression to the democratic will of the people as a whole and particularly its Black majority.

He describes very clearly the change in tactics that resulted from the banning of the ANC, and its shift from a reformist to a revolutionary programme:

Prior to 1960, activists in the liberation movement, of whom a large number were banned, operated on two levels, the open and the covert. They sat in offices behind desks and produced legal publications, but they also met other banned personnel in private. While this system made it possible to combine legal and illegal work effectively, it also gave leads to the police. After the declaration of a state of emergency this system was changed.

A movement which sets up an underground apparatus

has moved very far indeed from the position it held formerly. It requires a total reorientation in political outlook. The underground activist is a social outcast isolated in his network of close associates. He must shed his remaining illusions of political participation as an ordinary citizen.[8]

What is being described here? I suggest there are two very different issues in question. First, what is political action now like for the revolutionaries: the answer to this is careful and vivid, and a novelist who wanted to write about underground activists would be pointed in the right direction. Second, what will the eventual institutions of revolutionary democracy be like: there is no answer at all to this question, either in the passage quoted or elsewhere in the article. Would revolutionary democracy involve parliaments at all, would there be elections, would there be soviets, would it be military or civilian, who would take what decisions? A novelist who wanted to write about revolutionary democracy would get no help from Ben Turok. But then what novelist would want to write about that (unless she were writing a Utopia or a Dystopia) since it does not yet exist? Turok's article, it turns out, is more help to the novelist than to someone who wants to understand the politics.

For the novelist, revolution provides subject matter in the form of revolutionaries; for the poet, in the form of a call to or a celebration of political action. A revolutionary poem of the simplest kind would be Barry Feinberg's 'Ten Targets Reel under Rage of Vision', which ends like this:

Tomorrow,
maybe no game but combat coming.

Then,
that fast drop to knee
fierce burst of fire,
quick dodge and crawl
and back track to cover.

This,
a fine tuned, harsh handled man
hard as nails and head well guided;
no computer type reaction
no lathe like operation,
but thought out, mind planned,
hands trim on hair-taut trigger.
His eyes blaze down dead–still barrel.
ten targets reel under rage of vision.[9]

This is the celebration of heroism, in its simplest form: the exhilaration of fighting, the delight of one's own physical control, the ability to kill cleanly. Suppose we put this next to another celebration of heroism:

The fighting man shall from the sun
Take warmth, and life from the glowing earth. . .

And when the burning moment breaks
And all things else are out of mind,
And Joy of Battle only takes
Him by the throat and makes him blind. [10]

Here are two different cultures. The romantic pantheism of Julian
Grenfell, celebrating the pointless heroism of the 1914–18 war, tells
us, by its hunting imagery ('the kestrel hovering by day') and its
tightlipped diction ('the fighting man') that this is an officer's
poem, not a private's. The attempt at down-to-earth imagery by
Feinberg says (or tries to say) that this is a materialist poem, free of
gentlemanly ideals. Yet for all their differences, I ask whether there
is not a great overlap between the poems: whether Feinberg's too
could not be called 'Into Battle', whether the blazing eyes of the
freedom fighter are those of someone whom Joy of Battle has taken
by the throat.

A more interesting case is Oswald Mtshali's poem 'The Birth of
Shaka', perhaps the most famous single poem produced by the
Soweto poets, the so-called 'Generation of 1976':

His baby cry
was of a cub
tearing the neck
of the lioness
because he was fatherless.

The gods
boiled his blood
in a clay pot of passion
to course in his veins.

His heart was shaped into an ox shield
to foil every foe.

Ancestors forged
his muscles into
thongs as tough
as wattle bark
and nerves
as sharp as
syringa thorns.

His eyes were lanterns
that shone from the dark valleys of Zululand
to see white swallows
coming across the sea.
His cry to two assassin brothers:

'Lo, you can kill me
but you'll never rule this land!'[11]

Here Shaka, the Zulu warrior chief, is a Hercules figure, heroically
strong from birth; and the final cry is like the defiance of Marius in
prison, frightening the armed assassin by demanding haughtily
whether he would dare to kill Caius Marius, saving himself by
sheer strength of character.[12] But such classical parallels are not
really appropriate, because the poem is thoroughly, even ostanta-
tiously, African in setting and imagery. We would not be justified
in saying 'ostentatiously' if it were a Zulu song dating back to the
time of Shaka, and I am not competent to say how plausibly it
could be seen as a translation of such – in other words, how far its
origin in modern urban South Africa is incorporated into its
meaning. As we read it this way – reading it as a Soweto poem –
the African imagery becomes not something inevitable, but an
assertion. The penultimate paragraph then takes on historical
meaning: not only in the obvious symbolism of 'white swallows
coming across the sea' but in the suggestion that Shaka represents
the emergence of the Zulus from their homeland. But though this
ambiguity is suggestive there is, surely, nothing ambiguous about
the celebration of heroism: that, centrally, is what the poem is.

   To find such celebration in fiction, we can turn to the ending of
Alex La Guma's *In the Fog of the Season's End*, which relates two
days in the life of Beukes, an underground worker distributing
illegal pamphlets. One of his comrades is caught and tortured,
some others escape to join the freedom fighters. Beukes watches the
latter drive away:

The sun was brightening the east now, clearing the roofs of the suburb
and the new light broke the shadows into scattered shapes. . . Beukes
stood by the side of the street in the early morning and thought, they have
gone to war in the name of a suffering people. What the enemy himself
has created, these will become battle grounds, and what we see now is
only the tip of an iceberg of resentment against an ignoble regime, the
tortured victims of hate and humiliation. And those who persist in hatred

and humiliation must prepare. Let them prepare hard and fast – they do not have long to wait.[13]

Stirring stuff, in its predictable way: and not very different from a pamphlet, for the language of heroic action does not change much when it moves from exhortation to narrative: the leader's speech before battle can slide between the formalities of actual encounters and the ringing lines of epic without ceasing to feel at home, and both the short exhortatory poem and the heroic gesture at the end of a novel are easily tugged towards a rhetoric of oversimplification. For a more complex example, I turn to La Guma's novel *The Stone Country*, set in a South African prison. It has two claims to being thought of as a political novel. George Adams, the hero, is a political prisoner, arrested for distributing illegal pamphlets: what he has done would not be a crime in a liberal democracy, but here it has made him one of the 'forced inhabitants of another country, another world':

This was a world without beauty; a lunar barrenness of stone and steel and locked doors. In this world no trees grew, and the only shade was found in the shadow of its cliffs of walls, the only perfume it knew came from night-soil buckets and drains. . . The only music the regulations allowed was composed out of the slap-slap of bare feet, the grinding of boots, counterpointed by shouted orders, the slam of doors and the tintinnabulation of heavy keys. Anything else smacked of rebellion.[14]

In this other world, he is forced into contact with the dregs of society, with the strong and the brutal, and finds himself in physical danger from the other prisoners as well as from the warders; at the same time he is forced into solidarity with them, and in some cases he succeeds in breaking through the barriers of hatred and isolation. This is the second reason why the novel can be called political, that it shows prison as a microcosm of an oppressive society: the warders are white, the prisoners are non-white.

There are two simple views of the relation between radicalism and crime. To the naïve conservative, they are unconnected: the criminal is merely wicked, or pathological. To the naïve Marxist they are allies because both defy 'the system'. Neither simplification can apply to this novel, in which we constantly swing between the solidarity of prisoners under their institutional oppression, and the view that the worst oppression is that of some prisoners over others. This is the way La Guma sees non-white society in all his novels: both as imploding under self-destructive forces, and as resisting outside oppression.

If I am right in drawing a parallel between the underground workers and the non-whites – the voluntary and the involuntary exiles from the privileges of white South Africa – then every story about non-whites is at least potentially political. To test this, I will look at a collection of short stories by four coloured writers, called *Quartet*. Four of them are especially relevant to us. In 'Strike', by Richard Rive, two coloured men, Boston and Lennie, are (once more – it is clearly a favourite subject) distributing illegal pamphlets. Lennie turns into a booksellers to buy some drawing paper, saying he must paint over the weekend, though Boston is nervous, and tells him to hurry. It takes Lennie a long time to get served: it always does, if you are coloured. While he is waiting Boston turns over books in the shop, and attracts the attention of a suspicious assistant (you often do, if you are coloured). He is indignant when accused of stealing, but once he has become the focus of attention there is no way he can prevent his satchel being opened and the pamphlets discovered. In 'Out of Darkness', by Alex La Guma, the narrator is in prison, where he is fascinated by a fellow prisoner nicknamed Old Cockroach, who is gentle, educated and more or less mad, and whose story he finally learns: he'd been a schoolteacher, and in love with a girl whose skin was pale enough to pass for white, and who therefore jilted him, calling him finally a black nigger, and goading him to murder. In 'A Glass of Wine', also by La Guma, the narrator is in a pub with his drunken, loudmouthed friend Arthur, who teases a young boy about the obvious attraction between him and the proprietress' daughter Charlette, to the great embarrassment of both. The story ends with the narrator saying to Arthur:

'You know that white boy can't marry the girl, even though he may love her. It isn't allowed.'
'Jesus,' Arthur said in the dark. 'Jesus. What the hell.'

The non-South African reader might not have noticed that the boy was described as having 'beautiful red-gold hair combed in a high pompadour, and a pink-white skin', and the girl's skin was 'the colour of amber wine, and she had dark brown eyes, bright and soft, and around her oval face her hair was very black and curly'. Finally, 'The Park', by James Matthews, which has no plot, tells of the misery of a coloured boy shut out from the park, who comes

there after dark to use the forbidden swings, and is seen by the
attendant, who is also coloured but has to chase him away, and
indeed runs off for the police, while the boy goes on swinging,
higher and higher. 'At the entrance to the park the notice board
stood tall, its shadow elongated, pointing towards him.' (The
notice board says 'Whites only'.)[15]

Now the situation in all four of these stories has parallels outside
South Africa. The irony of 'Strike', by which the conspirator is
caught not because of his actual plot but through an irrelevant piece
of bad luck, could arise if a gunrunner were stopped for speeding,
or involved in a car accident through someone else's fault. Old
Cockroach could have committed his uncharacteristic act of
violence because the girl had been unfaithful, or developed a taste
for a richer life-style than he could offer her. The boy in 'A Glass of
Wine' might have been already married. The lad in 'The Park'
might have been shut out because the swings were on private
property, giving us a story about the rich and the poor rather than
the white and the black.

Could have . . . could have. . . Why should anyone want to
change the stories? Not, certainly, in order to improve them: in
every case, such a change would probably weaken them, though
some more than others ('Strike' and 'A Glass of Wine' would seem
to me to lose most, 'The Park' to lose least). This counterfactual
procedure is to help us establish just what the stories are about: how
far they are about the colour bar, how far that is just a local
manifestation of a more universal theme. It is not a matter of
replacing the political by the personal, since all the stories depict the
personal distress caused by something in the political situation; it is
rather a matter of deciding how specific the political is. I do not
indulge in this thought-experiment in order to influence the way we
read the stories, but to guide the way we think about reading them
and draw conclusions from them.

The stories were not written as a sequence, and are by three
different authors, but their presence in the same volume strengthens
them all: what grows steadily as we read is a sense of the lurking,
oppressive burden of apartheid, making it impossible for these
coloured people to do things that are quite reasonable in
themselves. In some ways this resembles a series of stories about
the looming inevitability of death, in another way it is quite
different, for what looms here is man-made and feels man-made
even as it feels, to the protagonists, inescapable. The tears of rage
and disappointment felt by the lad in 'The Park' cannot be replaced

merely by tears of compassion without dulling the effect: if it were a story about property, it would need readers who are as outraged by gross inequalities of wealth as most readers are by apartheid. If it is read by a reader who considers apartheid reasonable, it could have similar effect to the story about property on those who consider inequality inevitable. We can follow a similar train of thought with the others. 'A Glass of Wine' depends for its effect on our assuming the young couple to be perfectly ordinary, and perhaps it gains in power if we read it without noticing, first time round, the racial gap. If the obstacle were that Charlette or the boy is already married, it would only have the full effect on a reader to whom monogamy is as outrageous as apartheid.

Putting, now, the general question, how far are these stories political, I answer that they are so: not for the a priori reason that all stories about South Africa (or, for that matter, all stories) are political, but because removing the political element deprives them of part of their force.

Nadine Gordimer and the Critics

And now, to test the ground more thoroughly, I want a case where the political input of a writer's work shifts, so that we can ask what effect that has had on the literary product. An admirable example is provided by Nadine Gordimer, because of the contrast between her early and her later work, which most critics see as a result of her radicalization. We have already seen how she provides a classic example of the liberal dilemma in her first novel. We would not expect a writer of her sensitivity and intelligence to stand still, and her views on South Africa do seem, over the years, to have hardened, her political statements to have grown blunter. In 1965 she declared 'I am not a politically minded person by nature,' and though she went on to say that living in South Africa had forced her into political awareness, she was very emphatic that such awareness should feed the creation of art, not dominate it:

The artist must at all times follow his instinct, which makes art the most real thing, the most austere school in life and the last true judgement. The temptation to put one's writing at the service of a cause – whether it is fighting the colour-bar or 'the momentary renunciation of literature in order to educate the people', etc, is a betrayal.[16]

None of her later statements actually rejects this, but in more recent interviews she does not speak in the same way. 'I am a white South African radical,' she said in 1974. 'Please don't call me a liberal.'[17] 'As time went on,' she said in 1987, 'I felt I could not go on living in South Africa without moving to meet some of the demands of the time. . . . I wouldn't then (1960) take a public position on politics, as I am doing now.'[18]

Most of her critics, aware of this change, use it to describe what has happened to her fiction. Thus Michael Wade claims that she has moved from 'being a European writer born in exile' to 'placing South African reality firmly within the context of the post-colonial experience of the third world'.[19] Abdul R. JanMohamed divides her fiction into three phases, which he calls 'bourgeois', 'postbourgeois' and 'revolutionary'.[20] John Cooke says that in her later fiction she 'claims an African tradition as her own', centring her novels on the actions of blacks, treating 'black' as 'an answer'.[21] Stephen Clingman claims that in the later novels 'the very notion of change in itself implies the complete overturn of existing social reality'.[22] And so the novelist who above all others seemed the laureate of the white liberals is now seen as their scourge.

This looks very like an overlap between literature and politics, and a literary change that is also – indeed, that was caused by – a political change. But now we must pause: the united chorus of critics shows that when they look at Nadine Gordimer's work they all see the same thing, but that may be because they are all wearing the same spectacles. So I now turn to the novels, and for convenience I have chosen one early and one later one for comparison: *A World of Strangers* (1958) and *The Conservationist* (1974). In both these books we are shown three groups in white society, the tycoons, the liberals and the ordinary unquestioning believers in apartheid. Black society, however, is represented by the urban and the sophisticated in the earlier novel, by the rural in the later. In *A World of Strangers* the protagonist and narrator is Toby Hood, a young Englishman who has reacted against the left-wing pieties of his conscientiously political parents, and who arrives in Johannesburg as local representative of the family publishing firm. The four main characters he meets are arranged with some symmetry. Two are non-political and pleasure loving, a black man and a white woman who become, respectively, his best friend and his mistress. His friendship with Steven Sithole is completely spontaneous, containing none of the dutiful 'working among Africans' associated with white liberals. The other two, Sam and

Anna, once more a black man and a white woman, are earnest and politicized, aware of the injustices of apartheid. By the end of the book Toby has decided to stay in South Africa and is on the verge of becoming politicized himself.

The world of big business appears in the novel through the circle of Hamish Alexander, wealthy, hospitable, pleasure loving, and with hints of a tough ruthlessness when serious matters of finance crop up. The equivalent figure in *The Conservationist* is the protagonist (not, this time, the narrator), Mehring (he has only a surname, as fits someone who has no real friends) – wealthy, powerful, divorced, an international industrialist (his field is pig-iron), who buys himself a farm as a hobby: partly as a tax loss, partly as 'a good place to bring a woman', and partly out of a genuine love of nature. He leaves it in the hands of Africans, under the supervision of Jakobus, who cheats him in small matters, and with whom he has a genial, paternalistic relationship. His divorced wife lives in New York, his teenage son is worried about military service, and eventually decides, when on a visit to his mother, to stay there; his left-wing mistress has had to flee to England, and we learn about their continuing political arguments through Mehring's rehearsal of them in memory. Our glimpse of the run-of-the-mill prejudiced Afrikaners in *A World of Strangers* was of Toby's secretary, who gave notice indignantly at having to enter his office when it was full of black men, and the caretaker of the block of flats who complains furiously one night 'You can't bring Kaffirs in my building'. In *The Conservationist* they are represented by the jovial neighbours, the De Beers, who borrow Mehring's car, and tell him in breezy racial solidarity that Jakobus, the caretaker, drives round in the tractor when he's not there (but they return the car with the rear light broken, Jakobus causes no damage to the tractor).

And both novels show us the land. *A World of Strangers* has a shooting trip on which Toby goes with a group of white South Africans, from which he returns both exhilarated and repelled, having fitted into that very masculine world, but in a way that lays the foundation for a later rejection of it. In *The Conservationist*, the landscape, as Nadine Gordimer herself said, is more important than in any of her other books, and there is the inevitable relationship between absentee owner and resident manager. In both books, we do not see the land actually being farmed (South African farmers are of course white, and almost exclusively Afrikaners).

I have described these two novels in a way that brings out the very close similarity if we think about the picture they offer of

white South African society. But from the first page, they are
utterly different to read. *A World of Strangers* is a work of
straightforward realism, moving steadily forwards in narrative
time, using orthodox first person narration: we see, and know, as
much as Toby does. *The Conservationist* is largely (not exclusively)
written in stream-of-consciousness; it darts to and fro in time; it has
little if any conventional plot (most of the other white characters are
not even named, so that this sophisticated work sometimes looks
like the first English novels, those of Defoe); and as the story
proceeds, the interior monologue moves in and out of fantasy, so
that it is not easy to be sure just what happens. The girl to whom
Mehring gives a lift at the end may or may not be coloured, may or
may not be a prostitute, he may or may not seduce her (or let her
seduce him), he may or may not be beaten up by her friends (thugs?
policemen?) who may never have existed. Some critics (but they
seem to be mistaken) understandably thought that Mehring dies at
the end of the book. Certainly the African who was found
murdered on his farm at the beginning, who was buried hugger-
mugger by the police to save trouble, and disinterred by the floods,
becomes more and more important symbolically as the book
proceeds, and in the end is mysteriously identified with Mehring.
Indeed, it is such suggestive and hallucinatory mergings that take
the place of straightforward action as the book unrolls: Mehring's
New Year's Eve conversation with Jakobus, completely plausible in
its easy patronizing, the tough of cynical sycophancy, the touch of
man-to-man directness, turns out never to have taken place.

The change of narrative technique is so immediately striking
when we compare early with late Gordimer, that we can ask why
any other account of the difference is needed. Does this change
spring from a change in political stance? Some of the critics are so
concerned with political interpretation that they hardly seem to
notice the technical differences. I will take as an example Michael
Wade, whose reading seems the most directly political.

Pale freckled eggs.
Swaying over the ruts to the gate of the third pasture, Sunday morning,
the owner of the farm suddenly sees: a clutch of pale freckled eggs set out
before a half-circle of children. Some are squatting; the one directly behind
the eggs is cross legged, like a vendor in a market.

This is the opening of the novel. The farmer, as he is then called,
gets out of his car to investigate:

The eggs are a creamy buff, thick-shelled, their glaze pored and lightly speckled, their shape more pointed than a hen's, and the palms of the small black hands are transulucent-looking apricot-pink. There is no sound but awed, snuffing breathing through snotty noses.[23]

We begin with a beautifully delicate moment of perception. As we read on, we learn that the 'owner of the farm' is not really a farmer, he is a rich industrialist. His vain attempt to prevent the stealing of eggs is a recurrent theme – and provides the title. To Wade, Mehring's preoccupation with the eggs is trivial, and reveals the 'mistakenness' of his attitude to the earth and its inhabitants;

Total 'conservationism' plus mechanistic cultivation denies the bridge of a *human* dependency; and of course it is the black people on the farm – those whom he doesn't *see* as human – who are therefore denied this living interdependency relationship.[24]

How our political certainties change. In the 1960s, perhaps also in the 1970s, when this was written, only a few specialists were worried about ecology. Now the Greens are all around us, and we can no longer be sure that the interests of those who live on the land are more important than preserving the balance of nature. I must in fairness say that Mehring has no carefully thought-out ecological plan for his farm, but he has a genuine love for the non-human life on it – and incidentally, he does see 'his' black people as human: he treats them with careless, patronizing generosity, and arguably has a better relationship with them than with the hostesses of his own class whom he despises, sometimes fiercely.

Wade passes adverse judgement on virtually all Mehring's actions and thoughts. He tells us that Mehring cannot imagine that the black men exist as thinking beings, Mehring deludes himself about his own freedom; most striking are the arguments between him and his mistress, Antonia, the most explicitly political element in the novel. Mehring rehearses in memory this virtually non-stop discussion interspersed with their sexual encounters. 'Tremendously concerned about love, your kind,' says Mehring, 'although they hate so many and despise so much.' She goes to bed with him, he points out, 'while blacks do all the work'. She wants to 'change the world but keep bits of it the way I like for myself'. And he, she ripostes, when he sneers at her for calling South West Africa 'Namibia' without knowing anything about it: 'in what way is your concept of the place any more than an idea, . . . you who "know" the country? Little white baas who ran barefoot with the little black sons of servants.' To and fro they argue, each seeing the bad faith in the other with vicious precision, the fierce candour a kind of spice to their love-making. Above all, he recalls that when the police arrested her, she came to him for a good lawyer – 'a respectable, shrewd company lawyer; . . . it was no good being represented in court by one of her own set.' Bad faith, or sensible cynicism against a cynical system? The recurrent argument offers, as political background, a glimpse of white South Africa that no one could accuse of one-sidedness. Wade, hearing the argument, takes sides: Antonia 'is capable of understanding the historical dimension' and so sees through Mehring's position. I do not cite this to accuse the critic of incompetence, but to show that the novel will allow a committed critic to offer a committed reading. A pro-apartheid critic, with as little distortion, could offer a reading committed the other way.

Yet it is difficult to say where distortion begins. John Cooke, for instance, claims:

When the Forsterian 'only connect' proved unworkable, Gordimer was forced to stand apart from a society with which she found no way of connecting. Only by claiming an African tradition as her own in the early seventies did she find a new code and means for herself to identify with her world.[25]

The more I think about this claim, the less true it seems. There is no claim in the early work that 'only connect' is *workable*, in political terms: the liberals always lose. And it is hard to see the sense in which the later novels 'claim an African tradition': even *July's People*, in which the white liberal family take shelter from the revolution in their houseboy's village, and are steadily absorbed into the village way of life – even that novel sees the Africans overwhelmingly through white eyes, and is very careful, as is *The Conservationist*, not to idealize the life of the rural Africans, not even to exaggerate its self-sufficiency. To take a small but striking detail, when Mehring's farm is cut off by flood, Jakobus saves the life of a cow which had developed mastitis by finding the right medicine, filling up the syringe and injecting it 'the way he had seen the vet do'. For this, Mehring remarks that he really seems to have coped rather well, and Wade remarks on 'the sense of natural order evoked by Jakobus' actions' as part of his argument that the Africans are the real farmers. Mehring's version is certainly the more accurate, and Wade does not even mention that it is the white man's medical science that actually saves the cow.

If there is a novel by a white man that 'claims an African tradition as its own', it is surely *Cry the Beloved Country*.[26] This book is the *Uncle Tom's Cabin* of South African literature: it awoke the conscience of the world, and is now seen, by radicals, as failing to politicize its insights (though the politicizers are there, in the novel, and not unfairly handled). Its hero, an elderly African clergyman, is used as the centre of consciousness, and his trip to Johannesburg in search of his corrupted son makes him a kind of Wordsworthian Michael who instead of going on with his useless sheepfold, expresses his despair by leaving the pastoral world for the bewilderments of the city. The African tradition that Paton claimed as his own is one based on deference, and will not appeal to the radical; but then the African tradition that Nadine Gordimer's most recent novels display such interest in (if they do not quite 'claim it as her own') is rural and rather feckless, and largely without political consciousness. The critics who have set out to describe the changes in her fiction seem to me to have described (correctly, I presume) changes in her opinions, and then to have imposed these on the fiction.

Political Fiction: Political Readers

Most readers of South African literature approach it with political commitment. Ezekiel Mphahlele, a South African black in exile, wrote a short novel called *Mrs Plum*, which the blurb on the edition I have (published in East Africa) describes as 'one of the most damning and bitter indictments of the white "liberals" in South Africa yet printed.' Mrs Plum 'loved dogs and Africans, and said that everyone must follow the law even if it hurt'. The story is told by the young African woman who works for her as cook and washerwoman, and whom she pleases by insisting on calling her Karabo, when most white employers, for their own convenience, replace the African name by Jane or Dinah. Mrs Plum goes to protest meetings, and tries to make Karabo eat at table with her. She invites Africans to parties in her home, and Karabo remarks:

I did not like the black people who came here to drink and eat. They spoke such difficult English like people who were full of all the books in the world. They looked at me as if I were right down there whom they thought little of – me a black person like them.[27]

When two policemen turn up and start harassing her servants, Mrs Plum turns the hosepipe on them, refuses to pay the fine, and spends a week in prison. As the story proceeds, we learn more about Mrs Plum's weaknesses, which seem centred on her dogs: Karabo discovers that she uses them for sexual titillation; when a rumour spreads that African servants are plotting to poison their employers' dogs, Mrs Plum cannot stop herself believing it, and dismisses her houseboy. There is a dispute with Karabo when she wants to go home to her village because her uncle has died, which results in Karabo leaving her; Mrs plum follows her to the village to ask her to come back, and Karabo finally gives a grudging consent, insisting on better pay and noticing that Mrs Plum did not actually apologize to her. The story ends with a hint that Karabo is not going to allow herself to be patronized in future.

It is perhaps Karabo's story more than Mrs Plum's: the function of the title might be to locate the action, as if it were called 'In Greenside' (the Johannesburg suburb where it takes place). In so far as it concentrates on Mrs Plum, it begins with her liberal views, and goes on to show her weaknesses, and her vulnerability, and how her well-meaning acts sometimes produce the wrong effects. If this is a 'damning and bitter indictment' of a white liberal, as the blurb writer claimed, then to be shown as human is an indictment. That white liberals will find themselves unable to act consistently is inevitable: that is what it means to be a liberal in South Africa. That they will have petty or selfish impulses is what, to the novelist, makes them interesting. The blurb could be paraphrased to read: 'it shows that a white liberal is not an angel but a human being.'

La Guma's *And a Threefold Cord* appeared in East Germany (where a good deal of modern African writing, especially the more openly political, is published by Seven Seas Publishers) with an introduction by Brian Bunting, a political activist, which sets the book in its political context by describing the author's work for the South African Communist Party, his trial, and his house arrest under the Nationalist government. This introduction begins 'It is difficult to propound the doctrine of "art for art's sake" in South Africa', and ends with the hope that the publication of the book will achieve two results: win for La Guma the international reputation he deserves, and 'stimulate a worldwide campaign which will force the Verwoerd regime to restore to him and to all other prisoners their full freedom'.[28] Bunting does not discuss the book itself, so it is not clear whether this didactic purpose governs his reading in detail, but it happens that the university library copy I used offers Bunting a fair amount of support in the way of marginal jottings that point a political moral at every opportunity; and another annotator interpreted *The Stone Country* by gleefully pointing out that an attempt to escape unites the prisoners, by equating 'solidarity of the underworld' with 'threat to the system'. This tale of prison is seen as a boys' adventure story, in which goodies unite against baddies.

At this point I need to be careful. Bunting's dismissal of 'art for art's sake' seems to offer a simple contrast: either you care about the evils of apartheid and support those who write against it, or you retreat into an ivory tower. This chapter will have been written in vain if it does not succeed in overthrowing that crude contrast. Serious South African literature is likely to deal with politics, because politics are so urgent in that society. But we can ask how the political concern relates to the literary experience: is it the material out of which the book is made, or is the book the material out of which political action is to be made? The former is not 'art for art's sake' in any escapist sense, since no worthwhile book is likely to be made unless there is real involvement in the political issues. The latter position, however, encounters difficulties which I have already glanced at. The world-wide campaign now trying to destroy apartheid operates through propaganda, through sports boycotts and attempted economic boycotts, and merges into the 'violent alternative'. One can see why it wants the support of writers, and why writers want to support it, but are novels and poems very useful among its weapons? I have already suggested that though literature can expand our awareness, there is no real evidence for believing that it helps much in bringing about political change. I have suggested too that the novel which has done most for this movement is one whose outlook many of its keenest supporters would disown. It is to be hoped that there is no fervent Afrikaner nationalist waiting his opportunity to write the jingo song of apartheid.

My argument is based on the necessary ambivalence of a work of literature when it comes to passing political judgements; and I am suggesting a parallel between the second-rate novelist, who shuts down options in her own book by imposing too narrow a range of awareness (as did Millin because of her obsession with miscegenation), and the highly political reader or critic, who shuts off the resonances of a situation by extracting a single-minded political judgement, by approving of one character and condemning another. My student annotator treated La Guma as Millin treated her characters.

This may seem to some a complacent position, not giving the necessary priority to human suffering. What does the prisoner on Robben Island or the black woman shot in Soweto care whether we misread a novel, a long as we make an urgent political commitment. I have great respect for this objection, and though I have no difficulty in logic when it comes to finding an answer, there is a natural reluctance in wanting to win an argument against the sufferers. If anyone said he could not be bothered with literature because he had more important matters to get on with, I would in some circumstances feel humbled. But there are replies to be made, and I will make them. First, rejection is not the same as confusion: to regard literature as a luxury you have no time for is not the same as pretending that literary excellence is the same as political rightmindedness. And second, and more profoundly, I do not want a world in which being on the right side politically is the most important question: it presupposes a confidence about political rights and wrongs that leads easily to dogmatism, bullying and (if you take power) tyranny. The opening up of political judgements that good fiction provides, the resonance with which a good poem surrounds a clear message – these can be seen as *politically* valuable.

There is a parallel objection to be considered. To some, it will seem a barren academic exercise to separate one's political from one's literary response. To read *One Day in the Life of Ivan Denisovich* or *First Circle* is to be deeply moved by human suffering: why analyse how far we are responding to Solzhenitsyn's power as a writer, how far to the horrors of Russian communism, since the two reinforce each other? Here I have to say again, that if we are thinking of the reading experience itself, this objection is wholly justified: to be moved is to be moved. But if we are reflecting on that reading experience, beginning to theorize about it, beginning to write literary criticism, then the distinction becomes very important. First, for a very pragmatic and untheoretical reason, that not all readers will hold the same political views. Choosing South Africa as example obscured this, since there are not likely to be many enthusiastic supporters of apartheid among my readers (though you never know. . .). But readers will certainly be divided between the liberal and the radical and (no doubt in some cases) the moderately conservative position on apartheid. None of these groups is justified in claiming that the others are incapable of reading a novel.

Finally, there is the question of authorial intention. There is little doubt where La Guma (or, for that matter, every non-white writer) stands. Nadine Gordimer has been outspoken in her political comments, and might not care for my analysis of her fiction. For the most part, these authors have had the sense not to tell us how to read their books: the abdication of the author (known as the intentional fallacy) and his subsequent death in Paris has now permeated our literary culture, and the self-denying ordinance it has led to among writers has saved us from a good deal of misleading dogmatism. If the authors do try and tell us, we must hear but not necessarily obey. If we are ignorant about South Africa, and an appeal to the author can explain what might otherwise have been puzzling (translating bits of Afrikaans or Zulu, explaining how the pass laws works, explaining whether Antonia was in any real danger if she had stayed in the country), then it is foolish not to look for help. But when it comes to telling us whose political views are right and whose are wrong, we shall make up our own minds. The author has no power, not even over her own work. The better the novelist, the less power she can claim.

4

Play

What is a Game?

We need, to start with, a theory of play, and I shall take this from Huizinga. The general theory of *Homo Ludens* is summarized as follows:

Let us enumerate once more the characteristics we deemed proper to play. It is an activity which proceeds within certain limits of time and space, in a visible order, according to rules freely accepted, and outside the sphere of necessity or material utility. The play-mood is one of rapture and enthusiasm, and is sacred or festive in accordance with the occasion. A feeling of exaltation and tension accompanies the action, mirth and relaxation follow.[1]

The remarks on mood and feeling, though useful, can be regarded as consequences of the definition proper, which has three elements: play is limited and secluded, the rules are freely accepted, and it serves no useful or necessary function. The first and third are connected: just as the site of the game is detached from the time and place of ordinary work, so its purpose is detached from social usefulness. So there are two essential points, uselessness or detachment, and rules.

Child psychologists will perhaps point out that play is not at all useless: that children learn by playing to cope with situations that they will actually encounter in later life. This is true, and important, but can be accommodated in the definition: children are not interested in, not even aware of, the valuable part that play will have in their development, and to them the contrast between lessons (what they have to do in real life, in order to learn) and games (what they do spontaneously and so learn) is obvious and important. We can therefore regard learning as a byproduct of playing, and even if it is the most important consequence, and the (evolutionary) reason why playing does not die out, it need not form part of our definition, for the activity is not experienced as learning. And in the case of adults, it is not certain that games serve any such ulterior purpose.

I should also say that the view that Huizinga actually uses for most of the book places great emphasis on contest: a game is something you try to win. It is a competitive exercise of skill or luck. Now contest is only possible within a framework of rules, without which it would not be possible to know who wins. So once again, rules and detachment seem the two essential elements in the definition.

Freud discusses play in two works, *Beyond the Pleasure Principle* and *Jokes and their Relation to the Unconscious*. In both it is associated with childhood. In the former, the emphasis is on repetition, on the way a child will insist on an exact recapitulation of a story it knows, or drops its toy over and over in order to have it restored. Clearly this has a strong resemblance to sticking to the rules. There is no difficulty in accepting this observation without following Freud in his claim that the creature insists on surviving so that it can die in its own way, and on his wild path to unicellular organisms and the death instinct.[2] *Jokes* is a much more important contribution to the theory of play. It offers a continuum from word-play, through jest and innocent jokes, to the tendentious joke, in which the intense pleasure of a release of aggressive or erotic feeling is triggered by the forepleasure which the joke's mechanism provides.[3] We are here concerned only with this forepleasure, which Freud also postulates as the releasing mechanism of the wish fulfilments of art (though in 'The Relation of the Poet to Daydreaming' he regards that mechanism as mysterious:[4] Freudian aesthetics needs to supplement that over-simple essay with the more profound insights of *Jokes*).

Now if we follow Freud in tracing the pleasure of innocent jokes back to childhood release from the rule, imposed by the adult world, of making sense and being coherent, we seem to arrive at a contradiction with Huizinga. Both see play as detached and useless, but for Huizinga play depends on sticking to rules, whereas for Freud it depends on abandoning them. This contradiction, I shall suggest, points to a central paradox about play.

Word-games

An obvious transition between childhood games and literature is provided by nursery rhymes, which merge sometimes into sheer enjoyment of nonsense sounds. As a text for looking at nursery rhymes, I shall take the fifty-one rhymes present in *Mother Goose*, a collection published by John Newbery about 1750.[5] All are now at least two centuries old, and some must already have been old then. Let us arrange them on a scale.

There was an old man,
  And he had a calf,
  And that's half;
He took him out of the stall,
And put him on the wall,
  And that's all.

At one extreme comes pure nonsense – in this case, logical nonsense, sometimes even verbal nonsense, that is, not even made of recognizable words ('Hey, diddle, diddle'). If these jingles are corruptions of real narrative (if 'The cat and the fiddle' is Catherine la fidèle) this only turns it to sense for those who know (and are thinking of) the origin; it is still nonsense for those who have only the text.

O, my kitten, my kitten,
  And O my kitten my deary!
Such a sweet pet as this
  Was neither fat nor neary.

And here we go up, up, up,
  And here we go down, down, down
And here we go backwards and forwards,
  And here we go round, round, round.

In the second category I place those that organize a game, as this clearly does, along with (no doubt) 'One, two, three, four, five' and 'Great a, little a'. (Perhaps this is the moment to point out that the verbal shift from 'play' to 'game' is of no significance. Other European languages use only one word (Spiel/spielen; jeu/jouer), and the fact that the noun and the verb have different etymologies in English seems to have lost all semantic significance.)

Little Jack Horner
Sat in a corner
    Eating a Christmas pie;
He put in his thumb,
And pulled out a plum,
    And said, What a good boy am I!

In the third category I place those with a rudimentary story or moral. 'Pease porridge hot' is clearly about poverty. 'What care I how black I be' has a very neat counter-moral (counter to orthodox opinion), and 'Jack Horner' is elusively ambiguous. Is Jack the hero of an ethic of getting-on, or the villain of a more Christian ethic? Is the rhyme about table manners, or self-satisfaction, or greed? It has haunted enough generations for us to be sure it is about something significant.

Ding, dong, bell,
The cat is in the well!
Who put her in?
Little Johnny Green;
What a naughty boy was that
Who tried to drown poor pussy cat,
Who never did any harm,
And killed the mice in his father's barn.

Perhaps there is a subterranean meaning here, mocking our confidence that there must always be somebody to blame; certainly the explicit meaning is so neat that one suspects the editorial hand of Newbery, who added prose morals to all the rhymes, some almost absurd in their pompous inappropriateness ('This little pig went to market' teaches 'If we do not govern our passions, our passions will govern us'); though, to do Newbery justice, he often realized the irrelevance of his moral, and he does seem to have left the text alone.

This scale has nothing to do with the merit or authenticity of the nursery rhymes. It is clear that though they can accommodate a story or a gesture towards some social situation, no one can value them, in the first instance, for narrative skill or moral subtlety. This is parallel to the theory of jokes: a joke can accommodate tendentious impulses, and to the Freudian, tendentious jokes are the most powerful, but what makes it a joke in the first place is that it is a release mechanism for verbal play. The sound-patterning by which everyone recognizes a nursery rhyme leads an almost independent existence from the content, which may have its own interest, or be there simply as an excuse for the word-play, or may not even be there.

Now, to move further up the scale, let us turn to a real poet who uses word-play. I choose as example Christian Morgenstern, the most celebrated German writer of (to use his own preferred terms) 'Wahnwitz oder Tollheit oder dergleichen' (madwit or folly or something like that: he is objecting to the labels 'Bloedsinn oder Stumpfsinn' – silliness or stupidity).[6]

Palmstroem

Palmstroem steht bei einem Teiche
und entfaltet gross ein rotes Tashentuch:
Auf dem Tuch ist eine Eiche
dargestellt, sowie ein Mensch mit einem Buch.

Palmstroem wagt nicht sich hineinzuschneuzen, –
er gohoert zu jenen Kaeuzen,
die oft unvermittelt-nackt
Ehrfurcht vor dem Schoenen packt.

Zaertlich faltet er zusammen,
was er eben erst entbreitet.
Und kein Fuehlender wird ihm verdammen,
weil er ungeschneuzt entschreitet.[7]

(Beside the Pond

Palmbeck stood sniffing, frowned,
drew out his handkerchief, and shook.
And there, depicted on a scarlet ground,
appeared an oak, a man, a book.

Palmbeck stood hesitating; nor
did he dare to blow his nose.
The sight of beauty grips some folk with awe:
Palmbeck is one of those.

Tenderly he folded up again
what he'd unfolded. And am I alone
in thinking he was not to blame
to leave the pond wth nose unblown?)

This is instantly recognizable as *Tollheit*, though only two things distinguish it all that radically from a straightforward poem. First, it has no action: after Palmstroem's initial move, nothing happens. I do not just mean that he folds the handkerchief up again, I mean that the whole act, taking it out and not using it, sounds like the beginning of a story in which Palmstroem will take decisions or learn something; but the poem just runs into the sand as Palmstroem, in its odd diction, debouches with unblown nose. And second, it flaunts the fact that words are not chosen for their meaning alone. There is no reason for him to stand by a pond, or for the handkerchief to depict an oak, except that *Teiche* rhymes with *Eiche*. In that case the words are ordinary but, as the rhyme underlines, arbitrarily chosen; in the second stanza the rhyme is ingenious, even farfetched, and this again thrusts the arbitrariness at us. And in the third stanza we are invited to linger on the plausible but comic diction.

Looking at the whole, we can see that the poem behaves like Palmstroem. It unfolds its images like the handkerchief, then does nothing with them, and slips away wthout blowing its nose. That is one extreme of Morgenstern's *Wahnwistz*; here is the other.

Das grosse lalula

Kroklokwafzi? Sememi!
Seiokronto – praflipo:
Bifzi, bafzi; hulalemi:
quasti basti bo. . .
Lalu lalu lalu lalu la!⁸

No need to translate, since the poem is as incomprehensible in German as in English. Its metre and rhyme are impeccable, and continue so over three stanzas. Morgenstern amused himself by writing a mock commentary on this and twenty-five other *Galgenlieder* under the name of Jeremias Mueller, Dr Phil, Privat-gelehrter, and in this he claims that the poem conceals an endgame (Kroklokwafzi = k a 5, etc.); later he suggested that it is a heroic song in a lost Indian language.⁹ There are virtually no semantic clues to confirm or refute such readings, and the poem stands almost at the extreme of meaningless sound-play. Writers of nonsense verse often seem tugged to that extreme, even if they can't stay there for long. Edward Lear, whose word coinages in his verse are few and fairly clear in what they suggest, let himself go in prose:

Thrippsy pillivinz,
Inky tinky pobblebookle abblesquabs? – Flosky! beebul trimble flosky! Okul scratchabibblebongibo, viddle squibble tog-a-tog ferrymoyassity amsky flamsky ramsky damsky crocklefether squiggs.
Flinkywisty pomm.
Slushypipp[10]

Because our thirst for meaning is so strong, we deal with such nonsense by looking for associations: if we fail, boredom rapidly sets in. The attempts at interpretation which Morgenstern parodies are inevitable even though, in this case, almost infinite. The phonetic polish of the verse form, like the layout and punctuation of the Lear, carry us a certain distance, but sooner or later we will start our semantic sniffing. In *Lalula* we might begin to build on the suggestions of jungle life, in the Lear letter we will not get far, since its effect seems to consist in the contrast between the very careful syntagmatic pattern and the complete absence of anything para-digmatic that makes sense: the words fit wonderfully together, but have no connection with any alternatives.

It will be useful to turn to word coinage in an English nonsense poem.

Twas brillig and the slithy toves
    Did gyre and gimble in the wabe:
All mimsy were the borogroves,
    And the mome raths outgrabe.[11]

Here we have the advantage (if it is an advantage) of authorial glosses – in two stages, since Lewis Carroll explained much of the poem in his family magazine *Misch-Masch* when he first wrote it in 1855, and then gave similar (but sometimes much livelier) explanations to Humpty Dumpty when it was published in *Alice through the Looking-Glass* in 1872. Some of the words are simple portmanteaus (slithy = lithe and slimy; frumious, in a later stanza,

= fuming and furious; burble = bleat, murmur and warble). We might not have guessed these, but they are clear once explained – the first two, at least: if we are sceptical about 'burbled', we will read with a wry smile Carroll's admission 'I'm afraid I can't distinctly remember having made it that way'. Yet plausibility is not the same as conscious intention: 'mimsy' is clearly a portmanteau for flimsy and miserable, yet Carroll does not seem to have noticed this in 1855, and that explanation only appears in *Through the Looking Glass*.

Sometimes the explanation is itself a joke. 'Brillig' is a lovely word, and I have no difficulty in believing that it means four o'clock in the afternoon, but not, surely, because it is the time 'you start broiling things for dinner': the remote operation of preparing dinner seems to have little to do with it (it is not 'you', the Victorian child, but the cook, safely tucked away in the kitchen, who does the broiling); I would rather think it is we who are broiling, in the afternoon heat. 'Wabe' is interesting because it is given three glosses. Carroll's original definition was 'the side of a hill', from its being soaked by the rain (the verb to 'swab' or to 'soak'). Humpty Dumpty explains 'the grass plot around a sundial' because it goes a long way before and a long way behind. Here are two thoroughly unconvincing explanations: the former is only a portmanteau at one remove ('wabe' does not *mean* swab or soak), the latter is unconvincing semantically (why shouldn't the grass plot be narrow?) and phonetically ('wabe' clearly does not derive from 'way'). There may be an admission of all this in the fact that Alice finds she simply knows the meaning without any explanation. 'Wabe' looks like the kind of English monosyllable that has a precise meaning and an unobvious etymology (like 'furze', say, or 'lobe'), where you might suddenly remember what it meant without having any idea why.

The interest of 'Jabberwocky' does not lie in the story or the feelings but in language itself. Morgenstern, calling attention to the formal elements in his verse (phonetic, morphological, syntactical) and undermining the semantic, seems to lend support to the structuralist claim that the real subject of poetry is grammar. Lewis Carroll also emphasizes form, and to this we can add etymology, and how it functions both in and beyond our awarness. Etymology is close to meaning, but it does not prevent him, too, from undermining the semantic. He is concerned not with what words mean, but with how they mean. One of Morgenstern's poems could have been written expressly to confirm this point:

'Der Werwolf,' sprach der guter Mann,
'des Weswolfs, Genitiv sodann,
dem Wemwolf, Dativ, wie mann's nennt,
den Wenwolf, – damit hat's ein End.'

A werewolf comes to the grave of a village schoolmaster and asks,
'Bitte, beuge mich': inflect me, please. The schoolteacher gets up
(what does death matter when grammar's at stake?) and takes
advantage of the fact that *wer* means 'who'. The poem is in the
most obvious sense untranslateable, though there have been
attempts, using 'banshee' (banhers, banher) or hoopoe (whosepoe,
whompoe). The helplessness of nature before words is enacted at
the end of the poem: asking, now, for the plural forms, the
werwolf is told that though there are plenty of wolves, *wer* can be
used only in the singular. Since he has a wife and child, he is
heartbroken, but

Doch da er kein Gelehrter eben
so schied er dankend und ergeben

(But since the creature was no scholar
He humbly thanked the learned wallah.)[12]

I have already remarked on the arbitrariness of choosing words
for the rhyme: in at least two of Morgenstern's poems, this is
explicit:

Das aesthetische Wiesel

Ein Wiesel
sass auf einem Kiesel
inmitten Bachgeriesel.

Weisst ihr
weshalb?

Das Mondkalb
verriet es mir
im Stillen:

Das raffinier
te Tier
tat's um des Reimes willen.[13]

(The aesthetic Otter

An otter
lifted up its trotter.
The sun grew ever hotter.

Can you tell me why?

The mooncalf,
    descending from the sky,
    said, 'Don't laugh,

And I will tell you why:

The otter told me, "I'm
Doing it for the rhyme." ')

Since it is obvious that no weasel would sit on a heap of gravel
surrounded by the murmuring of a stream, for any other reason
than the rhyme, the effect is less successful here than in 'Das
boehmische Dorf', where Herr von Korf makes a perfectly
plausible appearance, and the parenthesis

– Auch von Korf (der nur des Reimes wegen
ihn begleitet) ist um Rat verlegen –[14]

is a given as a parenthesis, not produced like Jack Horner's plum at
the end, as if waiting for applause. But even this is not a trick that
can be played more than once.

Discussion of Morgenstern's poems tends to analyse and classify
the verbal devices used (concretizing, materializing, personification
of abstractions, metaphors, idioms and proverbs, displacement,
word-echoes of various kinds – the list can be made very long). I
shall fasten on only one point: how far the universe is a purely
verbal one, how far it is transitive. Meaning, marking the
movement from signifier to signified, is transitive, whereas the
Nasobem arose, we are told, only out of the poet's lyre.[15]

In a word-game, there is no transitive movement. In scrabble, or
in a crossword puzzle, there may be great argument on whether
such-and-such is a real word, but the argument only concerns its
admissibility *into* the world of the game. Once there, its doubtful
credentials cease to matter, and it will then do what all other words

do there, take part in a contest. In normal language, the transitive
movement may be referential (the text says something about the
world) or expressive (it conveys an emotion) or didactic.

Nein!

Pfeift der sturm?
Keift ein Wurm?
Heulen
Eulen
hoch vom Turm?

Nein!

Es ist die Galgenstrickes
dickes
Ende, welches aechzte
gleich als ob
im Galopp
eine muedgehetzte Maehre
nach dem naechsten Brunnen lechzte
(der vielleicht noch ferne waere).[16]

(No!

Who's whistling? the storm?
Who's nagging? a worm?
Does an owl
howl
from under its cowl?

Nope!

It's the gallows rope
Moaning in the air
Like a dead tired mare
hungry for the hay
that's still miles and miles away.)

This is obviously a word-game, yet it shows how difficult it is to
stay wholly within the world of play. Storms do whistle, in
common usage, but worms do not nag, by any usage. Owls do not
howl, but it is not impossible to think of a usage by which they did;

and they do live in towers. We are given enough reference to provide a framework within which the arbitrary can play.

The second half of the poem has virtually no referential content, but by now we can begin to wonder if it is expressive. Critics have not been lacking who relate Morgenstern's poems to early twentieth-century alienation, and find a frequently recurring atmosphere of gloom, night, loneliness, fear and death. It is no use going to Morgenstern himself to find out if this is their right context. By dedicating his poems to the child in man, by emphasizing the origin of the *Galgenlieder* in student pranks, he makes them out to be play; but he explained to a friend of his wife in 1910 that only the fundamental idea should be seen as grotesque: the treatment and development throughout are organic and consistent, which raises them to level of works of art, not mere frivolity (*Spielerei*).[17] Morgenstern, clearly, is inconsistent; and in remarks like this he seems in danger of assimilating the Wahnwitz to the serious poetry of which he wrote so much that the world has chosen to forget.

Form as Play

We can now address the paradox I mentioned earlier: play sticks to the rules, play breaks the rules. Sticking to the rules of the game is what licenses the flouting of more serious rules. Simply to utter a row of incomprehensible syllables would not constitute much of a release, since it is so cheaply purchased: it offers no kind of threat to serious thinking. But if we erect internal rules for our activity – the more difficult the better – we demand the same level of apparently earnest work as does real thinking or the tasks society approves, and thus we set up a rival task that both demands respect and announces itself as futile. That is why rhyme is so prominent in nonsense verses: it is on the one hand the most striking of verbal devices – flaunting its technical achievement – and on the other the most arbitrary and pointless. It is a verbal game in itself.

There is a connection between rhymes and puns: a rhyme is a phonetic pun, a pun is a semantic rhyme. The fact that 'guilt' and 'gilt', *nom* and *non*, 'boy' and 'buoy' sound the same is not very different from the fact that 'gilt' and 'silt', *non* and *son*, 'boy' and 'joy' sound the same, and it is not even easy to decide whether, for instance, the laboured jokes of the priest in *Walenstein's Lager* ('Der Rheinstrom ist worden zu einem Peinstrom') should be called puns or rhymes.[1] There has never, as it happens, been a verse form built on regularly recurring puns, as there has been on regular rhymes; if there were, then using puns would be thought of as a convention rather than a display of cleverness, and if rhyme had not become established we might think of the rhymester as a show-off, as we now think of the punster (and as we sometimes do think of the versifier who indulges in double and triple rhymes). For both the pun and the rhyme are ways of taking pleasure in an accident of resemblance.

If puns and rhymes are both word-play, so too is metre. That every line of a poem should have ten syllables is an arbitrary rule laid down like the rules of a game, and we admire and enjoy the skill of the poet who sticks to it, as we admire even more the skill that writes sonnets, villanelles or Spenserian stanzas. Can we not, I now want to ask, extend this to cover all the formal elements of poetry?

The fullest taxonomies of formal devices are those laid out in the Elizabethan rhetoric books, and of these the most thorough is *Puttenham's Art of English Poetry*. Puttenham divides the elements of poetry into two, proportion and ornament, corresponding to the division between phonetic and semantic figures: proportion, based on an analogy with music and with mathematics, includes all examples of regular recurrence, but excludes signification (as do music and mathematics). We naturally think of verbal patterns as phonetic, rhyme and metre as being essentially addressed to the ear. But a complicated rhyme scheme is addressed to the eye too (the ear alone would have difficulty in recognizing a Spenserian stanza or a sestina), and Puttenham recognizes this in his ocular figures, or shaped poems (the lozenge or rhombus, the square or quadrangle, the pilaster or cylinder, etc.).[2] So we ought to regard figures of proportion as patterns, addressed either to ear or eye. By ornament, Puttenham means figures of speech, 'which be the flowers as it were and colours that a poet setteth upon his language of art, as the embroiderer doth his stone and pearl or passements of gold upon the stuff of a princely garment.'[3] The long list of figures of both kinds makes of the treatise a Hoyle of poetry, a compendium of rules and advice on how to play word-games.

Form is a game. The formal elements of poetry are ways of playing games with words, and the best players are admired for their skill. As in all games, the good player can either show consummate skill in doing exactly what he is supposed to do, or he can devise elaborate obstacles in order to overcome them elegantly:

in the first case we have Dryden and Pope, masters of the heroic couplet, and in the second Donne, Herbert, Hardy, Auden, inventors of new and complicated stanza forms.

A single poem will help us explore the view that form as such is a game.

I on my horse, and Love on me, doth try
Our horsemanships, while by strange work I prove
A horseman to my horse, a horse to Love,
And now man's wrongs in me, poor beast, descry.
The reins wherewith my rider doth me tie
Are humbled thoughts, which bit of reverence move,
Curb'd in with fear, but with gilt boss above
Of hope, which makes it seem fair to the eye.
The wand is will; thou, Fancy, saddle art,
Girt fast by Memory; and while I spur
My horse, he spurs with sharp desire my heart.
He sits me fast, however I do stir,
And now hath made me to his hand so right
That in the manage myself take delight.[4]

The extended conceit of Sidney's sonnet is based on the analogy, explicitly stated at the beginning, between horsemanship and being 'ridden' by one's passion. It is the kind of analogy that can easily issue in word play (as in Schleiermacher's remark that *Leidenschaft –* passion – is what *Leiden schafft* – causes pain).[5] In the poem, the analogy issues in two main elements. First, there is the balanced placing of the parallel terms: 'A horseman to my horse, a horse to Love', which 'rhymes' aabb if a = literal and b = metaphorical, but abba if a = horse and b = rider. The next line ('And now man's wrongs in me, poor beast, descry') is ambiguous: the obvious reading, taking 'man's wrongs' as subjective genitive, says that he has now learned how much his horse had suffered at his hands; but if man's wrongs is an objective genitive, then he has learned about his own sufferings, and is cynically announcing that the parallel with horsemanship is a mere convenience of expression, showing no real interest in the horse. The second and third quatrains attempt to work out the details of the analogy. This is a favourite technique in extended conceits, much less skilfully done here than in (say) Richard II's soliloquy in prison ('I have been studying how I may compare / This prison where I live unto the world').[6] The final couplet, by a neat reversal, asserts that the exercise of skill is such a pleasure that he does not mind being ridden, and clearly implies that the horse does not mind it either. And this implication points to the invisible third item in the parallel: the writing of the poem. The skill with which the poet handles the analogy is itself a parallel to the horseman's skill and Love's (metaphorically) skilful horsemanship. The peculiarly satisfying last line, announcing the pleasure of being well-handled, makes explicit the reader's pleasure in the display of skill he has been shown. Any poem that sees itself as a game is likely, at some point, to offer an explicit parallel between some skill or elegance (or, in the case of Palmstroem, quirkiness) in the subject matter, and that displayed in the writing.

In so far as Sidney's sonnet is a way of throwing light on the experience of love, it is not a game; in so far as the theme of love is a mere excuse for the conceit, what matters is 'the manage', and our pleasure in reading is the spectator's pleasure in the display of skill. Here are two views of the relation between form and content; and the difference between them is very far-reaching.

Since play is detached and intransitive, serving no useful or necessary function, it can be praised as disinterested, or condemned as frivolous. Form – the play element in literature – can therefore be valued as the guarantee of self-sufficient beauty, or despised as cutting literature off from human values (or political seriousness). The latter will inevitably produce a rejection of form as in itself worthless. Total rejection – the demand for writing innocent of rhyme, metre, word-play, figures of speech and all forms of proportion and ornament – would be a rejection of literature, and a demand for functional prose, assuming a clear-cut frontier, and requiring us to emigrate. More interesting to us is the attempt to rescue form for an ulterior purpose, to value it but not for itself alone. To some extent, this has always existed, and we can find it in Puttenham.

In his discussion of ornament, Puttenham draws an important distinction. He tells us it is of two kinds, *Enargia*, which aims 'to satisfy and delight the ear only by a goodly outward show set upon the matter with words and speeches smoothly and tunably running', and *Energia*, which operates 'by certain inducements or sense of such words and speeches inwardly working a stir to the mind'. The first kind is ornament in the strict sense: they give delight without relating it to meaning. The second is functional, that is, ornament not for its own sake but in the service of meaning.[7] There is no doubt that Puttenham admires both: his tireless listing of metrical forms and rhyme schemes, of different figures of speech, reveals a fascination with the skill itself, but when he writes of style he insists on relating it to one of two things, either the mind of the author or the subject. He prefers the second, for although it is true that style can be seen as *mentis character*, it is more important to make it 'according to the matter and subject, and conformable thereto', and from this derives the well-known division into high, middle and base styles, according to the dignity of the subject.[8] With the Romantics, as we have seen, a clear shift has taken place from style as fitted to subject, to style as expressing the author, and the distinction which Puttenham designates as that between *Enargia* and *Energia* becomes of crucial importance. Once literature is seen as the expression of a state of mind or feeling, as the revelation of personality, all its technical devices become means to that end, and to linger on them for their own sake is superficial and mechanistic. Literature as expression dismisses literature as game.

As an example of this Romantic view (which of course is still with us today) we can revert to Middleton Murry. As we saw in chapter 2, *The Problem of Style* is totally committed to the expression theory, and from this follows his rejection of the view that style is applied ornament, a view that was, he considers, (just) defensible for the teaching of rhetoric, but that Murry now dismisses with contempt as a belief in 'fine writing',

a miserable procession of knock-kneed, broken-winded metaphors with a cruel cartload of ponderous, unmeaning polysyllables dragging behind them.[9]

Metaphors and polysyllables can only be justified if 'a strong and decisive original emotion' lies behind them. The opposite of this can be found in Auden:

Like Matthew Arnold I have my Touchstones, but they are for testing critics, not poets:

Do you like, and by like I mean like, not approve on principle:
1.   Long lists of proper names, such as the Old Testament genealogies or the Catalogue of ships in *The Iliad*?
2.   Riddles and all other ways of not calling a spade a spade?
3.   Complicated verse forms of great technical difficulty, such as Englyns, Drott-Kvaetts, Sestinas, even if their content is trivial?
4.   Conscious theatrical exaggerations, pieces of baroque flattery, like Dryden's welcome to the Duchess of Ormond?[10]

When Auden then tells us that he will trust a critic who can answer 'yes' to all this, he is of course emphasizing the play element in literature, the pleasure we take in seeing a completely useless task performed with great skill. In the fourth example, the task is not just useless but distasteful, but the argument is of course that if we are sufficiently caught up in the brilliance of the execution we shall lose all interest in the morality or otherwise of the activity, just as, if we are really enjoying the ponderous unmeaning polysyllables, we shall lose interest in the 'strong and decisive original emotion'.

To set these two views against each other, we need an example where both are plausible and both have been held, and I take the case of the sonnet, since it is an elaborate form which has been much discussed and much defended. Why has a sonnet got fourteen lines? And why is it divided either into eight and six, rhyming abbaabba cdecde (slight variations are permitted in the sestet), or into three quatrains and a couplet (abab cdcd efef gg)? There are two kinds of answer.

The first says that the number of lines was orginally quite arbitrary, but once established by the early Italian poets it constituted a habit which others followed. The sonnets of Dante and Petrarch are divided into octave and sestet, and it was the influence of these admired poets that kept the pattern going; then a number of Elizabethan poets employed a less complicated form, and because of the importance of Shakespeare this, too, caught on; then Milton reverted to the Italian form, and he had his influence too. . .

The second answer says that having made a statement in the first part of a sonnet, the poet qualifies or illustrates it in the second part: rather less space is needed for this, and the sestet is likely to be more compact because it can make use of the more leisurely exposition of the octave, or (to use another kind of language) the wave breaks and then, as it retreats, offers a less imposing height of water. It says that the natural way to work on your hearers is to make your statement three times (three parallel instances, or a general assertion followed by two illustrations) and then to draw the three units together with a succinct statement of ringing and memorable finality – a concluding couplet.

Examples abound of the sonnet being used in this way. Dante and Petrarch do not usually offer strong contrasts within a sonnet, but often pause and qualify, illustrate, or turn to direct speech in the sestet. Milton spends eight lines lamenting that he has attained his twenty-third year and hasn't achieved much, then, more succinctly and with more dignity, announces that he will accept what God decrees for him; or he praises Cromwell's military exploits in the octave, and then announces in the sestet that 'Peace hath her victories'/ No less renowned than war' – and the fact that the break comes after eight and a half lines is one of those deliberate untidinesses that serve to emphasize the firmness of the underlying structure.[11] Shakespeare makes constant and brilliant use of the three quatrains and a couplet – as, for instance, here:

How sweet and lovely dost thou make the shame
Which, like a canker in the fragrant rose,
Doth spot the beauty of thy budding name!
O, in what sweets dost thou thy sins enclose!
That tongue that tells the story of thy days,
Making lascivious comments on thy sport,
Cannot dispraise, but in a kind of praise;
Naming thy name blesses an ill report.
O, what a mansion have those vices got
Which for their habitation chose out thee,
Where beauty's veil doth cover every blot,
And all things turn to fair that eyes can see!
Take heed, dear heart, of this large privilege;
The hardest knife ill-used doth lose his edge.[12]

The young man is told three times that because he is so handsome it is difficult to blame him for his (unspecified) bad conduct. In the first quatrain this is conveyed by the image of the canker in the rose, in the third by that of a fair mansion; in between comes a wry comment on the censurers, clearly including the poet, who 'cannot dispraise but in a kind of praise'; then this mounting, ambivalent compliment is rounded off with an admonitory couplet that could be spoken either affectionately or bitterly.

There is no need to go on: any history of the sonnet will offer abundant examples of what can hardly surprise us, that the poets are able to make a structure seem the one inevitable form for what they are trying to say. That after all is what it is to be a poet. Yet however triumphantly poem after poem confirms the view that it compels language to conform to the mode of experience expressed, we have to remind ourselves of the obvious: that forms are not devised to serve this functional purpose, they are already there. Milton did not create the eight plus six sonnet because that was the perfect way to express his thought, he picked it up, ready made, and bamboozled us into feeling that he must have invented it. The organic, functional view of form is true when we are appreciating a successful poem. The view of form as arbitrary, as lying around for some one to use, is true when we are tracing its history.

Everything is Play?

Everything I have said about play assumes a contrast with something else. If play means contest, there are other activities which are collaborative or solitary. If play is limited, in terrain or duration or repercussions, there are other activities whose range is not so limited. If play is intransitive, the opposite will be serious, transitive activity. In the case of language, a word-game will be contrasted with a statement, or a command, or a question, or an illocutionary act. A statement can be true or false, but no one cares whether Peter Piper really did pick a peck of pickled pepper; a command instructs us to act, but no one ever started baking, or speeded up, because of 'Pat-a-cake, pat-a-cake, baker's man, Bake me a cake as fast as you can'; a question requires an answer, but Mary, Mary, quite contrary will not tell us how her garden grows; an illocutionary act can bind the speaker, but no one will be sued for breach of promise for saying 'Little maid, will you wed, wed, wed?'.

But even the most serious discourse can be invaded by the playful. Critics are always noticing verbal accidents: the huge philosophic contrast between 'casual' and 'causal', or between the charming young chimney sweeps of Charles Lamb who seem to be calling 'peep-peep' and the exploited children of Blake calling 'weep-weep'.[1] A universe of difference opens up between two letters. Is this just a quaint linguistic fact? Does the critic pause on it out of regret, hoping that it will turn out significant, not merely quaint? But can it be claimed that verbal resemblances like this constitute a kind of argument? Since such resemblances are clearly the stuff of games, we would then have had to call in question the distinction between reasoning and playing.

I have already proposed the paradox that play means both breaking rules and sticking to rules; this means that it can be contrasted either to sticking to rules or breaking them, and that seems to open the door to the view that any activity could count as play or not, depending on how we looked at it; and this in fact is a well-known view, maintained in a splendid piece of nineteenth-

century deconstruction by Mark Twain. Tom Sawyer, set by his
aunt to paint a fence, is pitied by his friends, and turns the tables by
feigning delight in the task, so that they will envy him and want to
do it; and this leads the author to observe that the difference
between play and work has nothing to do with the nature of the
activity: climbing mountains is play to the holiday-maker, work to
the guide, riding horses is play to the gentleman, work to the
jockey. The distinguishing criterion is whether you have to do it,
or do it voluntarily, and that is entirely a matter of context.[2]

And so, emboldened by Mark Twain, can we call into question
the clear contrast between play and seriousness, between word-
games and statements? This is precisely what Derrida has done.
A.D. Nuttall points out that the alliance of psychoanalysis and
post-structuralism leads to 'a set of mental toys'. Without the usual
purposes of language (truthtelling, expression, persuasion, performative acts, etc.), 'there is little for the first intelligences of Paris
and Yale to do but *play*' (his italics):

Occasionally, indeed, such play closes any gap which might once have
existed between European philosophy and parodies of it.

Nuttall then quotes Lacan's description of the child as an
'hommelette', that is, both a little man and a sort of broken egg,
lacking identity, and comments sternly:

He is not joking. Nor is he thinking. The difference between the two is
perhaps no longer apparent to him.[3]

Puns like this are common in Derrida and Lacan. The 'nom du
père' is the 'non du père'; 'un cheveu' is 'un je veux', Hegel is an
eagle ('Hegel'/'aigle'): the philosophers seem to have been reading
Joyce. Such a torrrent of puns as we find in *Finnegan's Wake* could
never pass for philosophy (or not yet), but in Derrida there is a
deliberate attempt to incorporate them into his thinking, to claim
that they are a contribution to theory. Can we take this seriously?
(the question, we shall see in a moment, is not one that Derrida will
allow).

The first problem is that a pun belongs in one language only:
would philosophy then become as untranslateable as poetry? We
might get round this by finding equivalents: 'le non du pere' might

be rendered by 'father'/'farther', and though we cannot pun on Hegel in English we certainly can (can't we?) on Kant. But what then of the reader who knows no English – or no French, as the case may be? We tell him that through linguistic serendipity, Hegel soars and Kant is full of cant (or we may try something more vulgar), Mill grinds us down with logic, Bacon sizzles with ideas, Whitehead is an old man's thinker. . . . Our reader happens to have read some of these philosophers (in translation, presumably), and doesn't agree: he wants Kant to sizzle, Bacon to be the logic grinder, and so on. He asks if we could find some alternative and more suitable puns, and if we can't he goes in search of another language. May there not be a language, somewhere in Turkestan or Kenya (and who will be so ethnocentric as to say that these are not appropriate languages for philosophy?), where the sound 'Kant' means 'bacon', where 'Mill' means 'eagle', where 'Derrida' means 'wisdom' – or nonsense, where 'true' means false?

But, it may be said, what matters is not the particular pun, but the fact of making them: the incorporation of the ludic principle into thinking, as it is already incorporated into poetry. So I will now turn to the most sustained and notorious example of this in Derrida, his attack on John Searle in the pages of *Glyph*. In 1977 Derrida published in this journal his essay 'Signature, Event, Context', a discussion of Austin's theory of speech acts. This theory points out that language is not confined to describing the world but can constitute a form of action, as when you promise something, or declare a couple man and wife, or name a ship. Austin calls these 'illocutionary acts', and in *How to do Things with Words* he offers a classification of them. Derrida's article was followed by a short reply from Searle, which claimed that he had misunderstood and misstated Austin's theory. Searle begins by confessing 'I did not find his arguments very clear and it is possible that I may have misinterpreted him as profoundly as I believe he has misinterpreted Austin.' In the first part of his article, he attacks the view that writing differs from speech by virtue of iterability or absence, and claims that the distinguishing feature is its relative permanence; and he defends the idea of intentionality, claiming that 'a meaningful sentence is just a standing possibility of the corresponding (intentional) speech act'. In the second part, he defends Austin's decision to rule out of the discussion those illocutionary acts which are 'parasitic' on the straightforward ones – those uttered by actors on the stage, or as jokes, or as quotations. Derrida in his article had written:

What Austin excludes an anomaly, exception, 'non-serious', citation, (on stage, in a poem, or a soliloquy) is the determined modification of a general iterability – without which there would not even be a successful performative.

Searle replies that these instances of parasitic discourse are not cases of citation, because they are cases where expressions are used and not just mentioned. More important, Austin's decision to hold in abeyance the set of questions about parasitic discourse until one has answered a logically prior set of questions about 'serious' discourse was obviously sensible, and doees not prevent us from proceeding subsequently to these. Searle denies that the idea of 'parasitism' involves some kind of adverse moral judgement: it refers simply to logical dependence. Searle traces the misreading of Austin to Derrida's confusion between iterability, citationality and parasitism.[4]

So far, this looks like the kind of argument that often crops up in philosophical journals, the tone, perhaps, a bit sharper than usual. But *Limited Inc* takes us into (shall we say?) a different ball game. To describe, let alone to summarize, this astonishing document is daunting. It begins by tossing around the idea that it should have pretended to begin with a false start; then, turning to Searle's article, it remarks on the words 'Copyright © 1977 by John R Searle', and looks for reasons why this apparently harmless formula could be considered misleading: because Searle claims that his article sets out universally accepted truths (so how can it belong just to him?), because Searle, who acknowledges his debt to 'H Dreyfus & D Searle' in a footnote, may not be the sole author (and so Derrida christens the author SARL, acronym for 'Société à Responsibilité limitée), and, most teasingly, because in the course of his article Derrida manages to quote the whole of Searle's paper, and so throws down a kind of challenge to sue him for infringing copyright, suggesting that he might in his speech for the defence be able to spell out the implications of the debate more fully than he has had space for. By lingering on this apparently extraneous piece of text, Derrida is taking a kind of revenge for the fact that Searle ignored part of *his* text – for instance the 'signature' appended at the end. This rebuke (which Searle would clearly consider trivial) alternates with the much more conventional rebuke that Searle has ignored or distorted the main thrust of his argument.

In a book on frontiers, we should prick up our ears to find someone raising the question of whether some of the words lie inside or outside the text; and the questions raised by *Limited Inc* resemble the issues I shall be addressing in the last part of the book, where I look more literally at edges. But for the moment, let me go on with the impossible task of summarizing Derrida's essay. It is full of verbal games: thus, having renamed Searle 'Sarl', he then refuses to claim unequivocally that he, Jacques Derrida, is the author of the original article, which he refers to as 'Sec' (another acronym: and there had been an unobtrusive joke in the original about its dryness). Yet at the same time it is an exposition of some of Derrida's central beliefs (I have to use this term, though Derrida attacks the very idea of centrality): it calls in question all the clear-cut distinctions that Searle uses, not only between use and mention, but also normal/abnormal, intrinsic/parasitic, serious/non-serious, literal/non-literal, and several others; it refuses to allow parasitic speech acts to be held in abeyance as a special case, for it refuses to admit the distinction between holding in abeyance and actually dismissing. The possibility of a speech act being feigned, cited or otherwise parasitic is part of the determining structure of iterability that produces every such act, including the straightforward ones:

Si un certain 'break' est toujours possible, ce avec quoi il rompt doit être necessairement marqué dans sa structure par cette possibilité.

(If a certain 'rupture' is always possible, that which it breaks with must necessarily be marked, in its structure, by this possibility.[5]

The question I need to ask about *Limited Inc* is whether it is a game or a serious philosophical argument: but this is precisely the question it sets out to subvert. If the possibility of parasitic language (including jokes and games) is marked in the structure of 'serious' language, then we cannot separate the two any more than, in biology, we can separate parasite from host. Derrida believes that since a philosophy of speech acts will itself contain speech acts, a theory that no such theory should marginalize the playful must present itself playfully. Joking then becomes a consistent way of being serious. It is an elegant paradox, but every reader of poetry knows that you can enjoy the elegance by a willing suspension of disbelief without being converted to the detachable conclusions. If I can respond to Donne's Holy Sonnets without accepting his theology, to Hardy's 'Loss of the Titanic' without believing in an ironic Fate, and to Yeats's 'Byzantium' and 'The Gyres' without believing in a cyclical view of history, can I not enjoy Derrida's brilliant paradoxes and then go on to ask whether, as a logocentrist, I believe he has been serious?

For he has. This is clearest at the points where he considers himself to have been misrepresented. That Searle does misrepresent Derrida, I have little doubt: Derrida is very difficult to read, and his fireworks have misled Searle into attributing to him several positions that he certainly does not hold; often Searle's replies come closer to what Derrida believes than the view he believes himself to be attacking. (Indeed, there is a good deal of agreement between them, though this is not a fact either feels moved to emphasize.) Now if Derrida were wholly consistent (but perhaps he doesn't believe in consistency), he ought not to mind being misrepresented, since he could regard this as a game that Searle is playing with him. But instead, he protests: he points out that Searle is quite unable to quote chapter and verse for the implicit position he attributes to Derrida (that 'illocutionary intentions if they really existed or mattered would have to be something that *lay behind* the utterances'), and he refers meticulously to his own text to show how Searle has got it wrong. When it comes to his own essay, Derrida is as logocentric as the rest of us, and I can scarce forebear to cheer.

I will go further. *Limited Inc* is not only serious in its concern that Derrida's own position should not be misstated, it could also be said to have a serious expressive purpose. Let us pause to notice one or two facts about it. In reply to a twenty-page attack, Derrida has written an eighty-page reply, in which he pours scorn on his opponent's understanding, makes fun of his name, and indulges at great length in the strategy of 'Look, I didn't say what you say I said'. It sounds like every scholar's dream: most people have the self-control to resist it, and those who haven't are restrained by their editors, or denied publication. Derrida actually tells us why he is going on at such length: he is delighted at the invitation to reply, he is enjoying the whole thing, some of Searle's sentences give him enormous pleasure. Who am I to accuse him of bad faith here? But he can scarcely object if, treating these remarks as attempts to link the essay to its origins, I observe that 'a written sign carries with it a force of breaking with its context, that is, the set of presences which organize the moment of its inscription', and then say that the written signs of *Limited Inc* sound as if they might well be the work of someone who was hurt and angry. For they make use of virtually every device by which the controversialist sneers at his opponent. 'A plusieurs reprises, passant d'ailleurs trop facilement de

l'intention à l'intentionnalité (mais laissons cela), Sarl attribue. . .':
let's leave that aside – a way of indicating that your opponent has
got so much wrong that it's not worth pausing on his minor errors.
'Je connais bien cet argument': let him not imagine that his points
haven't been made a dozen times before. 'Avec une attention plus
active et présente, Sarl aurait pu remarquer un passage comme
celui. . .': he couldn't even read my essay carefully – followed a
page later by 'Suivons donc la *Reply* au plus près': but I shall read
him with care. And most striking: ' "Intentions must all be
conscious". Devant cette phrase, je dois avouer que j'ai écarquillé
les yeux. Avais-je rêvé? mal lu? mal traduit? . . .': the mock
astonishment when your opponent attributes to you what you'd
never dream of saying. I, too, rubbed my eyes when I read that in
Searle, but since I am not taking part in the controversy I can say
this without being suspected of defensiveness or irritation. The
cumulative effect of the rhetoric of *Limited Inc* suggests that it might
well be an outburst of rage and self-vindication, the jokes springing
from bottled-up indignation.

To separate the game from the serious purpose (expository or
expressive) of this essay is extremely difficult, and seems rather
philistine. It is the most entertaining piece of Derrida I have read
(though some of its jokes, especially the copyright joke, begin to
wear a bit thin as it goes on), and it goes against the grain to subject
it to this dissection. But it has to be done, in the interests of
logocentrism: of my belief that a text can refer to something outside
itself. Having suspended disbelief in order to enjoy the joke, I must
pull back from the deconstructive brink before being swept over.
The moment before a text charms and bamboozles you into
accepting what you don't believe is the moment to be philistine. If
your enjoyment of Hopkins or Evelyn Waugh leads to your being
told that you must now join the Roman Catholic church, if your
enjoyment of Pound and Eliot leads to an invitation to join an anti-
Semitic brotherhood, then it is time to draw back. Of course there
is a paradox in this. The doctrine that *Limited Inc* may bamboozle us
into accepting is precisely the doctrine that there is no reality
outside text. If we do not intend to be swept into this, we must stay
inside this text. In the interests of logocentrism, we must
deconstruct this deconstruction.

And so, after this glorious digression, I reassert what I began by
taking for granted: play is great stuff, but it's not the same as being
serious.

5

The Body of Literature

The Book

If a work of literature is like a human being (the analogy is old and familiar) then it has a soul and a body: a purpose and a material existence. The idea of the ghost in the machine has fallen out of favour, since we have grown sceptical whether either soul or body can exist separately. We ought then to replace it with a view that does not in any literal sense detach them from each other, but distinguishes function from material extension. What we think and feel and do, our identity and character as individuals: that is what, today, we call the soul, or the self. The embodiment of this self, which has size, weight, extension, which grows and decays and dies, is the body: no longer thought of as a garment or a person or a container, since that too implies the possibility of taking off the garment, or walking out of the prison, which (in any world we can know) does not happen.

This book so far has been concerned with the soul of literature; but every poem or novel also has a physical embodiment as book, and it is to that I now turn.[1] A different analogy is available, for those who don't like soul/body; that is software/hardware. If a work of literature is seen as a programme, then to be put into operation it needs a computer, made not of metal but of paper. In one respect at least this is a better analogy. Your soul can only inhabit the one body, but books, like programmes, are condemned to metempsychosis: my tattered paperback edition, your handsome privately printed edition, Thomas Thorpe's edition of 1609, all of which exist in multiple copies: these are all Shakespeare's *Sonnets*. Your own body can lose a limb or acquire contact lenses or even an artificial heart, and the surgeons of literature, whom we call textual critics, and the midwives, whom we call printers, can similarly tinker with the literary body; but neither you nor the *Sonnets* will lose your identity as a result.

Pick up a book, and open it at the beginning. What do you find?

THE FAERIE QUEENE. / Disposed into twelve books, / Fashioning / XII. Moral virtues. / (Then an oval drawing, showing a hand descending from a cloud, holding an anchor intertwined with leaves, and the motto *Anchora Spei* (the anchor of hope.) Then, *London* / Printed for William Ponsonbie. / 1596.

Or you find:

A MASKE / PRESENTED / At Ludlow Castle, / 1634: / On Michaelmasse night, before the RIGHT HONOURABLE JOHN Earle of Bridgewater, Viscount BRACKLEY, Lord President of WALES, And one of HIS MAJESTIE'S most honourable Privie Counsell / Eheu quid volui misero mihi! floribus austrum perditus (Alas, what wretchedness I intended to myself when I exposed my flowers to the south wind) / LONDON / Printed for HUMPHREY ROBINSON, at the signe of the Three Pigeons in Pauls Churchyard / 1637.

Or you find:

TRAVELS / INTO SEVERAL Remote Nations OF THE / WORLD / IN FOUR PARTS, / By LEMUEL GULLIVER, first a SURGEON and then a CAPTAIN of Several SHIPS. / VOL I / LONDON: / Printed for Benj Motte, at the Middle / Temple-gate in Fleet-street / M,DDCC,XXVI.

Or you find:

THE DUNCIAD, / VARIORUM. / WITH THE / PROLOGEMENA OF SCRIBLERUS. / (Then a picture of a donkey carrying a load of books, on which sits an owl, and the motto *Deferor in vicum vendentem Thus et Odores*) / LONDON. / Printed for A Dod. 1729.

Or you find:

CLARISSA. / OR, THE / HISTORY / OF A YOUNG LADY; / Comprehending / The most Important Concerns of Private LIFE. / And particularly shewing. / The DISTRESSES that may attend the Misconduct / Both of PARENTS and CHILDREN, / In Relation to MARRIAGE. / Published by the EDITOR of PAMELA. / Vol I. / LONDON: / Printed for S Richardson: / And Sold by A MILLAR, over-against Catharine-

Street in the Strand (plus three other booksellers, with addresses) / MDCCXLVIII

Or you find:

SHELLEY / POETICAL WORKS / EDITED BY THOMAS HUTCHINSON / A NEW EDITION, CORRECTED BY G M MATTHEWS / OXFORD UNIVERSITY PRESS / LONDON OXFORD NEW YORK.

Or you find:

VANITY FAIR / A Novel without a Hero / By WILLIAM MAKEPEACE THACKERAY / (the title shown on cards strung on a line between two rickety posts, underneath a jester sits on the ground, looking into a cracked mirror) / LONDON / BRADBURY & EVANS, BOUVERIE STREET / 1848

Or you find:

Lord Jim, / A Tale / By JOSEPH CONRAD / 'It is certain my Conviction gains infinitely the moment another soul will believe in it' – NOVALIS / WILLIAM BLACKWOOD AND SONS / EDINBURGH AND LONDON / MDCCCC / All Rights Reserved.

It is quite clear that books have no standard way of announcing themselves. For us, the two basic pieces of information about a book are the title and the author: that is how librarians classify them and we describe them (Milton's *Comus*, Conrad's *Lord Jim*). But for a long time title pages did not know this: often they did not name the author, or only pretended to ('Lemuel Gulliver' is really part of the title), sometimes they did not give a title ('A Masque' is merely an indication of genre), or they give one so long and clumsy that abbreviating it will clearly be left to us ('Travels. . .'). And there is other information on title pages. Publisher is something we still allow, for commercial reasons, though the book trade is now so well organized that it's no longer necessary to direct us to the sign of the Three Pigeons in Pauls Churchyuard. Yet we know well that this is not part of the book: a reissue by another publisher would be the same book. In one case, the patron takes pride of place: the Earl of Bridgewater dominates the title page of the masque presented in his honour, and the epigraph could be taken to mean that the poem was really only for him, not for us, the mere readers. Epigraphs are still quite common, but the function of Spenser's elaborate pictoral emblem, or the book-laden ass of the *The Dunciad*, has been taken over by the book-jacket.

Turn the page: there are still plenty of preliminaries before we can be sure the book has started. In the case of *The Faerie Queene*, we shall find a dedication To the most high mighty and magnificent empress Elizabeth, fulsome in addressing her and in humbling the poet, then a Letter of the Authors to Sir Walter Raleigh, 'expounding his whole intention in the course of this work', a series of Commendatory Verses, the first by Raleigh (though we are not told this), the rest signed with initials or pseudonyms, and seventeen dedicatory sonnets, signed ES, to various noblemen who we presume could hardly object to having been squeezed out of the main dedication by the high and mighty empress. In the case of *Comus* (I will restore its now usual title) we have a dedication to the Earl of Bridgewater's son by Henry Lawes, who wrote the music, which makes it clear that he had acted in the first performance (as had Lawes, in the part of Attendant Spirit), and which mentions that the poem is 'not openly acknowledged by the author'; then a commendatory letter to the (still unnamed) author from Henry Wootton; and then a list of the Persons, and the direction 'The first scene discovers a wild wood. The Attendant Spirit descends or enters.' It is clear that this is a masque, in which visual effects are far more important than in an ordinary play, and for which future producers may or may not have the equipment to bring the Attendant Spirit down from the starry threshold of Jove's court by machinery.

In the case of *Gulliver's Travels* (again I will restore the familiar title) there is a Letter from Captain Gulliver to his Cousin Sympson, passionately complaining that though his book has been out for six months there has been no noticeable reformation of the world's wickedness; then a note from the Publisher to the Reader, earnestly – and patronizingly – telling us about Gulliver ('the author, after the manner of travellers, is a little too circumstantial'); and then a detailed Table of Contents before the matter-of-fact beginning of the story proper: 'My father had a small estate in Nottinghamshire.'

The preliminary material in the case of the Variorum *Dunciad* is enormous. An Advertisement promises us that this edition is 'a much more correct and complete copy of *The Dunciad* than has hitherto appeared' and defends the critical apparatus with mock solmnity. A long Letter to the Publisher from one William Cleland is really a defence of the poem and an elaborate compliment to Pope in terms very like those he uses about himself in his Satires ('He has lived with the Great without Flattery'): from the first, Pope was suspected of writing this himself, even of inventing the figure of Cleland, and the exact truth is still uncertain. Testimonies of Authors concerning our Poet and his Works, by Martinus Scriblerus, occupy more than twenty pages, and include hostile as well as favourable comments (though pointing out that the favourable come from those who know him, the unfavourable from those who don't). Also by Martinus Scriblerus (this was a communal pseudonym of the Pope-Swift-Gay-Arbuthnot circle) is an essay on the poem, that defends it for sticking to the best classical models and imitating a lost work of Homer. Then come the Arguments to the three books, and then at last we turn the page to begin the poem

- Books and the Man I sing, the first who brings
  The Smithfield Muses to the Ear of Kings –

and no sooner have we realized, from the first phrase, that this is a parody of ancient epic, than we see it almost disappear in a vast swamp of footnotes – beginning with a tortured discussion whether it should be spelt Dunceiad, and signed Theobald: Theobald being the King of Dullness and main butt of the poem, and a sentence by him defending punctiliousness about single letters is actually included in the note.

We have looked at the preliminaries of two of the great ironic masterpieces in English, and one thing is clear: if the work itself is ironic, and the purpose of the introductory material is to tell us, objectively, what the work is (title, author, date, perhaps dedicatee), then all this apparatus has been swallowed up by the work. Yet not swallowed up completely, for it does, somehow or other, get a good deal of this information over to us, even if in a voice that speaks from within the text.

The rest of the examples are, by comparison, blessedly simple. In *Clarissa* there is an Author's Preface. In *Vanity Fair* there is a preface called 'Before the Curtain', developing the analogy between author and Manager of the Performance at the theatre, and then we come to Chapter I, 'Chiswick Mall'. In *Lord Jim* an Author's Note appears in the 1917 issue.

One item in our list is anomalous. Shelley's *Poetical Works* is not a single book but a posthumous collection, and strictly speaking I should here have put *Queen Mab* or *Prometheus Unbound*: but this, along with anthologies, is the way we now read poetry, at least when the poet is dead and famous. In this case, there is not really a title, simply a statement of genre: 'Poetical works' corresponds to 'A Tale' or 'A Masque', and it is the individual poems that have titles.

This anomaly is also the norm: unless we are bibliophiles, we no longer read any of these books in the original editions that I have described. We read them in popular or scholarly reprints (nowadays these two categories have begun to merge), in which a good deal more preliminary material appears: the editor's introduction, some bio- and bibliographical information, and as like as not some notes at the end, and even textual apparatus. We might associate all this with editors, and detach it clearly from the atuhor's book, but that too is a distinction that blurs, as we have very vividly seen from *The Dunciad*. *Clarissa* too has notes by the author.

As for the introduction, in order to separate what the author wrote from what his editor adds, we sometimes distinguish the synonyms Preface, Foreword, Introduction, keeping the last for what the editor writes; but this is not consistent, especially since a Preface could as easily be a commendation by a friend, a distinguished writer or 'Richard Sympson'. And of course the editor's introduction may be partly 'by' the author: it may quote remarks which the author herself made in letters, or extracts from her notebooks; indeed, the textual apparatus, it could be argued, is entirely by the author, though not in any form she would recognize.

Textual apparatus: nothing makes the edge of a book more ragged than the fact that an author can, and does, change her mind. Usually she will tidy up the text for publication, but an editor may come along and untidy it. He may print rejected versions (at the foot of the page; in notes at the back), and may wonder whether they really were rejected. The usual criterion is that the author's final thoughts should provide the authoritative text, but any textual critic knows that this is easier said than done. In some cases the author did not finish revising, leaving us with half a final text and the whole of an earlier version (Sidney's *Arcadia* is a well-known instance). In some cases, we suspect that the final version was imposed on the author against his will. The New Oxford Shakespeare calls Falstaff 'Oldcastle' on the grounds that Shakespeare was forced to change the name to Falstaff by the descendants of Sir John Oldcastle, and there is no reason to believe that he wanted to do this. This raises obvious borderline cases: that change may be imposed on an unwilling author before or after publication – should those be distinguished? Sometimes the final thoughts may have been announced but not executed ('I'm going to alter that if there's another edition', we find in a letter – or are told – on what authority? – was said in conversation). And even when the changes are clear and unambiguous, we may, if they are carried out, consider them disastrous. 'My God what genius I had when I wrote that book,' said the old Swift, looking through *A Tale of a Tub*: but how many authors have reacted with less searing honesty, and revised away their early genius? We possess the manuscript of Wordsworth's 1805 *Prelude* as well as the text printed after his death in 1850, and it has become common to print them on facing pages, so that readers can choose which version they prefer: this is an admirable practice, but its implications will not stand up for a moment. A complete Wordsworth cannot be made 200 pages longer by printing both versions in full, and then longer and longer still as we add both versions of anything else the poet happened to rewrite, or of which the revisions happen to survive. And anyway, it is an oversimplification to divide the *Prelude* into two distinct versions: Wordsworth revised it continually over thirty years or so, and it is arguable that the difference between the original 1799 text, of only 978 lines, and that of 1805, of some 8400 lines, is far more important than anything that happened subsequently. The existence of an '1850 Prelude' and an '1805 Prelude' is itself an artificial idea imposed on the material by editors, and it has not even the advantage of corresponding to the author's intention.

And notes? Notes, that is, by the author, which he intended, or may have intended, to be printed with the book. I will take one example, short but by no means simple. When Stendhal writes in the margin of *Lucien Leuwen*: 'Modèle: Dominique himself. Ah! Dominique himself', he presumably did not intend it to be printed (we cannot be sure, since he did not live to publish the book; but there's a good deal in the margin of *Lucien Leuwen*). The fact that he calls himself by a nickname, and half dodges into another language, inserts an element of role-playing into this personal admission, that seems to reach out and attach it to the text: he is on the way to calling the book 'Dominique'. Are such notes part of the book today? The Pleiade edition prints them at the back, a paperback will omit them.

It is growing clearer and clearer, as we proceed, that there is no clear boundary between the text and the rest of the world: that the edges are ragged, and that there is a good deal of no man's land along the frontiers. If you are beginning to wonder whether there is such a thing as the text, stop. Read this:

If I were a dead leaf thou mightest bear,
If I were a swift cloud to fly with thee,
A wave to pant beneath thy power, and share

The impulse of thy strength, only less free
Than thou, O uncontrollable; if even
I were as in my boyhood, and could be

The comrade of thy wanderings over Heaven,
As then, when to outstrip thy skyey speed
Scarce seemed a vision, I would ne'er have striven,

As thus with thee in prayer in my sore need.
O lift me as a wave, a leaf, a cloud.
I fall upon the thorns of life! I bleed!

A heavy weight of hours has chained and bowed
One too like thee, tameless and swift and proud.

You have just read the fourth section of Shelley's *Ode to the West Wind*. There is no doubt that it is by Shelley, and no doubt what poem it comes from, and no doubt about the text. The seasoned reader of Shelley will have no difficulty in recognizing it (he may well know it by heart) and in pointing out how typical it is of Shelley's poetry – the surge of emotion, conveyed by rhythmic parallels and images of being blown along; the underlying conviction that youth is the time of most intense living; the self-pity of the poet who is exhilarated when he can feel misunderstood by the world. The seasoned literary historian will have as little difficulty in pointing out how typically Romantic it is, comparing it to Wordsworth recalling his youth 'When like a doe / I bounded o'er the mountains', or Lamartine lamenting 'De mes jours palissants le flambeau se consume, Il s'éteint par degrés au souffle de malheur', and showing how the use of *terza rima* in this intensely ego-centred poem both announces an allegiance to Dante and asserts a deep historical rupture. The biographcially-inclined critic will be able to relate it to Shelley's sojourn in Italy; other kinds of critic will relate its enthusiasm to Shelley's Platonism, or to his political enthusiasms and perhaps to the political tensions in English society, or will point out how often the Romantics liked to use that apparently very eighteenth-century and impersonal form the Ode, or will show how the principle of equivalence has been projected from the axis of selection into the axis of combination.

Reading the poem, untroubled by doubts about just what you are reading, is central to our experience of literature. Discussing the issues I have just listed – and many more – is central to literary criticism. Both of them presuppose that the statement 'This is the fourth section of Shelley's *Ode to the West Wind*' is unproblematic. And now, once again, we have two extreme positions, essentialist and deconstructionist. The essentialist will have no truck with these ragged edges of uncertain status. Ontological problems about the text must either be settled by a few sound Johnsonian kicks, or such territory must be given up to those who enjoy theoretical quibbling, while we retreat to the undisputed heartland of literature, where the West Wind blows, and the heavy weight of pedantry and scepticism will not chain us. The heart of the deconstructionist, on the other hand, leaps up when he beholds the ragged edges: following his favourite paradox, he wishes to put the edges at the centre. The process of eating away at the concepts, once begun, cannot be stopped, and our doubt about the edges is not a special but a representative problem. And once again, this book will try to steer its path between these two extremes.

How shall we arrange these very miscellaneous edges and border territories, for without some sort of arrangement we cannot begin to discuss them? There are two possible principles of classification, corresponding once again to body and soul, to extension and function. First, where are they? Second, what are they doing?

Where do they come? There is the title, which comes first; the author's name, which usually comes next; the various kinds of subtitle, which will include epigraphs, chapter headings, and epigraphs to individual chapters; the dedication; the various kinds of preface (foreword, introduction, epistle); the notes; the various kinds of epilogue or conclusion (injunctions to heed the message of the book or not to take it too seriously, to wait for and buy the sequel, to destroy what you have just read), culminating in the illocutionary assertion, 'The End'. Then there is the material clearly external to the text, which can be divided into that by the author (textual variants, comments) and that by the editor. The material by the author can be further subdivided according as it is or is not accompanied by some kind of announcement that it really belongs in the book.

I shall single out two items in this list for special treatment. The two most prominent places are, obviously, the beginning and the end, so I shall devote a section to titles, and then, in conclusion (where else?) a section to conclusions, or rather to that one radical conclusion (which, as we shall see, does not have to come at the end) which no book is proof against. In between, I shall make an attempt to arrange the edges of the text according to their function.

Titles

If structuralism has taught us any one thing, it is the importance of the act of reading: that the meaning of a literary work must be located not simply 'within' it, as if the reader merely received passively an already completed message, but in the interaction between the work and the competence of the reader, on the analogy of any linguistic act of understanding, in which the act of constituting the meaning depends on the activity of the hearer, as well as on the words themselves.

If you only know one language, there is no need to know what language it is: every comprehensible statement will necessarily belong to it, and need not be further identified. But the polyglot needs to know whether he is hearing, say, 'nine 'ere' (put number eight over there), or 'nein, ihr' (it's not we who have to do it, but you). None of us is a poetic monoglot, who speaks and hears nothing but poetry; on the contrary, we speak mostly prose, and some speak only prose. So the first condition needed for reading a poem is to know that it is a poem; if we don't know this, certain necessary preconditions for constituting the meaning in the appropriate way will be missing. And so Jonathan Culler rewrites a newspaper report to make it look like a poem, in order to show how this can alter our expectations, and thus our interpretation.[1] True, but perhaps trivial: the expectation that we are going to read a poem is so general that it does not tell us much. The title 'Poem' (popular in mid twentieth century) is too minimal to be of any help (though it is slightly more use than the self-refuting practice in exhibitions of labelling a painting or a photograph 'Untitled'). Titles, fortunately, can do much more than this.[2]

O joy of creation
To be!
O rapture, to fly
And be free!
Be the battle lost or won,
Though its smoke shall hide the sun,
I shall find my love – the one

Born for me!
I shall know him where he stands
All alone,
With the power in his hands
Not o'erthrown;
I shall know him by his face,
By his godlike front and grace;
I shall hold him for a space
All my own.

It is he – O my love!
So bold!
It is I – all thy love
Foretold!
It is I – O love, what bliss!
Doest thou answer to my kiss?
O sweetheart! What is this
Lieth there so cold?[3]

A first response to this poem might observe the use of romantic clichés, and think of it as a gushing and derivative love poem; but we may also notice a puzzling narrative element – why should 'he' fall dead at the moment of contact? All is explained when we add the title, 'What the Bullet Sang', and the poem becomes both perverse and interesting: nothing can restore the details from the tarnish of cliché, but the odd purpose they are being put to makes the effect of the whole altogether more striking. 'Be the battle lost or won', which might have been a stale metaphor for love's encounter, suddenly and startlingly becomes literal. Here the title makes so radical a difference that the purpose of the poem seems to be that we should discover it or, if told in advance, savour the difference it makes. In fact we are told in advance, for Bret Harte, the author, published it with its title at the top; yet this 'informed' reading seems far more effective if imposed, with a shock of surprise, on a previous first reading; this would make it into a riddle.

Heaven–Haven
A nun takes the veil

I HAVE desired to go
    Where springs not fail,

To fields where flies no sharp and sided hail
  And a few lilies blow.

  And I have asked to be
    Where no storms come,
Where the green swell is in the havens dumb,
  And out of the swing of the sea.[4]

Another short poem, this time better known. It has both title and
subtitle, and they perform quite different functions. The subtitle
corresponds to the title of Bret Harte's poem. By omitting it we
can leave the reader uncertain; he might then see it as a death wish.
(Poems about entering a convent are, after all, much less common
than poems about ceasing on the midnight with no pain.) This
possibility could be disturbing to the pious reader (or poet): hence
the main title, which is really a value judgement. Imagine that the
main title was 'Rest' or 'Escape', or 'The Coward': this would
invite a very different judgement on the nun's act. Indeed 'The
Coward' is so explicit that, followed by so delicate a poem, it
would probably be taken as ironic, so let us stick to 'Rest' or
'Escape'. Now an earlier version of this poem was actually called
'Rest'; this is milder than 'Escape', but all the same it omits the
verbal echo that appears like objective confirmation that God has
blessed the renunciation, and instructs us to read the poem as an act
of affirmation, not of cowardice. If Hopkins had left the earlier
title, would not commentators have felt more strongly the need to
tell the reader that he was a Jesuit priest? The lack of a clear-cut
instruction from the title could stimulate the need for external
information as a safeguard against what might be seen as a wrong
reading (or even a different poem). And the irreligious reader who
detested monasticism might of course *prefer* the title 'Rest' or
'Escape', claiming that it helped to rescue the poem from the poet's
deplorable opinions.

The wind billowing out the seat of my britches,
My feet crackling splinters of glass and dried putty,
The half-grown chrysanthemums staring up like accusers,
Up through the streaked glass, flashing wth sunlight,
A few white clouds all rushing eastwards,
A line of elms plunging and tossing like horses,
And everyone, everyone pointing up and shouting![5]

This poem, by Theodore Roethke, is called 'Child on Top of a Greenhouse'. Of the two important pieces of information in the title, the second could perhaps be guessed without great difficulty. The fact that the speaker appears to be on glass, and can see down to the chrysanthemums, makes any other kind of building much less likely. If we are not told in advance that it is a greenhouse, our pleasure comes, as in a riddle, from the skill with which clues are offered us; if we are, it comes from the felicity of observation and metaphor ('staring up like accusers'). But the first piece of information, that the speaker is a child, is not so obviously deducible from the text. He could be an escaping criminal, a sleepwalker suddenly awakened, a madman or a stunt man (though perhaps he is too excited for this last). In the other cases, the first two lines will probably be an expression of fear, and the last line will convey an unwanted, even distressing experience. If it is a child, however, then we have a piece of bravado: the first line will express exhilaration, and the last line his excitement at being the centre of attention.

Would the rather different poem we would read if the speaker were an escaping criminal be more or less successful artistically? The striking verbal strategy of this poem (a series of noun phrases, every one with a present participle, and no main verb), which conveys so well the intensity and isolation of an experience that seems to be outside time, would be equally appropriate to both; and in both cases the final line, which forms the climax of the escapade, also contains the threat of its termination. But the climax is a more complex one for the child. For the criminal, becoming the centre of attention is in every way unwanted. The child however wants to be spotted and pointed at, yet he does no want (or part of him does not want) to come down: the desired climax is at the same time the undesired termination. This will make it a better poem (or better reading) if we believe that complex experiences are more rewarding to express than simpler ones. And there is another closely connected argument, the complexity of our response. No doubt we can feel a sort of identification with the escaping criminal in a well-written thriller, or at the end of *Oliver Twist*, but for most of us it is a rather strongly literary identification; whereas we have all been children, and can recognize in the climbing of the greenhouse the sort of thing we did, or consciously refrained from doing, or watched our friends do. The child poem, it could be argued, invades the self of the reader more directly than the criminal poem.

Of course we would expect the poem Roethke actually wrote to be better than the rather different poem we turn it into by changing the title, but though common sense urges this it is not logically necessary. In particular, when the reader's position has changed through the passage of time – when the title would lock the poem into a past situation from which we would like to remove it – then a change of title may be to the poem's advantage. I shall return to this point.

We cannot unfortunately stay with examples that are short enough to quote in full, and I turn now to a more complex case. The title of Andrew Marvell's 'Horation Ode upon Cromwell's return from Ireland'[6] also performs two functions, and could easily be turned into title and subtitle: 'Upon Cromwell's Return from Ireland: an Horatian Ode'. The main title relates the poem to a particular political event, and the effect of removing it would be to conceal the fact that it is about Cromwell. Of course we'd have to remove Cromwell from the text too, along with other proper names like Charles, Carisbrooke and even perhaps Ireland. Since the poem is filled with particular references, we could not possibly turn it into a wholly general poem about a victorious and usurping general without totally destroying it. Its strategy is totally different from, for instance, Charles Wolfe's poem on 'The Burial of Sir John Moore after Corunna':

– Few and short were the prayers we said,
   And we spoke not a word of sorrow;
   But we steadfastly gazed on the face that was dead,
   And we bitterly thought of the morrow. . .

Slowly and sadly we laid him down,
From the field of his fame fresh and gory;
We carved not a line and we raised not a stone,
But we left him alone with his glory.[7]

This could easily be retitled 'In the Hour of Victory', or 'Burying the Leader', to give us a poem that could apply to virtually any general killed in a victorious battle. As could many such poems, and Whitman followed such a policy in entitling his funeral elegy 'O Captain, my Captain' instead of 'On the Death of Abraham Lincoln'. The only way to do anything similar to Marvell's poem would be to replace its numerous proper names with Latin names:

So restless *Martius* could not cease
In the inglorious Arts of Peace

This would, after all, only carry further the poem's own strategy:
on one occasion it refers to Charles as 'Caesar', and makes
prominent use of parallels from Roman history:

So when they did design
The Capitol's first Line,
A bleeding Head where they begun,
Did fright the Architects to run.

If however we did this, it would look as if the poem was in code (as
are parts of Pope's Satires), and there would be an invitation to the
knowledgeable to 'solve' it, and those without the knowledge
would think of it as a poem that others could solve. There is no
way we could turn it into a poem like the following:

(1) Did the people of that land
    Use lanterns of stone?
(2) Did they hold ceremonies
    to reverence the opening of buds?
(3) Were they inclined to rippling laughter? . . .

(1) Sir, their light hearts turned to stone.
    It is not remembered whether in gardens
    stone lanterns illuminated pleasant ways.
(2) Perhaps they gathered once to delight in blossom,
    but after the children were killed
    there were no more buds.
(3) Sir, laughter is bitter to the burnt mouth.[8]

In this case I have removed not the title but a crucial word from the
first line. The poem (here abridged) by Denise Levertov, is called
'What were they like? (Questions and Answers)'; the sort of
information that would usually come in the title is conveyed by the
first line, which actually reads 'Did the people of Viet Nam'. In
future years, if this poem is reprinted in a school anthology, it will
doubtless be necessary to mention the date (1966) and to supply
information about American involvement in Vietnam and the
protests against it. And if there are similar wars in those future

years, there will be no difficulty in applying this poem to them
with much more ease than, say:

A *Caesar* he ere long to *Gaul*,
To *Italy* an *Hannibal*,
   And to all States not free
   Shall *Clymacterick* be.

Marvell's poem will not easily submit to the surgical operation I am
proposing, but the reason for this is the way it is written. It is clear
that such an operation is in principle possible, and can be performed
on other poems. But why should anyone want to do it to this – or
any – poem? The answer is, I hope, obvious: in order to establish
how far the poem is specifically about Cromwell, and that in its
turn will be crucial to our reading. For if the sense in which it is
'about Cromwell' is central to its significance, then all the
knowledge about the English Civil War that we can feed in will be
relevant to our response. Specific knowledge (that Charles was
imprisoned in Carisbrooke Castle) will help us to understand the
references, but this is of minor importance. What matters much
more is the politics. If one reader considers Cromwell as an
enlightened statesman who pacified England, established religious
toleration and made her respected abroad, and a second regards him
as a narrow-minded bigot who murdered thousands of Irishmen,
can they read the poem the same way (or, if we prefer, are they
reading the same poem)?

To answer this we must obviously ask what judgement the poem
passes on Cromwell, and at this point the other title becomes
relevant. What is a Horatian Ode? Only to a casual glance will this
four-line stanza look like the alcaics and sapphics of Horace, and in
any case poets choose metrical patterns not just for their own sake
but to join the poem to one tradition or another. What is relevant
therefore is that Horace wrote a number of patriotic odes praising
the courage and *virtus* of famous Roman soldiers, and that he wrote
with unsurpassed grace and elegance. An Horatian Ode on
Cromwell can therefore suggest two things, praise of his heroic
virtue, and a highly polished and sophisticated treatment: this is
exactly what we find in Marvell's poem, and of course they clash
with each other.

The reader who knows his Horace will think of examples when
they clash in Horace too, just as he will recall how differently
Horace (the self-confessed bad soldier) behaved from the 'forward

youth' of the poem's opening stanzas. These parallels and ironics enrich the reading, but at the moment I am concerned with relating the poem not to Horace, but to Cromwell. For that purpose, 'Horatian Ode' announces an emphasis on tradition and a poise in the writing, which is exactly what we have. Cromwell is seen as an irresistible force, compared to the lightning, which ignores rules and causes destruction, in order to obey the force of angry Heaven, and the poem ends with a couplet that could be either straightforward or sinister:

The same *Arts* that did gain
A Power must it maintain.

The king, in contrast, is compared to an actor, who plays his part with impeccable dignity on the scaffold. Cromwell belongs to the world of action, Charles to that of performance. Explicitly, the poem praises Cromwell, but it behaves more like Charles.

What political position does this imply? On one level, it is a panegyric to the now established ruler, but so written that the royalist can read it and nod. By giving a slightly different emphasis to the similes of destruction

– Then burning through the Air he went
   And Palaces and Temples rent –

by remembering that kingship is essentially a form of role-playing, the royalist will be able to read Marvell's complex, balanced poem with a great deal of sympathy, for it is a poem that does not take sides as much as it seems to. The Cromwellian and the anti-Cromwellian will differ in the significance they attribute to the poem, but the poem accommodates that difference. This also means that the careful reader of the poem who knows nothing of Cromwell is not likely to be led to any conclusion he will subsequently reject.

A sudden blow: the great wings beating still
Above the staggering girl, her thighs caressed
By the dark webs, her nape caught in his bill,
He holds her helpless breast upon his breast.

How can those terrified vague fingers push
The feathered glory from her loosening thighs?

And how can body, laid in that white rush,
But feel the strange heart beating where it lies?

A shudder in the loins engenders there
The broken wall, the burning roof and tower
And Agamemnon dead.
                    Being so caught up,
So mastered by the brute blood of the air,
Did she put on his knowledge with his power
Before the indifferent beak could let her drop?[9]

How can there be any doubt about the title of Yeats's 'Leda and the Swan'? It is a narrative poem, or at any rate a poem based on narrative, and the story is mythical and well known. Yeats's own note, however, can give us pause:

I wrote Leda and the Swan because the editor of a political review asked me for a poem. I thought, 'After the individualist, demagogic movement, founded by Hobbes and popularised by the Encyclopaedists and the French Revolution, we have a soil so exhausted that it cannot grow that crop again for centuries.' Then I thought, 'Nothing is now possible but some movement from above preceded by some violent annunciation.' My fancy began to play with Leda and the Swan for metaphor, and I began this poem; but as I wrote, bird and lady took such possession of the scene that all politics went out of it. . .

It was intended to be a poem, we realize, about Yeats's apocalyptic, cyclic theories of history, of the same kind as 'The Gyres', in which the violence of our own times is assimilated to that of other times ('Hector is dead and there's a light in Troy').

How can this point be conveyed to the reader? Yeats published this poem in *A Vision*, in the section entitled 'Dove or Swan', and that context immediately directs us to the issues raised in the note: indeed Yeats once described that whole section of *A Vision* as '40 pages of commentary' on the poem. Yet for one reader who reads the poem in *A Vision* there are many thousands who read it in an anthology or in the Poems of Yeats, and even those who read *A Vision* almost certainly know the poem already. As the object of a reading act, the poem's existence outside *A Vision* is far more important than its existence within it; and it was originally written as an independent poem. There is therefore no escaping the question, can we indicate to the reader *of the poem* that it is about

the need for some violent annunciation today? – that is, can we do
this by means of retitling? One possibility would be to take an
image from the poem itself as title ('The Broken Wall', say, or
'Brute Blood'). Since there are sufficient clues in the text to lead the
well-informed reader to the Leda story, this would have the effect
of delaying our awareness of the subject, and so (perhaps)
suggesting that this is not the true subject, but a metaphor. But that
'perhaps' is a futile hope: readers would simply take the delay as a
characteristic modernist strategy. To convey the point made in the
note, it would be necessary to use a title that explicitly introduced
our own age: 'A Fable for our Time', or 'After Hobbes' or 'After
Thirty Centuries'. But since nothing in the poem ties on to this
point, it might then be necessary to insert into the text some
reference to the cyclic theory of history involved, and it would then
seem natural to use that as the title, which would give us 'The
Gyres'. In the poem of that name, written some years later, Yeats,
by singling out the system itself in the title, calls attention to it, and
opens the possibility of our not taking it wholly seriously –
especially since the poem contains such a nice ambiguity as (my
italics):

And all things run
On that *unfashionable* gyre again.

If we wanted to give this dimension to 'Leda and the Swan', we
would have to suggest that the 'knowledge' of the penultimate line
is of the ending of the Hobbesian era, or that the destruction
'engendered' by the sexual act is of our civilization, but it is very
doubtful whether the mere act of retitling could lead any reader to
do this. As Yeats all too clearly says, 'all politics went out of it', so
that there is simply nothing in the text that would enable us to
derive the contents of that note. Retitling can change our
expectations, but there is a limit to what it can insert into the
meaning.

I now take two very different poems in order to make a common
point. Edwin Muir wrote a poem beginning 'The angel and the girl
are met', which describes the timeless ecstasy of their encounter:

See, they have come together, see,
While the destroying minutes flow,
Each reflects the other's face

Till heaven in hers and earth in his
Shine steady there.

The rapt attention described is mutual: not only the girl's joy but
also the wonder of the angel is described. This mutual delight
sounds like the experience of love, when a new dimension of
experience seems to have opened up, and seized both parties:

But through the endless afternoon
These neither speak nor movement make,
But stare into their deepening trance
As if their gaze would never break.[10]

Could that not describe two lovers, sufficient to each other, like the
lovers in Donne's 'Ecstasy'? The angel has come from 'far beyond
the farthest star': could this not be the image a girl in love might
use for the transfiguring sight of her lover? We have here a religious
poem that uses the analogy of sexual love: could it not equally be a
love poem using a religious analogy? The question is settled by the
title, 'The Annunciation' – unless that too is a metaphor.
    Sylvia Plath wrote a poem beginning 'An old beast ended in this
place',[11] which describes the decomposition of a dead body, and
includes the lines 'A monster of wood and rusty teeth', 'The rafters
and struts of his body' and 'The coils and pipes that made him run'.
Are we reading a poem about a dead animal that uses images of
building and of machinery, or a poem about a building that
compares it to a body? Once again the title, 'The Burnt-out-Spa',
settles the question (this time surely beyond any doubt). In both
these cases, an extended conceit takes us to the point where there
could be uncertainty about which is tenor and which is vehicle – if
it were not for the title.

My true love hath my heart, and I have his,
By just exchange, one for another given.
I hold his dear, and mine he cannot miss.
There never was a better bargain driven.
My true love hath my heart, and I have his.

His heart in me keeps him and me in one;
My heart in him his thoughts and senses guides:
He loves my heart, for once it was his own;

I cherish his, because in me it bides.
My true love hath my heart and I have his.[12]

This time I want to postulate a particular situation, in order to see
the possible definitions of the poem's subject as a process. Let us
imagine this poem being sung at a wedding (a church wedding,
today): it is after all clearly a poem about sexual love. But if we
turn to the original context we can be quite certain that it is not
about married love. It comes from Sidney's *Arcadia*, where it is
attributed (by one of the characters) to a shepherdess making an
assignation with an ugly (and married) old man: the context is
adulterous and comic. But the poem soon became a favourite in its
own right, and the context ought therefore perhaps to be more
general: the poetic tradition it belongs in rather than the *Arcadia*
itself. This tradition is the poetry of courtly love, and in particular
the sixteenth-century English lyric driving from it: the first is
almost entirely and the second largely adulterous. There is however
nothing in the poem itself to make the adulterous situation explicit,
and a very similar love vocabulary is used in Elizabethan love
comedy during courtship. It is not difficult to imagine a real-life
Elizabethan lover chastely wooing a lady by singing her this song.
The implication would be 'Look, I'm offering you in an honourable
way the sort of stuff that sophisticated courtiers offer to their
mistresses.' It is however much harder to transfer such poetry to a
wedding. Impossible, perhaps, in the case of a poem that uses (as
do most of Dante's sonnets and many of Petrarch's) the love–
religion analogy, since a church wedding is itself a religious
occasion, in which Christianity is explicit and so cannot be
metaphorical. Today, of course, the conventions that lie behind the
poem will be less present to the minds of the hearers, and we can
therefore imagine a number of different reactions among them.
  First there is the pious Christian who believes it is a poem about
married love. He will have no difficulty fitting it into the
ceremony, and may find it moving, but he is to some extent
mistaken about the poem: certainly about its context, arguably
about its meaning. He may call the poem 'Wife to Husband'.
Second there is the pious Christian who knows it is about romantic
love, and comes from a tradition of adulterous love poetry: he will
object to its being sung at the wedding, and may call it 'The False
Goddess'. Third, there is the believer in romantic love who knows
its history and approves: that it began in adultery, shifted to
courtship, and then shifted to marriage. He will be delighted that

the poem is being sung at a wedding, and may simply call it 'True Love'. Fourth is, say, Denis de Rougemont, who knows the history of romantic love and strongly disapproves: he considers that the attempt to base marriage choice on so irrational a passion is a piece of modern vulgarity, an escapist attitude to a serious institution; de Rougemont can provide his own contemptuous title for the poem, 'Marrying Iseult'.[13] Finally the modern radical, who disapproves of marriage, and considers the decision of the lovers to get married at all – let alone in church – a compromise with respectability. If he is well-informed he will welcome the song as an outbreak of subversion, and may call it 'For How Long?', or 'A Touch of Constancy'.

I would have liked, as a parallel to this discussion of the titles of poems, to discuss the titles of novels. There would be one fundamental difference: The experience of reading a novel is on such a large scale, that the initial instructions are likely to be submerged in the actual reading. The impact of the title of a lyric may control the intense, brief experience which succeeds, but whatever we are told by the title of a novel will not reveal its full importance until we are well on in the book, by which time we have been told a great deal more. The title of a novel is therefore better seen as an instruction on how to look back on the reading experience, how subsequently to arrange and understand it. Examples of this would be *A la recherche du temps perdu*, which sums up our own gradual discovery as we read; or Conrad's *Chance*, an act of bravado inviting us to reflect on the use of coincidences. Such a discussion could also contrast the function of titles that name the theme (*The Return of the Native, Pride and Prejudice*), that relate the book, perhaps ironically, to a tradition (*The Old Wives' Tale, Far From the Madding Crowd*), that single out a central symbol (*The Rainbow, The Bell-jar*), that name the place or setting (*Mansfield Park, Framley Parsonage*) or that name the hero or heroine (and here the form of address may be important: *Sir Charles Grandison, Emma, Redgauntlet*). Even as I sketch such a discussion it becomes clear that my space would never run to it, and I shall therefore turn to painting instead, where there is an example that very neatly raises the central issues I wish to address.

There is one kind of painting that necessarily bears a title, and a title which refers to the outside world; this is the portrait. A portrait is not painted only for the subject, but if it is looked at by someone who neither knows nor cares who the subject is, he is not treating it as a portrait – and so is misreading it. Now the viewer's awareness of the subject can vary greatly.

Let us begin with those cases in which it is not certain, or not explicit, that we are looking at a portrait. Inserting portraits into a painting without admitting it has always been fairly common, never more so than in the Italian Quattrocento: Masaccio, Lippi, Perugino and many others inserted friends, patrons and themselves into large religious pictures. This adds a piquant element to the response of those in the know (friends then, and scholars now), but can it be regarded as part of the subject? This will depend on whether the uninitiated realize it is a portrait. They can be told this in conversation, or by what we may call a 'pedagogic title': 'Baptism of Christ, containing Giovanni Basso della Rovere and members of his family', by Perugino. If they realize it, then an element of realism is being fed into the response, an invitation to believe (like Browning's Fra Lippo Lippi) that capturing individual traits – 'homage to the perishable clay' – is another way (perhaps a better way) of depicting the act of worship.

The one case where such recognition is officially invited is that of the donor who appears in the devotional picture he has paid for – at first modestly tucked away in a corner, and, after Masaccio, lifesize and prominent, even (as in Van Eyck's 'Chancellor Rolin before the Virgin and Child') dominating the picture, both because of his placing and because of the greater realism of his treatment. This picture offers such a strong invitation to recognize (or, if we are strangers, inquire about) Rolin, that it virtually presents itself as a portrait.

In all these cases, the 'portrait' is inserted into a larger composition, but there can be uncertainty in the case of a single figure too. Compare for instance, Magnasco's picture of 'A Writer' (*c*. 1700) with Tiepolo's portrait of Antonio Riccoboni (1745). Both are on the borderline between portraits and genre paintings. The nervous grip of Magnasco's writer on his bulky folio of papers, the tight lips, the suggestion of bitter introspection, all say 'writer and scholar' as clearly as the emblematic row of tall books behind his left shoulder; yet it is very obviously a portrait of an individual. Riccoboni has the same emblems (books and pen) yet he too is clearly an individual; and the fierce regard he turns on us, as if he were the one doing the scrutinizing, could suggest the anger of somebody disturbed at his work by an importunate caller. Both pictures are so finely balanced between the individual and the general, that much will surely depend on how we are invited to view them; and both invitations turn out to be ambiguous. We do not know if the title 'A Writer' goes back to Magnasco, and we do not know the identity of the sitter: there is no certainty how we are intended to see it. Antonio Riccoboni was certainly a real man, but he died a century or more before Tiepolo was born; so the invitation to view his picture as a portrait is a kind of lie. The fact that both paintings figured in an exhibition on 'Le portrait en Italie au siècle de Tiepolo' (Petit Palais, Paris, 1982) imposed on the viewers one way of looking: we can regard this as a title bestowed by the exhibition. If the one painting had figured in an exhibition of Magnasco (called, shall we say, 'A Modern Man before his Time'), and the other in an exhibition on sixteenth-century humanism, where it would have been described as an idealized picture of a Renaissance scholar, we would view them with quite different instructions, and would constitute their significance differently. Restored respectively to their private owner and the Pinacotheca de Rovigo, they would stand deprived of any title save what the curator attached to them, and the viewer might lack instructions.

Turning now to the portrait as such, we can say that two interacting factors determine the way we look at it: whether we are told that it's a portrait, and of whom; and how much that information tells us. For we may or may not know about the sitter, and for various reasons. He (or she) may be a nonentity who derives immortality from the fame of the painter (the Mona Lisa); he may be someone who was once famous but is now forgotten (the cardinals and dukes of Mantegna and – in the future – most of Graham Sutherland's subjects); or the viewer may realize that he is looking at a figure of great historical importance (Titian's Charles V, Clouet's Francois I) but reflect ruefully on his own ignorance. Further what we do or don't know about the sitter may concern his character, his biography, or his appearance (the latter of increasing importance since the invention of photography).

In the case of public figures, the kinds of knowledge that are relevant will be altogether fuller and more complex, so let us consider two public portraits by great painters: Titian's Charles V and the Doge Leonardo Loredano by Giovanni Bellini. We can begin from an observation of Berenson's about the latter:

In the portraits of Doges which decorated the frieze of its great Council Hall, Venice wanted the effigies of functionaries entirely devoted to the state, and not of great personalities, and the profile lent itself more readily to the omission of purely individual traits.[14]

We do not need to take the question of the profile very seriously, not only because it was widely held in the fifteenth century that a profile actually made it easier to capture individual traits, but also because there happen to be two portraits of Loredano, a profile by Gentile Belleni, and a full face by Giovanni, either of which would serve us for the ensuing discussion. Of greater importance is the fact of hanging in the great Council Hall: this too is halfway between the world of the art work and the world outside. If we look at a reproduction, it might be with or without this information, as it might be with or without the title. It is essential, for the full understanding of this picture, that we realize it is of a public figure (if, for instance, we are given no instructions, we might – just – mistake the official cap he is wearing for a quirk of personal taste). But it is also a public *portrait*: that is, it depicts individual traits. If (as Berenson seems to be suggesting) these were completely omitted, we would have an icon, incorporating emblems of the office of Doge, and the portrait of one doge would differ from another in purely conventional ways (that is, not connected with what they looked like). This might be the case in a Byzantine portrait, where the omission of individuality is part of the convention, but in Bellini's work the subordination of personal to public is inserted into the painting itself. If we imagine a portrait of a doge commissioned by the family to hang in their own house, we would expect it to differ subtly from that in the Council Hall: it will still be made clear that he is doge, he may still be wearing the cap and the insignia, but this public element will now be seen as contributing to his personal distinction.

Titian's portrait of Charles V (or, say, Holbein's of Henry VIII) is just as public as the Loredano: if he were not king (or emperor) it would be quite a different painting. To place these portraits in their social context could lead us to an almost endless study of sixteenth-century history, in which detail after detail of Henry's divorce or Charles's political manoeuvring accumulated; if we try to control this endlessness by asking which elements in this knowledge are relevant to the viewing of the painting, we must surely fasten on the difference between a doge and a king as crucial. Charles and Henry are supreme rulers, whose individuality is of public importance, just as the tantrums of Queen Elizabeth (or King Lear) were public events. Loredano is a ruler chosen by his peers, who holds office temporarily in a republic. The Bellini portrait does not need to bear the name of an individual, but it can; the Titian and the Holbein do need to, not primarily so that we can bring into play our detailed knowledge of Charles and Henry, but so that we can see that such knowledge, whether or not we have it, might matter.

The literary equivalent of a portrait is in many respects an epitaph; and the same distinction between private and public applies there. Here, for instance, are two epitaphs:

Good bless our good and gracious King
Whose promise none relies on;
Who never said a foolish thing
And never did a wise one.[15]

The Lady Mary Villiers lies
Under this stone; with weeping eyes
The parents that first gave her birth,
And their sad friends, laid her in earth.
If any of them, Reader, were
Known unto thee, shed a tear;
Or if thyself possessed a gem
As dear to thee, as this to them,
Though a stranger to this place
Bewail in their thine own hard case;
For thou, perhaps, at thy return
Mayst find thy darling in an urn.[16]

The first poem has two contemporary titles, whose implications are very different: 'Impromptu on Charles II' and 'Posted on Whitehall Gate'. The first title may imply what legend certainly asserts, that it was composed by Rochester in the king's presence; the second suggests anonymity and surreptitiousness. The first makes it a relaxed joke or a piece of really bold bravado; the second a more tense joke, with possible hints of censorship and even tyranny. Meaning in the strict sense remains the same for both, but the emotional quality is very different.

The modern reader will clearly savour the poem more richly if he knows it is about Charles II, and knows something about Charles's acts and character, though he will learn a good deal of what matters from the poem itself, short as it is. Perhaps the main reason we need the title today is to make it clear that it was written about a real king, during his lifetime (both titles imply that) at a time when kings were dangerous. This makes it a truly political poem.

Thomas Carew in contrast expects to have readers who know nothing about Lady Mary Villiers, and has designed his poem for them. The apparent care with which he assures certain readers that the poem is meant for them can lead us to ask if anyone at all is

being excluded. The reader who did not know Lady Mary, nor any
of her family and friends, nor has a beloved daughter, is perhaps, in
strict logic, not being addressed, but that is not the intended effect.
The 'gem' does not have to be a daughter, and the rhetorical impact
is surely that we all have someone we care about sufficiently to
appreciate the parents' grief. The poem has to be called 'Epitaph on
the Lady Mary Villiers' to guarantee its genuineness, but it disowns
its title, saying to us 'This is about you'.

We can sum up the discussion of portraits as follows. Any
portrait must bear a name, if we are to know that it is a portrait.
('Portrait of an author' is a kind of metaphor: it really means 'genre
painting with one person only'.) Once it bears a name, the
information that the viewer can feed into his response is
theoretically unlimited: in practice, it will be very large in the case
of famous public figures, and people we know personally. But the
required information may be about their public office rather than
about them as individuals: to call the Bellini picture 'Doge' and the
Titian 'Emperor' would actually convey enough information, but it
would not do because it would not make it clear that they are
portraits.

The usual way for the title to control our reading is by narrowing
the subject: not 'In the Hour of Victory' but 'The Burial of Sir John
Moore after Corunna'. Sometimes it simply changes it: not a love
poem but 'What the Bullet Sang', not a beast but a spa. It is less
likely to broaden the subject. This can only happen if the text
contains specific references, and the title is more general: perhaps
this is sometimes the case with Yeats. And of course it can
announce firmly that the subject is meant to be universal: 'Any
Wife to any Husband'. But in a rather different sense, any literary
work broadens its subject by the sheer fact of being fiction, or
belonging to a genre; so that the kind of subtitle that serves as
generic indicator ('a novel', 'a tale', 'a novel without a hero')
prepares us for more than the particularities of history. Some
generic titles may set out to mislead. How dull it seems just to tell
your reader this is a novel, so we have '*Middlemarch*: a Study of
Provincial Life'. That does not really mislead (we all realize it is a
novel), but some tricks are less easy to see through. Not all readers
realise that *The Autobiography* of Mark Rutherford is actually a
novel, *The Autobiography of Mark Rutherford*, by William Hale
White. If we read an intensely personal story in ignorance of the
fact that it is a novel, as Edgar W. reads *Werther* in Plenzdorf's *Die
neuen Leiden des jungen W.*, then we are on the same frontier that the
first chapters of this book tried to explore, and the announcement

that it is a work of fiction, which changes our expectation, can be said to bestow a kind of generality on the subject.

Broadening the subject: for a long time, it was a commonplace that literature transforms the local and the particular into something of universal significance. That quondam commonplace has now become highly controversial. Matthew Arnold saw the function of criticism as 'a disinterested endeavour to learn and propagate the best that is known and thought in the world', and thought that this was best pursued by maintaining one's independence of the practical spirit: 'let us think of quietly enlarging our stock of true and fresh ideas, and not, as soon as we get an idea or half an idea, be running out with it into the street, and trying to make it rule there'.[17] The ideal of disinterestedness is now, by Marxist and Foucaultian alike, attacked as conservative; the attempt to assemble the best that is known and thought in the world into a timeless order transcending the circumstances that produced it, is now seen as mystification, obscuring the inescapable historicity of all discourse, the political interest that, overtly or covertly, it always serves:

'Materialism' is opposed to 'idealism': it insists that culture does not (cannot) transcend the material forces and relations of production. Culture is not simply a reflection of the economic and political system, but nor can it be independent of it. . . A play by Shakespeare is related to the contexts of its production – to the economic and political system of Elizabethan and Jacobean England and to the particular institutions of cultural production (the court, patronage, theatre, education, the church).[18]

So Dollimore and Sinfield, in the Preface to their *Political Shakespeare*, defend the doctrine of cultural materialism. Stephen Greenblatt's article in the same volume displays this method at its most intelligent:

Art's genius for survival, its delighted reception by audiences for whom it was never intended, does not signal its freedom from all other domains of life, nor does its inward articulation of the social confer upon it a formal coherence independent of the world outside its boundaries. On the contrary, artistic form itself is the expression of social evaluations and practices.[19]

Both Arnoldian disinterestedness and cultural materialism raise problems. To the Arnoldian, we can object that dehistoricizing can turn works of beautiful complex particularity into a kind of vague uplift ('high seriousness'); and disinterested withdrawal from the practical spirit can (and in Arnold sometimes did) turn into a simple defence of the status quo. Of course there are replies to these objections: it is possible to concede the need for historical placing in order to be sure we have understood a text correctly, without conceding that its value for later readers is confined to the act of historical understanding; and the difference between disinterestedness and commitment is not simply the same as that between conservative and radical. There is active, committed conservatism; and there are forms of disinterestedness very useful to the radical – oppressive systems are often challenged in the name of freedom, dignity and other universal-sounding concepts.

To the cultural materialist we can object that an 'expression' of social practices that is 'not simply a reflection' of them, may well offer a rather good account of other, later social practices as well. To insist on referring it back to its particular historical origin is to show a certain lack of curiosity. To this too there are replies: for instance, that Arnoldians do not believe in historical transcendence just as a matter of historical curiosity and willingness to generalize, but as a deeply held ideological position, behind which lies class interest or structures of power. And to these replies there are replies, and so on and so on.

I believe (this must by now be obvious) that the two positions are unlikely to convince each other by rational discussion. I also believe that each position, as it makes necessary concessions, and is formulated with increasing care, grows more like the other, and that to refine one's own position in this way is more fruitful than to attack the other. And this is where the discussion of titles bears on the ideological dispute. Instead of asking how far a poem's significance is governed by the conventions in which it originated, I preferred to ask what possible titles we can give to 'My true love hath my heart'. This enables us to postulate a particular modern reader in plausible circumstances (as it happens, I did once hear the poem sung at a wedding, in church), and to ask what elements in the original convention can, should, can't, shouldn't, be shaken off.

Since the function of a title is more often to restrict than to enlarge, the process of 'universalizing' is more likely to be done by removing (or changing) than by adding a title; but 'Leda and the Swan' is perhaps a contrary case, and a particularly interesting one. By referring us only to the legend, that title underlines the omission of politics and of the 'after Hobbes' argument, and thus announces that the poem has broken free of its origin. The interest of the example lies in the fact that the poet himself has admitted what the

Marxist critic often triumphantly discovers and tendentiously asserts, the political origin of a myth (or of one version of it). At the same time, he tells us that this origin did not find its way into the final text; and our difficulty in retitling the poem confirmed this.

It is a vain hope, no doubt, to think that an ideological issue can be settled on a technical level; but to inject a technical element into the discussion can only make for (to borrow terms from both camps) sweetness and light, rigour and excitement. Instead of asking how universal the subject of a literary work is, we can ask how universal it can be made. Instead of asserting – or denying – that all works are connected with a particular social situation, we can ask what other times and places they can, without distortion, be applied to. To see the broadening of the subject in this way as a process means that we can then devise methods of monitoring the process, and keeping it in touch with the text – methods like, for instance, altering the title.

Exploring the Edges

I turn now to my promised attempt to arrange the borderline material, or paratext, by function, and for this I propose four main functions: Information, Control, Apology and Indecision.

As used by geneticists, information means the same as control, whereas in ordinary language information in itself does not *do* anything, or cause anything to get done. Which is the better usage in the case of a text? To provide your reader with information is no doubt to exert a kind of control, since it will be difficult for him to ignore it, and read as if he did not know; but it is the mildest and most indirect form of reader control, and therefore I treat it separately.

Conveying information is the usual function of the footnote, and the notes to any annotated edition (school or scholarly) of a Shakespeare play are there to tell us what we may not know but ought to, either because contemporaries knew it, or because we are students, not mere readers, and should therefore be aware of echoes and anticipations of other texts. Do footnotes by the author serve the same purpose? The most sustained and even monstrous example of authorial footnotes must be the *Variorum Dunciad*, and it is not easy to give a straightforward answer to any question about them. Pope published the first version of *The Dunciad* in 1728, and printed the names of the poets and booksellers he lampooned with only the

first and last letters. The following year he brought out the
Variorum, in which the text is almost buried in what Pope himself
described as 'Proeme, Prolegomena, Testimonia Scriptorum, Index
Authorum and Notes Variorum'. The initials are now expanded to
surnames, and there are lengthy more-or-less-truthful biographical
notes: thus

Hence springs each weekly Muse, the living boast
Of C---l's chaste press, and L----t's rubric post,[1]

appears in 1729 as 'Curl's chaste press and Lintot's rubric post', and
a note says: 'Two Booksellers, of whom see Book 2. The former
was fined by the court of King's-Bench for publishing obscene
books.' Curl appears in Book 2, taking part in the mock-heroic
games, and in the course of a race with Lintot slipping on a pile of
excrement ('Which Curl's Corinna chanc'd that morn to make'), he
rates a much longer footnote, beginning 'We come now to a
character of much respect, that of Mr Edmund Curl,' which calls
him 'the envy and admiration of all his profession' because

He possest himself of a command over all authors whatever; he caus'd
them to write what he pleas'd; they could not call their very names their
own.[2]

Is all this part of *The Dunciad*? It is not certain how far the notes
were written by Pope: he disclaimed authorship, but this may have
been a feint on his part (he loved to deceive on such matters), and
there is no doubt that he planned them, and urged his friends to
contribute.

Does any poem require – can any poem tolerate – such a mass of
factual encumbrance? *The Dunciad* is utterly untypical of other
poems: perhaps it is the one poem that can. The issue is one of
which Pope was very conscious: should satire lash the vices and
follies of mankind in general terms, or should it name its targets? In
the *Epilogue to the Satires* a friend is made to say 'Spare then the
person, and expose the vice', to which Pope replies:

Come on, then, Satire! general, unconfined
Spread thy broad wings, and souse on all the kind.
Ye statesmen, priests of one religion all!
Ye tradesmen vile, in army, court, or hall!
Ye reverend atheists. F. Scandal! name them, who?
P. Why that's the thing you bid me not to do.

As so often in Pope, the really significant effect comes not so much from the explicit joke as from an underlying ambivalence. The couplet 'Come on, then, Satire' could express delighted approbation of the wide reach of satire, a sense of exultation at the power of poetry, as easily as the mockery it apparently intends, and it is by no means certain who wins this argument. Pope's usual method, as is well known, was to use, for his main targets, fictitious names that everyone would see through: Sappho for Lady Mary Wortley Montague, Atticus for Addison. That this will stimulate rather than remove curiosity is wittily shown two lines later:

The poisoning dame.   F. You mean –   P. I don't.   F. You do.
P. See now I keep the secret, and not you.[3]

If *The Dunciad* had referred to Cibber as 'Lauratus', say, or 'Roscius', it would not have kept him anonymous: all Grub Street would have guessed, and the thin disguise would have added to the piquancy. Indeed, in the year between the first edition and the Variorum, two unauthorized keys to the poem were published.

By now of course we have another level of notes. Scholarship could never be expected to leave *The Dunciad* alone, and the Twickenham edition now does in earnest what Martinus Scriblerus did in jest; typographical devices have to be used to mark off the notes of Scriblerus from those of the modern editor (the real notes? But which ones are more real?). As we read, this typographical device is internalized, and we tell ourselves that James Sutherland's notes are clearly not part of the poem, but the Variorum notes possibly are. And if they are – strengthened, even, by the scholarly prop under that pointed bracket – will they push the poem away from satire and towards mere vindictiveness?

It is arguable that the answer is no: not only because the disguise was so thin to begin with, but because of sheer force of numbers. All those bad poets and unscrupulous booksellers are a flock of birds, deafening us by their agitating wings, clustering together in what the ethologists call mobbing. Such a flock of details loses individuality, and no longer seems personal. It's as if so many facts add up to fantasy: as if so many particulars make of Grub Street a richly invented realm, fit abode for the Goddess of Dullness. In this way, the notes do not destroy the imagined creation, and even Professor Sutherland's careful annotating becomes part of the mountains of heaped casuistry, and helps restore the great Anarch's ancient reign.

Now I turn to the opposite extreme, the poems where information is at the minimum, of which there are many: for the withholding of information is a central device of modernism,. Once poetry has shed the functions it shares with prose – narrative, exposition, description – as since Mallarmé and Valéry it has become almost an orthodoxy it should do – it ceases to have a subject in the clear-cut way that Gray's *Elegy* or *The Scholar Gypsy* has a subject. Modernism, seeking to render the fluidity and uncertainty of experience itself, will need to protect its poems against both title and notes.

The first of Ezra Pound's *Cantos* is a version of Andreas Divus' translation of Book 11 of the *Odyssey*; the seventeenth is in some way about the building of Venice; but neither has a title, or is annotated by the author. The first conveys the information, cryptically but not impenetrably, in the text, and could be said to have a delayed and hinted title; the second has not even got that, though there are one or two clues. In so far as the subject of Canto 17 is not the building of Venice but 'the state of mind in the builder immediately before the idea crystallises,' as Donald Davie admirably puts it,[4] we are clearly dealing with a modernist poem. It is still, however, possible to ask whether as we read we are meant to realize that the idea which has not yet crystallized is the idea of Venice. Will any reader discover this unaided? If he does not discover it, should be be told? Here is the bad faith of modernism. Explanation is kept out of the poem, as a matter of principle; that explanation can be conveyed through the edges of the text – notes or title. By having no title and no notes, the poet appears to want to conceal the information; but of course the reader will get hold of it, because his teacher will tell him. Modernism belongs to the age of the academic study of literature, when an acute or well-informed reader, or a reader with inside knowledge, will find out what the poem is about, and pass this on through the commentators: soon the student in the modern poetry class will be expected to know it. The claim that the poem is self-sufficient, that its subject is experience, not a story, not a situation, not Venice – this claim is sustained by the fact that there are others around to whisper to us what the poem disdains to say.

The second function of the borderline material is apology. This is the explicit purpose of a dedication. As he pays compliments to the various noblemen addressed in his dedicatory sonnets, Spenser naturally refers to his poem as 'the unripe fruit of an unready wit', as 'this base poem', as 'rude rhymes, the which a rustick Muse did weave / In savage soil, far from Parnasso mount'[5] (that last, of course, may not just be modesty; it can also be a hint to someone with influence that the chance to come back from Ireland would not be unacceptable). Along with the dedications come the commendations: sonnets not by but to the author, in which it is acceptable to say what a good poem it is, telling the author (and us) that 'some sacred fury hath enriched thy brains', that the dead poets are envious now that he is stealing their glory.[6] And no one minds being publicly modest if others will praise him.

There is true modesty as well as false: genuine conviction that one's writing is inadequate, along with a need to say so. This is likely to surface not in the formal self-deprecation of a dedication, but in something more urgent and direct. Milton wrote fifty-six lines of his poem 'On the Passion', probably when he was twenty-one, and then added:

This subject the author finding to be above the years he had when he wrote it, and nothing satisfied with what was begun, left it unfinished.[7]

A poet as intensely self-conscious and ambitious as Milton may well have come to feel that. The very fact that he published the unsatisfactory lines is, in an odd way, evidence that he was sincere in his note, for his reluctance to waste anything is another aspect of his reluctance to complete what is not doing him justice. And we notice that he published not only the fragment but also the note.

Shelley attached a similar note to his prose fragment 'On Love'. After describing love as (inter alia) 'not only the portrait of our external being but an assemblage of the minutest particles of which our nature is composed', he added in the margin: 'These words are ineffectual and metaphorical. Most words are – no help!!'[8] How like Milton's disclaimer in content, how different in tone! Instead of Milton's dignified, self-centred sentence, a cry of despair. Instead of a clear-cut excuse ('above the years he had'), a generalized awareness that expression has failed, as it always does.

The mind in creation is as a fading coal, which some invisible influence, like an inconstant wind, awakens to transitory brightness.[9]

That is the most famous, but by no means the only, attempt in Shelley's essay *A Defence of Poetry* to describe the difficulty of articulateness in the face of the 'evanescent visitations of thought and feeling', whose footsteps 'are like those of a wind over a sea, which the coming calm erases, and whose traces remain only, as on the wrinkled sand which paves it'. This idea, so central to Romanticism, leads to the cherishng (and publication) of fragments, since the coal fades before a work is completed, and to such agonized marginal notes as that just quoted. Milton, whose insistent concern with his own poetic career provides a kind of anticipation of Romanticism, is the one earlier poet we would expect to share this awareness.

These two apologies are extraneous to the text, but they also find their way inside. The poem 'On the Passion' anticipates its marginal note. It is a highly self-conscious poem, full of reflections on its own composition ('For now to sorrow must I tune my song'; 'to this Horizon is my Phoebus bound'), telling us not only how different the task is from his recent 'Nativity Hymn' (which he did manage to finish) but how the subject itself puts obstacles in his way ('Though grief my feeble hands uplock' – a line of almost mimetic awkwardness). And Shelley's awareness of incapacity also finds its way into his poetry:

– In the world unknown
  Sleeps a voice unspoken. . .
  O follow, follow!
  Through the caverns hollow,
  As the song floats thou pursue.[10]

–   My thoughts arise and fade in solitude,
     The verse that would invest them melts away
     Like moonlight in the heaven of spreading day.
  How beautiful they were, how firm they stood,
  Flecking the sky like woven pearl.[11]

Formal essay, marginal note, achieved poem, fragment: the apology is everywhere, for the pain of inarticulateness is everywhere in Shelley. We are even left uncertain whether it has been (or can be) overcome. Milton was more sure about this: his apology implies a confident claim that the subject of, say, the 'Nativity Hymn' was not above his years. But does that five-line fragment of Shelley's actually 'invest' his thoughts? The lines say no; but they are not the sort of thoughts one would elaborate in reasoned discourse; to express them would be, precisely, to say that they stood 'Flecking the sky like woven pearl'. 'These words are ineffectual and metaphorical': for a poet, those two terms ought not to be synonymous, the realization that most words are meta-phorical could be a cry of triumph rather than of despair. Shelley's evident longing for the literal is a longing to transcend language itself. By all normal criteria, the fragment does invest the thoughts, does what it claims not to do. Just as the mind in creation did catch the fading coal long enough to find that image.

We are on the edge here of a poem's invitation to us to reject it: there will be more of this in the last section. I turn now to my next function, control.

Every author is a Frankenstein, bringing into existence a text that will not obey him, that may run away and wreak havoc of a kind it was never meant to. Understandably, the author may issue instructions on how his text is to behave – that is, on how we are to make it behave as we read. Genette claims that the very existence of a paratext implies a belief in intentionality, a belief that the author 'knows best' what his work means. He knows of course that this naïve view is now questioned, and makes mild fun of its rejection:

Cette opinion, partagée presque sans réserve pendant des siècles, est aujourd'hui, nous la savons, battue en brèche pour des raisons assez diverses, où une certain formalisme ('il n'y a pas de vrai sens d'un texte') et une certaine psychoanalyse ('Il y a un vrai sens, que l'auteur ne peut connaitre') font un paradoxal bon ménage. Ce debat me laisse personnell-ment assez perplexe, sinon indifferent. . .

(This opinion, held almost without reservation for centuries, is today, as we know, assailed for varied reasons, among which a certain formalism ('There is no true meaning of a text') and a certain psychoanalytic theory ('There is a true meaning, which the author cannot know') join together paradoxically. This debate leaves me personally perplexed and even indifferent.)

The view that the author is not in charge of his text receives, according to Genette, a kind of ritual assent nowadays that means little:

la justesse du point de vue auctorial (et, accessoirement, éditorial) est le credo implicite et l'idéologie spontanée du paratexte.[12]

(the correctness of the author's point of view (and as a corollary that of the editor) is the implicit credo and the spontaneous ideology of the paratext.)

It is rash to disagreee with a critic who chooses his words as carefully as Genette; but without dissenting from anything he actually says, I reply that authorial control is not, perhaps, quite so easily reinstated. The issue is complicated by the distinction between discursive and fictional texts. The author was never deposed from the discursive text with the same thoroughness as from literature: certainly the Wimsatt-Beardsley intentional fallacy was intended to deal with imaginative literature, and even the structuralist death of the author seems mainly to concern poets and novelists. Genette recognizes that notes are much commoner in discursive texts, and that when they do occur in fiction it is usually in novels of impure fictionality, overlapping, for instance, with history (Scott is his main example of this, and his discussion would fit well into my first section). His only example of notes intended to control the reader's moral response is taken from Stendhal, as with his famous 'C'est un mécontent (ou "un republicain") qui parle'. Now Stendhal (as Genette himself has brilliantly shown elsewhere) is too tricky a customer to serve as example of control. It is always hard to judge the exact nature of Stendhal's irony, but there does seem, somewhere, an awareness that his notes are reductive of the novel. A more clear-cut case will be that of Samuel Richardson.

Because *Clarissa* is very long and was published in parts while still being written, Richardson knew how his readers were responding, and knew that their response was not what it ought to be. In particular, they were much too fond of Lovelace.

I told you in my first Letter that he had some good Qualities given him in Compliment to the Eye and Ear of Clarissa. But little did I think at the time that those Qualities . . . would have given Women of Virtue and Honour such a liking to him, as I have found to be the case with many. I thought I had made him too wicked, too Intriguing, too revengeful . . . for him to obtain the Favour and good Wishes of any worthy Heart of *either* sex. I tried his Character, as it was first drawn, and his last Exit, on a young Lady of Seventeen. She shewed me by her Tears at the latter that he was not very odious to her. . . . I was surprised; and for fear such a Wretch should induce Pity, I threw into his Character some deeper Shades.[13]

If *Clarissa* is a properly didactic novel, then Lovelace must attract at first and disgust in the end, not because the author has changed his mind, but because the reader has seen through the good qualities and realized that you cannot trust a rake. But the old problem recurs: readers, especially female readers, refuse to turn against Lovelace; as readers, especially male readers, of *Emma* refuse to turn against Mary Crawford. What then does the author do? Richardson's response to the young lady of seventeen suggests all too clearly that he might simply change his mind, and impose depravity on his helpless creation. But Richardson's imagination had a stubborn integrity, and so Lovelace had to be attacked through footnotes. The first of the anti-Lovelace footnotes 'reminds the reader' that Lovelace is insincere in his suggestion that Clarissa could take shelter with Mrs Howe when she runs away, for he had 'artfully taken care, by means of his agent in the Harlowe family . . . not only to influence her family against her, but to deprive her of Mrs Howe's, and of every other protection'. This has the air of a specific accusation, but it will not stand up for a moment. The Harlowes are not helpless puppets, Mrs Howe can hardly be controlled very easily by an 'agent in the Harlowe family', and when we turn up the letter to which the note refers us (the first of Lovelace's letters) it soon becomes clear that the note's summary of its high-spirited, free-ranging plotting is as reductive as that of any preacher. The next footnote, attached to the next letter, in which Clarissa describes the tyranny she is enduring from her family, runs as follows:

These violent measures, and the obstinate perseverance of the whole family in them, will be the less wondered at, when it is considered, that all the time they were but as so many puppets danced upon Mr Lovelace's wires.[14]

By now all pretence of documentation has gone, and the wonderfully meticulous descriptions of what is going on in the Harlowe household have been forgotten. If a student were to treat Lovelace in the cavalier fashion in which the author here treats him, he would be accused of slovenly reading and/or lack of literary sensibility. It is clear that a conflict between Richardson's didactic purpose and the imagination that created Lovelace has here risen to the surface, and that the former has imposed itself in a series of limpet-like annotations to the text. Now here we have to admit that Richardson was unlucky. Because he wrote an epistolary novel (for which we are profoundly grateful, the form suited his genius perfectly) there was no easy way for him to pass the sort of judgements that Thackeray never scrupled to offer about his characters. The pressure that forced the comments into footnotes may have acted to make them more reductive than they would otherwise have been.

The behaviour of a text, as we have seen, is a matter of interaction with the reader; if the text breaks its didactic reins and takes the reader for a gallop, the desperate author can only shout instructions after them.

The best-known statements of the conflict between imagination and didactic purpose are those of D.H. Lawrence, who wrote

It is such a bore that nearly all great novelists have a didactic purpose, otherwise a philosophy, directly opposite to their passional inspiration. In their passional inspiration they are all phallic worshippers. . .

O give me the novel! Let me hear what the novel says. As for the novelist, he is usually a dribbling liar. [15]

This formulation is more valuable as a way into *Clarissa* than into Lawrence's own novels. Lawrence could be as much of a dribbling liar as anyone, and his lies are mostly about phallic worship. Richardson's lies are conventionally moral, and though I cannot see Lovelace (much less Richardson!) as a phallic worshipper (his greatest attraction is his wit, for which the phallus is not noted), the tension here depicted is very like that we have been analysing. It is the tension whose most famous statement comes from Lawrence too: 'Never trust the artist, trust the tale.'

As far as theoretical clarity goes, Richardson's bad luck is our good luck. There are plenty of novelists who degrade their own characters, through didactic anxiety, by explicit moral comment (Hawthorne is a notorious offender) or by a crudely imposed image (as when Mary Crawford, in her last interview with Edmund, is suddenly seen as Satan). In order to rescue tale from teller, we have to impose our own judgement of what is quick and what is dead in a novel. Without this courage, though it means abandoning the neutrality of theory, the critic is prevented from making points that may be essential to treating literature as literature. In the case of Richardson, our task is easier because he has had to step into the paratext: we can watch him interfering with his own book, committing what we can in the fullest sense call a transgression.

Finally, the function I have named indecision, the opposite to control. Not all novelists tell their story in a manner that unleashes 'Les monstres glapissants, hurlants, grognants, rampants, Dans la ménagerie infame de nos vices'[16] – that whole gruesome menagerie of vices out of which so much modern literature makes its flowers of evil; such writers can sometimes be seen desperately patching the edges of their text, trying to reassert control. But there are also novelists who tell their story with carefully controlled subtlety, in a way that may exclude some of the rich uncertainty out of which it grew. I will take *Vanity Fair* as an example. Amelia the submissive heroine, whom most modern readers detest (as did some contemporaries), has married a selfish, blackguardly husband whom, as is her nature, she worships. She does not notice (she does not allow herself to notice?) that he has grown tired of her, as was inevitable, and has made an assignation with Becky (whom Amelia considers her friend; and indeed Becky is her friend, when there is nothing more important at stake). What saves George for Amelia is the irony of war; in one of the most famous chapter endings in fiction,

No more firing was heard at Brussels – the pursuit rolled miles away. Darkness came down on the field and city; and Amelia was praying for George, who was lying on his face, dead, with a bullet through his heart.[17]

Such an astonishing mixture of good and bad luck fills us with awe; but something is missing from the irony. To see what, we can turn up Thackeray's letter to his mother in which he tells her 'of course you are quite right about *Vanity Fair*, and about Amelia being selfish', and having admitted a more explicitly pejorative judgement on her than he ever allows himself in the novel itself, he promises that she will be humiliated 'when her scoundrel of a husband is well dead with a ball in his odious bowels'.[18] This remark is like the tearing of the delicate paper on which the book is printed: suddenly, one of the novel's silences is broken. There is no getting round the fact that this is not, strictly, part of the novel, and indeed it tells us so by the phrase 'well dead', which is in the voice of the author who has in front of him the task (to which he is looking forward) of killing George. But once we have read it, how can we fail to incorporate such a sentence into our experience of *Vanity Fair*? – all the more for the firmness with which it was kept away from us while we were reading.

I take a very different example of indecision from *The Faerie Queene*. To publish an unfinished work is asking for textual trouble: the temptation to make changes in the light of what you subsequently write may prove irresistible, and the earlier version will continue to exist as a hostage you cannot simply kill.

Books 1–3 of *The Faerie Queene* were published in 1590, Books 1–6 in 1596. Book 3 ends with the rescue of Amoret. Britomart, the heroine, disguised as a knight, finds Sir Scudamore lamenting on the ground because his beloved Amoret has been taken prisoner by Busirane, an allegory that is clearly about lust, though whether it means that Scudamore or Amoret (if either) is being reproached is uncertain. Britomart persuades him to join her in trying to enter the House of Busirane; the 'flaming fire ymixt with smouldry smoke' at the entrance turns him back, but she gets through. Inside, she sees allegorical tapestries and a masque of Cupid, then finds Amoret being tortured by the 'vile Enchanter'; she fights Busirane, frees Amoret, and tells her that Scudamore is waiting outside. In the first edition he looks up eagerly (once again he is lying on the ground lamenting) when they return, and they are reunited:

Lightly he clipt her twixt his armes twain,
And streightly did embrace her body bright,
Her body, late the prison of sad pain,
Now the sweet lodge of love and dear delight:
But she fair Lady overcommen quite
Of huge affection, did in pleasure melt,
And in sweet ravishment poured out her sprite,
No word they spake, nor earthly thing they felt,
But like two senseless stocks in long embracement dwelt.[19]

It is difficult to overstate the importance of this stanza for the poem as a whole. All the main characters of *The Faerie Queene* are in love, chastely if good, licentiously if wicked. All these loves look forward to consummation in the twelfth book, when (we assume) all the tangled threads of narrative will be drawn together, but our experience as we read is one of constant postponement. Even when Spenser was alive, readers may well have doubted if there would ever be twelve books. There are virtually no marriages in the poem, just the promise of marriages. But here, at the end of the first unit, is a happy ending. Even its ambiguity seems to fit it for so ambivalent a poem, for it is not clear if this is a description of sexual intercourse (how literally are we to take 'melt', 'ravishment', 'poured out'?). Britomart, the most prominent character of all, who has seen her Artegal only in vision and at one tournament, is moved to something like envy by the embrace, but is reassured, as are we, by the reminder that consummation is waiting as reward for the virtuous.

Our purchaser of the poem in 1596 has, let us assume, already read the first three books. He may begin again at the beginning, or he may (this seems slightly more probable) carry on from Book 4. Before long he will discover that Amoret_ and Scudamore are separated again. In puzzlement, he turns back to the end of Book 3, and finds the only important textual change from the first edition: Scudamore was not there when they emerged from the House of Busirane:

His expectation to despair did turn
Misdeeming sure that her those flames did burn.[20]

Scudamore is a pretty spineless character, and this change will not help him in our eyes; but, more seriously, it will change the poem. Three more books to read, with nothing to bring us near to marriage. (In fact, we shall have an allegorical wedding, of the Thames and the Medway, in Book 4, and the wedding of Florimell and Marinell in Book 5, but neither of these has the centrality of the triumphant original conclusion to Book 3.) The reader, surely, is as betrayed as Amoret: she came out of the castle, and found Scudamore gone; he comes back from his reading, and finds the stanzas gone. True, Spenser is in charge, for he wrote the poem; but he has no control over the reader's memory, and nothing can totally destroy those after all once published stanzas.

The function of the frontier areas of the text – all of those discussed – is to exert pressure on the reader in the act of constituting meaning. Supplying information, exerting (or diminishing) didactic control, apologizing (or boasting): all these are aspects of that pressure. Now I must say once more what has leaked out over and over during the discussion, that instructions on how to read can exist wholly outside the text, or wholly within it. They need not even come from the author, for anyone can give such instructions. 'Now children, this is going to be a really *funny* song.' 'The next poem is perhaps the most beautiful love lyric in the language.' 'To illustrate my point about neo-classic *imitatio*, let me read you a few lines of Pope.' Of course we will only listen to the instructions if we feel that whoever gives them has some authority for doing so, and we would normally feel that no one's authority can equal the author's. Yet all these three speakers clearly possess a kind of authority; a scholar editing a fragmentary and anonymous text may have very great authority, almost amounting to that of an author.

As well as being wholly outside, instructions can be wholly inside the text, to the point when it becomes impossible to excise them. We might for instance say that metanarrative and all forms of self-consciousness about the telling of a story are instructions on how that story should be read, less obviously but just as truly as moral judgements on the characters. The self-consciousness of Tristram Shandy, or of Salman Rushdie's narrative in *Midnight's Children*, is so prominent that to remove it we would have to tear the book in half, and it might not be the worser half that we threw away.

And now, in conclusion, a word on conclusions: on the one fatal marginal comment that can await any book.

Murdering the Text

It is said that when Virgil lay dying he gave instructions that the *Aeneid* should be destroyed. His friend Varius being reluctant to do this, he asked for the manuscript in order to burn it himself, but no one would bring it; and when he then bequeathed it to Varius and another friend under the condition that they publish nothing which he had not published, the Emperor overruled them and insisted that the public interest prevail over the author's reluctance.[1]

How fortunate, we may think, that the eccentricity of a dying man did not deprive us of a masterpiece. Eccentricity? It is striking how often legend, or even documentation, attributes such a destructive wish to old or dying writers: such tales are told of St Augustine and Bede, Ruskin and Ibsen, Tolstoy and Kafka. Authors, it appears, are often reluctant to let their offspring outlive them.

Legends, dying words, letters: these can at least be kept separate from the works they mention; we can weigh the authority they possess against the value of the book we are asked to destroy. But what happens when the instruction to destory the work is incorporated into the work itself? When Serenus Zeitblom, the narrator of Thomas Mann's novel *Dr Faustus*, receives Adrian's crucially improtant letter from Leipzig, describing the visit to the brothel that lies at the base of his syphilis and his genius, he disobeys the instruction to destroy it for two reasons.

I did not obey it, in the first instance because I felt the need to read again and again a piece of writing at first run through so quickly; to study it, not so much read as study, stylistically and psychologically. Then, with the passage of time, the moment to destroy it had passed too; I learned to regard it as a document of which the order to destroy was a part, so that by its documentary nature it cancelled itself out.[2]

The first reason might simply be a reason for not destroying it immediately; the second is a version of the famous logical paradox of the blackboard that contains the sentence 'Every statement on this blackboard is false' – which also cancels itself out. What I want to show is that Zeitblom was not just being disingenuous: his reasoning shows a profound understanding of the instruction, Burn this.

Such an instruction, incorporated into the text, was familiar in the Middle Ages: they called it a retractation, or palinode. One of the most famous examples is the treatise on courtly love of Andreas Capellanus, the *De Arte Honesti Amandi* (translatable as 'The Art of Courtly Love', or 'How a Gentleman should Love'). After two books on the rules and procedures appropriate to love, it contains a short third book, called *De Reprobatione Amoris* (on the condemnation of love), which is a systematic attack on all that the first two books assume, offering a long list of reasons why love should be renounced by the wise man: God has condemned extra-marital sex, love leads us to harm our neighbours, whom we are commanded to love, love destroys friendship, love pollutes both body and soul – the list goes on and on, culminating in a scathing denunciation of woman quite incompatible with the idealization of her implied (and even explicit) in the account of love's procedures.[3] Medieval scholars have offered various solutions to this puzzle: that the first two books are ironic, or that the last book is an afterthought and shows a change of heart (there is no textual evidence for either of these suggestions), or that the two viewpoints represent lay and clerical, humanist and Christian views of love (no doubt true, but this just restates the problem).

The most famous medieval retractations are those of Chaucer, who appends one both to *The Canterbury Tales* and to *Troilus and Criseyde*. *The Canterbury Tales* ends with the 'Parson's Tale' and this is followed by a postscript entitled 'Heere taketh the makere of this book his leve', which begins:

Now preye I to hem alle that herkne this litel tretys or rede, that if ther be any thyng in it that liketh hem, that therof they thanken oure Lord Jhesu Crist, of whom procedeth al wit and al goodenesse. And if ther be any

thyng that displese hem, I preye hem also that they arrette it to the defaute
of myn unkonnynge.[4]

The 'litel tretys' must be the 'Parson's Tale', not *The Canterbury
Tales* as a whole; and since that is not a tale but a sermon ('what is
Penitence, and whennes it is cleped Penitence, and in how manye
maneres been the acciouns of werkynges of Penitence'), it seems
appropriate that if any part of it is successful it should be ascribed to
our Lord Jesus Christ. But as the text proceeds, its completely
conventional prayer 'that Crist have mercy on me and foryeve me
my giltes' leads into a list of what those 'giltes' are: 'and namely of
my translacions and enditynges of worldly vanitees, the whiche I
revoke in my retracciouns'. Then comes a list of Chaucer's works,
including 'the tales of Caunterbury, thilke that sownen into synne'
that concludes with 'and many another book, if they were in my
rememberance'. He then thanks the Lord and his blissful mother for
his virtuous writings ('the translacion of Boece de Concolacione')
and ends with a prayer that 'I may be oon of hem at the day of
doom that shulle be saved'.

The retractation of *Troilus and Criseyde* is not separated off as a
postscript in this way: it makes up the last twelve stanzas of the
poem. It contains a farewell to the poem ('Go, litel bok'), a modest
reference to the superiority of the ancient poets, a prayer that his
text should not be corrupted, and then tells us that after Troilus was
slain his spirit looked down on earth in contempt at human
vanities, and laughed at the woe 'of hem that wepten for his death
so fast' – that is, laughed at the reader for being moved by the
poem! Such was the end of Troilus and his love; then comes an
appeal to the 'yonge fresshe folkes, he or she' to despise the passing
joys of the world and love him who died on the cross. After a
stanza pointing out that the poem is full of 'payens corsed olde
rites', the text appeals to 'moral Gower' and 'philosophical Strode'
to correct whatever needs to be corrected, and concludes with a
prayer for eternal life.[5]

Chaucer ends his two masterpieces with a statement that the
poems are wicked and that he needs forgiveness for writing them.
For a long time, scholars asked whether these passages were
genuine, and, if genuine, whether they were sincere. The
authenticity not only of 'Heere taketh the makere of this book his
leve' but of the 'Parson's Tale' itself has been questioned, but it is
found in all the manuscripts; and no one has seriously doubted that
the ending of *Troilus* is by Chaucer. Did he mean what he said? The

question is unanswerable unless we have access to some criterion of sincerity, which means we must have principles for reading and understanding a palinode.

My next example comes two hundred years later. Spenser's *Four Hymns* were published with a dedication to the Countesses of Cumberland and Warwick, which runs in part as follows:

Having in the greener times of my youth, composed these former two Hymns in the praise of Love and beauty, and finding that the same too much pleased those of like age and disposition, which being too vehemently carried with that kind of affection, do rather suck out poison to their strong passion, than honey to their honest delight, I was moved by the one of you two most excellent Ladies, to call in the same. But being unable so to do, by reason that many copies thereof were formerly scattered abroad, I resolved at least to amend and by way of retractation to reform them, making in stead of those two Hymns of earthly or natural love and beautie, two others of heavenly and celestial. . .[6]

At first glance, this seems straighforward enough. He cannot suppress the two earlier poems, so to undo the 'poison' which they give to 'strong passion' he has written two antidotes. Let us give Spenser the benefit of the doubt on the 'reason that many copies were scattered abroad' (we've heard that one often enough from authors); let us grant that he couldn't call them in; we have still to notice that he is not publishing two hymns but four, that whatever refutation of the earlier poems is offered seems to need their continued existence.

As indeed it does. The first two hymns, in honour of beauty and in honour of love, are Neoplatonic, and the relation between the two pairs of poems therefore involves the relation between Platonism and Christianity in the sixteenth century: a complex and tricky question, of which we can say that it is neither a matter of complete assimilation nor one of simple opposition. Christianity could be syncretic, incorporating Pagan wisdom as a foreshadowing or partial revelation of true religion, or it could be puritan, rejecting all other religions as devil worship – and Spenser was a deeply syncretic poet, with strong Puritan leanings. So when we read:

For Love is a celestial harmony
Of likely hearts composed of stars' consent,
Which joyn together in sweet sympathy,

To work each others joy and true content,
Which they have harbour'd since their first descent
Out of their heavenly bowers, where they did see
And know each other here belov'd to be.[7]

– we can be genuinely uncertain whether the terms are Christian or not. In fact this comes from the 'Hymne in Honour of Beauty' (the difference between Love and Beauty is as fluid as that between Platonism and Christianity), and we must therefore conclude that 'heavenly bowers' is being used loosely (and that 'descent' is perhaps being used precisely, referring to a Platonic doctrine of pre-existence). In the third hymn, of Heavenly Love, we read:

With all thy heart, with all thy soul and mind,
Thou must him love, and his behests embrace;
All other loves, with which the world doth blind
Weak fancies, and stir up affections base,
Thou must renounce and utterly displace,
And give thyself unto him full and free
That full and freely gave himself to thee.[8]

Knowing the context, we have no difficulty in finding this more explicitly Christian, especially if we look back six stanzas to see that 'him' refers to 'that dearest Lord of thine'; the 'other loves' we are asked to renounce will then be not just earthly but all non-Christian loves, and will include the love celebrated in the previous, Platonic hymn. We can tell this if we have the context, but by themselves the two stanzas are very similar: the Platonic speaks of 'celestial harmony', and the inferior love that the Christian stanza refers to could, after all, be the lower Venus of the *Symposium*.

With so intimate a relation between the two kinds of love, we can see why the relation between the poems cannot be one of simple rejection. The two later hymns are as much an invitation to reread the earlier ones with a different understanding, as they are attempts to replace them. It is hard to believe that they really offer 'poison', or that anyone could take them to celebrate mere lust, but one can see that it is part of the project of the Christian poems, and thus of the whole sequence, to offer that as a possible reading.

When Robert Herrick published *Hesperides*, a collection of epigrams, love poems and other secular lyrics, it was bound up with a much slimmer sequel, *Noble Numbers*, of which the second poem runs as follows:

His Prayer for Absolution

For Those my unbaptized Rhimes,
Writ in my wild unhallowed Times:
For every sentence, clause and word
That's not inlaid with Thee, (my Lord)
Forgive me God, and blot each Line
Out of my Book, that is not Thine.
But if, mongst all, Thou findst here one
Worthy thy Benediction;
That One of all the rest, shall be
The Glory of my Work, and Me.[9]

If we ask of this poem the naïve question – does he really mean it? – then the answer has to be, yes and no. Taken as a real prayer, this should have led Herrick to destroy most of the *Hesperides*, which includes plenty of poems that could not possibly be thought of as 'inlaid' with God. There was no practical obstacle to destroying them, since they had not previously been published. We must, clearly, take this poem as an invitation to read *Hesperides* in a particular way – a very different way from the invitation they themselves issue. God is being asked to cast his editorial eye over them, and pick out the ones inlaid with him. If we extend the invitation to ourselves, then what we're being given is an interpretation of the previous volume.

The same can be said about the retractation at the end of *Troilus and Criseyde*. Its two most important and eloquent stanzas both use the same comparatively simple rhetorical device, the repetition of the same two words at the beginning of five of the seven lines:

Swich fyn hath, lo, this Troilus for love!
Swich fyn hath al his grete worthynesse!
Swich fyn hath his estat real above,
Swich fyn his lust, swich fyn hath his noblesse!
Swich fyn hath false worldes brotelnesse!
And thus began his lovyng of Criseyde,
As I have told, and in this wise he deyde.[10]

This is ineluctantly ambivalent. To the worldly reader, who wept for Troilus' death as did the Trojans, such an end to his great worthiness is tragic, an example of the 'brotelnesse' of the false world. To the devout reader, Troilus himself is an example of such brutalness, because of his carnal appetite, and 'grete worthynesse' must be ironic. Both readers need to be reminded of the essential elements in the story by means of a device that permits either way of reading it. To call this 'ambivalent' is to use the vocabulary of New Criticism, to call it 'disjunctive' would use that of post-structuralism; as we shall see, there is something to be said for the more drastic term in this case. The invitation to read the work in a particular way is played against the knowledge that we have already read it another way.

The parallel stanza to this one attacks the pagan setting, which Chaucer had made far more prominent than it was in Boccaccio:

Lo here, of payens corsed olde rites,
Lo here, what alle hire goddes may availle;
Lo here, thise wrecched worldes appetites;
Lo here, the fyn and guerdoun for traveille
Of Jove, Appollo, of Mars, of swich rascaille!
Lo here, the forme of olde clerkis speche
In poetrie, if ye hire bokes seche.[11]

This seems cruder than the previous stanza, announcing unequivoc-ally that the paganism is cursed, though the second line can, surely, be read as tragic – and the first could be read ironically by a reader who loved 'payens olde rites', as Chaucer had seemed to. There seems some gusto, too, in calling the pagan gods 'swich rascaille'. Both these stanzas repeat a phrase ('swich fyn', 'Lo here') that is used ostensively, and so permits alternative interpretations. Of course Chaucer 'really means' us to impose a puritanical Christian reading on the tragic one; but at the same time he cannot really mean it as a pragmatic instruction, since we need the earlier reading we are being invited to destroy. Retractation means reinter-pretation.

So far we have looked at cases where the retractation is clearly separate from the rest of the text; but things are not so simple in the case of this poem by George Herbert:

Jordan II

When first my lines of heav'nly joy made mention
Such was their lustre, they did so excel,
That I sought out quaint words, and trim invention;
My thoughts began to burnish, sprout and swell,

Curling with metaphors a plain intention,
Decking the sense, as if it were to sell.

Thousands of notions in my brain did run,
Off'ring their service, if I were not sped:
I often blotted what I had begun;
This was not quick enough, and that was dead.
Nothing could seem too rich to clothe the sun,
Much less those joys which trample on his head.

As flames do work and wind, when they ascend,
So did I weave myself into the sense.
But while I bustled, I might hear a friend
Whisper, How wide is all this long pretence!
There is in love a sweetness ready penned;
Copy out only that, and save expense.[12]

This is a self-confuting poem, just like the statement on the
blackboard. For in the first place we cannot establish a list of poems
that are here being retracted, and replaced by plainness: Herbert's
poems do not divide into two groups in that way. It is not, though
it appears to claim that it is, a liminal poem, i.e. one announcing a
new series. It does not stand at the entrance to *The Temple*, nor at
the conclusion, nor does it mark any crucial break. And that point
should have been clear from the poem itself, for it enacts what it
rejects. This enables us to ask whether this poem itself is a
'pretence', whether it seeks out quaint words and trim inventions,
whether it curls with metaphor its plain intention. Of course it
does, and the fact that it does so is not a sign of weakness but of
strength. What makes it a poem rather than a mere statement about
poetry is precisely the fact that it enacts the process of recantation,
which means it must offer us the material of which we are meant to
perceive the 'pretence'.

Is the same true of the following?

The Coronet

When for the thorns with which I long, too long,
    With many a piercing wound,
    My Saviour's head have crown'd,
I seek with Garlands to redress that Wrong
    Through every Garden, every Mead,

I gather flow'rs (my fruits are only flow'rs)
  Dismantling all the fragrant Towers
That once adorn'd my Shepherdesses head.
And now when I have summ'd up all my store,
  Thinking (so I myself deceive)
  So rich a Chaplet thence to weave
As never yet the king of Glory wore:
  Alas I find the Serpent old
  That, twining in his speckled breast,
  About the flow'rs diguised does fold,
  With wreaths of Fame and Interest.
Ah, foolish Man, that wouldst debase with them,
And mortal Glory, Heav'ns Diadem.
But thou who only couldst the Serpent tame,
Either his slipp'ry knot at once untie,
And disentangle all his winding Snare:
Or shatter too with him my curious frame
And let those wither, so that he may die,
Though set with Skill and chosen out with Care.
That they, while Thou on both their Spoils dost tread,
May crown thy Feet, that could not crown thy Head.[13]

The corresponding question on this poem is whether it has the serpent wound about its flowers. It announces a shift from the secular poetry that Marvell had so far written to religious poetry, and then announces that the shift retains the taint of being the work of fallen man. The new poem too will be the work of a sinner, and must be destroyed. Now is 'The Coronet' itself that new poem? If so, why is it here in front of us, and not destroyed? If not, why will it be any different from the one he ought to destroy (?has destroyed)? It is therefore not possible, in this case either, to regard the poem as liminal: we cannot be satisfied that there really is a new series which it introduces.

The most profoundly ambiguous word in the poem is perhaps 'dismantling'. Has he dismantled his earlier poetry? If poems were physical objects, then he could quite literally make the new ones out of the flowers that were used for the old. For the writer, this can seem a true account: as he puts the earlier materials to new use, he will feel that he is eliminating them from his *œuvre*. But for the reader, the old poems are still available. Even if the writer used scissors and paste to write his new poem, he would not be cutting up the old poem, simply a copy of it.

Here is a third and final example of a seventeenth-century poet writing a poem to mark the transition explicitly

Of the Last Verses in the Book

When we for Age could neither read nor write
The subject made us able to indite.
The Soul with nobler Resolutions deckt,
The Body stooping, does Herself erect:
No Mortal parts are requisite to raise
Her, that Unbody'd can her Maker praise.

The Seas are quiet, when the Winds give o'er
So calm are we, when Passions are no more:
For then we know how vain it was to boast
Of fleeting Things, so certain to be lost.
Clouds of Affection from our Younger Eyes
Conceal that emptiness, which Age descries.

The Soul's dark cottage, batter'd and decay'd,
Lets in new Light, thro' chinks that time has made.
Stronger by weakness, wiser Men become,
As they draw near to their Eternal home:
Leaving the old, both Worlds at once they view,
That stand upon the threshold of the New.[14]

If there ever was a liminal poem, surely this must be it, since it explicitly announces that in old age the poet is shifting his subject from secular to religious. Once again, external evidence speaks against this interpretation, for the meaning of the title is that this is the last poem Waller wrote, and his son annotated it to that effect. If the subject has made him able to indite, it is not a form of writing that can be recorded on earthly paper. Not only are there no subsequent religious poems introduced by this one: we must add that this poem is being offered us as not really 'by' its author.

What are the fleeting things of the second stanza? If they are the things of this world (which they are) then the statement is no different from what could be found in any sermon. If they are the qualities of poetry (which they also are) then the poem is telling us that the author's previous poems were about things of no importance; this one is about something of great importance, but cannot deal with it. The most brilliant image, that which opens the last stanza, converts decrepitude from a weakness to a strength. In announcing a new beginning, it announces too that, qua poet, he cannot begin. Logically, there are only two courses open to the poet who has made this discovery. The first is to fall back on the praise of God that does not depend on mortal poets, that is, on the text of Holy Scripture: to paraphrase it, as closely as possible to the original – in the end, perhaps, to copy it out as it is. The other course is silence. The moment of falling silent produces the truest eloquence, for he has made the discovery that about God there is nothing to say. The most profound recognition of the nature of God becomes indistinguishable from atheism.

This was the poem that drew from Johnson his celebrated rejection of the possibility of religious poetry:

Contemplative piety, or the intercourse between God and the human soul, cannot be poetical. Man, admitted to implore the mercy of his creator, and plead the merits of his redeemer, is already in a higher state than poetry can confer.[15]

In one sense, Waller's splendid poem, simply by its existence, disproves Johnson's dictum, as do those of Herbert and Marvell; yet it also confirms it. For Waller, by asserting that poetic talent must be abandoned when religion is treated, has given us a poem that can only be written once: the discovery having been made and stated, will it not, in future, have to be obeyed? This is a liminal poem only in the sense that it introduces what it subverts, as it subverts itself. When a transition like that from secular to religious is involved, that is the only kind of threshold there is.

The parallel with deconstruction is so close that it now needs to be made explicit. To deconstruct a position is to reject it, but only in a way that depends totally on the formulation which is being undermined. Derrida writes: 'We have no language – no syntax and no lexicon – which is foreign to this history: we can pronounce not a single destructive proposition which has not already had to slip into the form, the logic and the implicit postulations of precisely what it seeks to contest. . . The *paradox* is that metaphysical reduction of the sign needed the opposition it was reducing. . .'[16] Poets are very familiar with this paradox:

Be shelled, eyes, with double dark
And find the uncreated light:

This ruck and reel which you remark
Coils, keeps and teases simple sight.

Palate, the hutch of tasty lust,
Desire not to be rinsed with wine;
The can must be so sweet, the crust
So fresh that come in fasts divine![17]

Derrida is writing of his assault on metaphysics, Hopkins of the habit of Christian renunciation: yet how perfectly the first passage describes the second. This renunciation of sensuous pleasures needs the 'postulations of precisely what it seeks to contest'; the only way it can assert that religious experience is finer than that of the senses is to present it as a kind of sight, a kind of taste, at the same time as saying that it enables us to do without sight, hearing, taste. It is the same paradox as Derrida's, and requires us to say that the nature of Hopkins's rejection of earthly pleasures is of a special kind, that cannot be stated except by using what it denies. 'Transgression', says Derrida, 'implies that the limit is always at work.'

From this Derridian paradox is derived the idea of using terms *sous rature*, which was explained in Chapter 2. Perhaps the perfect example of an expression that has to be used, and has to be used under erasure, is 'Burn this book!'

It is no accident that all the examples so far have been from religious poems. Having invoked the aid of Derrida for his concept of the deconstructive process totally dependent on what it assails, I now need a very different view of religion from his. He is inclined to see theology as the ultimate backing behind assertions of the rationality and knowability of the world, behind what he called the metaphysics of logocentric presence, the authority of God being the ultimate sanction behind our belief (which he wishes to subvert) in the authority of reason independent of text. In contrast to this, I suggest, it is possible to see religion as our profoundest way of dealing with the metaphysics of absence, as subversive of rational certainty and confidence, as 'a new and shocking revaluation of all we have been'. But simply because of the nature of the subversion it practices, it is dependent on the discourse which it subverts.

I would like to ask, finally, whether the palinode is necessarily linked to the religious. Are there any other shifts in discourse that involve the same subversion of a previous system? I suggest there may be one: the shift from the personal to the political.

Translations

You show me the poems of some woman
my age, or younger
translated from your language

Certain words occur: *enemy, oven, sorrow*
enough to let me know
she's a woman of my time

obsessed

with Love, our subject:
we've trained it like ivy to our walls
baked it like lead on our ankles
watched it through binoculars as if
it were a helicopter
bringing food to our famine
or the satellite
of a hostile power
I begin to see that woman
doing things: stirring rice
ironing a skirt
typing a manuscript till dawn

trying to make a call
from a phonebooth

The phone rings unanswered
in a man's bedroom
she hears him telling someone else
Never mind. She'll get tired –
hears him telling her story to her sister

who becomes her enemy
and will in her own time
light her own way to sorrow

ignorant of the fact that this way of grief
is shared, unnecessary
and political[18]

For all its modern dress Adrienne Rich's poem is, for the most part, very traditional. Love has always been seen as woman's subject, even though the love poems have been written by men: 'Man's love is of man's life a thing apart, / Tis woman's whole existence', said Byron. And as often as not, this has been seen as the cause of woman's suffering as much as her happiness. That man who won't pick up the telephone belongs to woman's folklore. Suppose the poem ended:

One after another,
Trudging, bleeding,
To solitude or pain.

Uninspired, no doubt, but familiar. But the actual ending refuses this elegiac note: what was central to the presentation of female suffering is suddenly rejected. Once we have read the ending, we can of course spot subtle anticipations of that refusal scattered through the poem, but I doubt if anyone would so interpret them without the shock of the last lines. These lines are a palinode: they insist on shifting us from the elegiac, the acceptance of suffering as inevitable by the very act of expressing compassion, to the political, telling us – as Brecht so often tries to tell us in the endings of his plays – that it is not inevitable to see suffering in terms of tragic inevitability.

For a sustained example from drama, however, I will turn instead to Ibsen. *A Doll's House* is a picture of nineteenth-century bourgeois marriage: the husband regards his wife as part of his possessions, the wife accepts her playful helplessness, and within this expected relationship they are fond of each other. The fact that Nora has in the past shown herself resourceful and even needed is buried from awareness, and even described as crime; the fact that Torvald's concern for her disappears when his own interests are threatened is only brought to the surface in the last act, and provides the climax of the action. Watching this play, what sort of ending did the original audience expect? We know that what really shocked people was the ending: when Nora closed the door, the sound echoed through the theatres of Europe, and critics amused themselves by devising alternative endings for the play (as well as the serious alternative that respectability imposed on some early productions).[19] If there were any conservative philistines – any Torvalds – in the audience, they no doubt expected that Nora would realise she was making too much fuss, and would allow motherhood to prevail over political awakening: this was in fact the alternative ending, and it was also written ironically by Israel Zangwill and Eleanor Marx.[20] Sensitive members of the audience expected Torvald to admit the error of his ways by means of a process of self-discovery: if the ending was to be happy, this would lead to reconciliation and a truer marriage, if tragic, Nora would drown herself (as she is tempted to do in the existing text) and Torvald would have his Aristotelian recognition too late (Walter Besant's alternative ending is a variant of this).[21] But Ibsen did none of these. Instead, Nora comes on to the stage dressed to go away, shocking us as much as she shocks her husband: the play is almost over, and she is now *beginning* something. Our attention is shifted from Torvald's tragedy to her situation, and it is seen as a socially conditioned situation, not as individual crisis: she needs a new kind of marriage, and is going out to find it. Shaw declared that the technical innovation in an Ibsen play was the discussion: the audience is meant to go out of the theatre arguing rather than moved and resigned – just as Brecht meant his audiences to go out of the theatre. Shaw found this element in all Ibsen's plays, as if they were really plays by Shaw, but on *A Doll's House* he was not mistaken.[22] The audience's conventional expectations have been cheated: Nora walks out of the play. The point is made by a shattering of dramatic form, as if we were being told that our dramatic expectations were posited on the belief that this is a personal tragedy, and the shift to the political cannot be contained within the expected form.

Both the shift from the secular to the religious, and that from the personal to the political, can be described in terms of the Hegelian dialectic: the former way of seeing things both is and is not abolished, it is 'aufgehoben' or suspended in the new. To some, this will be proof that there is, ultimately, no such things as the secular, or the personal; to some, it will be a mistaken rejection of the level of experience that really counts. To many of us, both these positions are oversimplifications. The palinode is needed when one level of experience is being replaced by another that cannot abolish it, that cannot even exist without it.

Finally, I return briefly to the question of the logical status of the palinode. I have already compared it to the blackboard dilemma, which is self-refuting. A closer parallel would be with the censor's dilemma. How can you defend rationally the banning of a book? If the book is as corrupting as you say, then no one for whose welfare you are concerned ought to read it; but no one who doesn't read it can judge whether you were right to ban it. This is also the syllabus-maker's dilemma. A syllabus is of necessity a pedagogic act, a selection of what is considered most valuable for the student to read. Since the number of available books (on any subject) is enormously greater than any student can read, syllabuses are essential (the alternative would be to leave things to chance), and books will be omitted because inferior. But education is not a matter of rote learning: the concept of what is worth studying is not one which the good student will take on trust, he will understand, criticize and (eventually) apply it for himself. The question of what should and shouldn't go into the syllabus is one to which he too must address himself. Therefore he ought not to accept the syllabus as finished product, but interrogate it, which requires him to read books which are not on it. It is no use claiming that a good syllabus will have a few works deliberately placed on the edge in order to give the student that experience: the really good student will want to interrogate the edge of that edge. The syllabus itself has to be treated under erasure: we need to understand this, and understand that this does not abolish the need to have a syllabus. Every syllabus ought to be followed by a palinode.

Here the Maker of this Book Takes his Leave

Now I pray to all them that have read this little treatise, that if there be anything in it that pleases them, and helps them in their reading and understanding, that they give thanks and tell their friends; and if there be anything that disgusts them and seems of evil effect, that they forgive the author and bear no ill-will. And most of all I pray to all readers that, having paced the frontiers of the fairest and most delightful territory known to language, that they fling my book away and spend a while with Dr John Donne, Dean of S Paul's, with John Berryman and his friend Henry, with Morgenstern, Marvell and Mark Rutherford and all besides whose acquaintance they desire to pursue: flinging away along with this all similar books, and this very note besides in which I exhort them and myself to repentance.

Notes

Introduction

1 Paul Valéry, 'Questions de poésie', *Variété* III (1936), p. 43.
2 Jacques Derrida, 'Force and Signification' in *Writing and Difference* (1967; trans. 1978).
3 See Terry Eagleton, *Literary Theory* (1983, 'Introduction: What is Literature?'; and the articles on 'What is Literature?' in *New Literary History*, vol. V, no. 1 (Autumn 1973), by Tzvetan Todorov, Christopher Butler and Alvin B. Kernan, and that on 'The Limits of Literature' by Henry Markiewicz in vol. IV, no. 1 (Autumn 1972).
4 Valéry, 'Je disais quelquefois à Stéphane Mallarmé', *Variété* III (1936), p. 9.
5 See (e.g.) F.R. Leavis, Introduction to *Determinations: Critical Essays* (1934); and Eagleton, *Literary Theory*.
6 E.D. Hirsch, *Validity in Interpretation* (1967).
7 Richard Rorty, 'The Historiography of Philosophy' in *Philosophy and History: Essays in the History of Philosophy*, ed. Rorty, Schneewind and Skinner (1984).

Chapter 1   History

Fiction and Autobiography

1 See Jacques Derrida, 'Semiology and Grammatology', in *Positions* (trans. 1981); Jonathan Culler, *On Deconstruction* (1982), esp. 2:5.
2 This view is now widespread in literary criticism, especially in narratology: as we can see from Paul Ricoeur who, though not himself in sympathy with it, sees literary criticism as able to ignore the difference between fiction and history 'inasmuch as it does not take into account division of narrative discourse into two large

classes', *Time and Narrative* (trans. 1984), vol. I, part i, ch. 3, p. 64.

3   Daniel Defoe, Preface to *Roxana* (1724).
4   See L.J. Davis, *Factual Fictions: the Origins of the English Novel* (1983).
5   John Forster, *The Life of Charles Dickens* (1872), Book I, ch. 2.
6   Charles Dickens, *David Copperfield* (1849–50), ch. 11.
7   Ibid., ch. 12.
8   Rudyard Kipling, *Something of Myself* (1937), ch. 1.
9   See Charles Carrington, *Rudyard Kipling* (1955), ch. 2; Roger Lancelyn Greene, *Kipling and the Children* (1965), esp. ch. 2; Mrs A.M. Fleming, 'Some Childhood Memories of Rudyard Kipling by his Sister', *Chambers Journal*, March 1939. The first chapter of *The Light that Failed* (1890) is also claimed by Carrington as a version of the childhood at Southsea, but its relation to the autobiographical material is slight.
10 'Baa Baa Black Sheep' in Rudyard Kipling, *Wee Willie Winkie and Other Stories* (1890).
11 Kipling, *Something of Myself*, ch. 1.
12 Kipling, *'Baa Baa Black Sheep'*.
13 George Eliot, *The Mill on the Floss* (1860), Book I, ch. 5; and see also her sonnet sequence, 'Brother and Sister' (1869).
14 C.S. Lewis, *Surprised by Joy* (1955).
15 Laurie Lee, *Cider with Rosie* (1959), ch. 1; Dylan Thomas, 'The Peaches', in *Portrait of the Artist as a Young Dog* (1940).
16 Dylan Thomas, 'The Fight', ibid.
17 Dan Jones, *My Friend Dylan Thomas* (1977), ch. 3.
18 For anyone discussing recent literary theory there is at least one problem of terminology tricky enough to require a note. Criticism that derives from the work of Saussure, Levi-Strauss, Foucault, Althusser, Barthes, the Russian formalists and Derrida can, in the broadest sense, be regarded as a school, and so requires a name (using such a name need not, of course, deny the obvious differences). The two possible labels are 'structuralist' and 'post-structuralist', and the question whether these terms are more like synonyms or antonyms is a hot controversy, with distinguished names on each side. Is post-structuralism a rejection of structuralism, abandoning its faith in system in order to open us to speculation, experiment and scepticism? Or is it a building on structuralist insights, developing the open-ended questioning that structuralism necessarily enables? I suspect the term owes much of its popularity to this ambiguity. On the argument that when used in a general sense terms should be widened rather than narrowed, I have chosen to use 'structuralism' as the all-embracing term; the reader can if he prefers usually read this as 'structuralism/post-structuralism'.

The Famous Mr Joseph Addison

1 Peter Smithers, *The Life of Joseph Addison* (1954).
2 William Makepeace Thackeray, *Henry Esmond* (1852), Book II, ch. 11.
3 Joseph Addison, *The Campaign* (1705), lines 287–292.
4 Addison, 'Note on Ovid's *Metamorphoses* (Book II Fable ii)', in *Miscellaneous Works*, ed. Guthkelch (1914), vol. I, p. 143.
6 Thackeray, *Henry Esmond*, Book II, ch. 5.
7 Samuel Richardson, *Clarissa* (1747–8) *passim*: e.g. Everyman edition, vol. II, letter 41. And see Esmond's own reference to his man, 'honest John Lockwood', Thackeray, *Henry Esmond*, Book III, ch. 9.
8 Thackeray, *Henry Esmond*, Book III, ch. 9.
9 Ibid., Book II, ch. 9.
10 Lewis Carroll, *Through the Looking Glass* (1872), ch. 4.
11 Thackeray, *Henry Esmond*, Book III, ch. 3.
12 R.G. Collingwood, *The Idea of History* (1946), part V, section 1, p. 213.
13 Horace Walpole, Letter to George Montagu, 16 May 1759, in *Correspondence*, vol. 9, p. 236.
14 Edward Young, *Conjectures on Original Composition* (1759).
15 Lord Macaulay, 'The Life and Writings of Addison', *Edinburgh Review*, July 1843; reprinted in Macaulay's *Miscellaneous Essays*.
16 Joseph Spence, *Anecdotes*, ed. James M. Osborn (1966), no., 157.
17 *Dictionary of National Biography* (1909), s.v. Mohun, Charles. The article is by Thomas Seccombe.
18 Thackeray, *The English Humourists of the Eighteenth Century*: Steele (1853).
19 Alexander Pope on 13 December 1730, in Spence, *Anecdotes*, no. 148.
20 Pope, *Epistle to Arbuthnot (Prologue to the Satires)* (1734), lines 193–214.
21 Pope, *Epilogue to the Satires*, Dialogue II (1738), lines 12–13.
22 See Pope, *Minor Poems*, ed. Norman Ault (Twickenham edition, 1954, Vol. 6, p. 143).

The Condition of England

1 Dr John Simon, *City Medical Reports*, nos 1 and 2 (1849, 1850), in *Human Documents of the Victorian Age*, ed. Royston Pike (1967), 6 (3). Elizabeth Gaskell, *Mary Barton* (1848), ch. 6.
2 Charles Dickens, *Dombey and Son* (1848), ch. 47; John Simon, ibid.
3 For instance, 'The criterion of literary specificity does not depend on the greater or lesser discursiveness of the mode but on the degree of

consistent "rhetoricity" of the language', Paul de Man, *Blindness and Insight* (1971), p. 137.

4 Friedrich Engels, *The Condition of the Working Classes in England in 1844*, tr. F.K. Wischnewetzky (1885; repr. 1952), pp. 45, 49, 57.

5 Dickens, *The Old Curiosity Shop* (1841), ch. 45.

6 Dickens, *Hard Times* (1854), ch. 5.

7 John Ruskin, Letter to Charles Eliot Norton, 19 June 1870, in *Works*, vol. 37 (1909), p. 7.

8 See *Bleak House* (1852–3), esp. chs 28, 63; *Little Dorritt* (1855–7), esp. chs 10, 23.

9 Dickens, 'Chatham Dockyard', *The Uncommercial Traveller* (1861) no. 26.

10 Charles Kingsley, *Alton Locke* (1850), ch. 1.

11 Engels, *The Condition of the Working Classes*, 'Results', p. 115.

12 Ibid., 'The Great Towns', pp. 23–4.

13 Ibid., p. 118.

14 Dickens, *Hard Times*, Book II, ch. 2; *Bleak House*, ch. 63 (and see chs 7, 18).

15 Karl Marx, 'Contribution to the Critique of Hegel's Philosophy of Right', Introduction (1844). Taken from Karl Marx and Friedrich Engels, *On Religion*, (Moscow, 1955), p. 42.

16 Charles Kingsley, 'Letters to Chartists', II, in *Politics for the People*, no. 4, 17 May 1848.

17 I hope I may be allowed a self-reference here. In an essay on 'The Bourgeois Imagination' in *The Literary Imagination* (1982), I quoted this extract from *Alton Locke*, but without realizing that Kingsley had made a remark very similar to Marx's. In incorporating that short discussion here, I am able to put right the omission.

18 Steven Marcus, *Engels, Manchester and the Working Class* (1974). I have for convenience used the first, briefer version of Marcus's discussion, an article called 'Reading the Illegible' in *The Victorian City*, ed. Dyos & Wolff (1973). Though the expanded version adds much that is fascinating, the original article presents the points relevant to my discussion in admirably terse form.

19 Marcus, 'Reading the Illegible', p. 265.

20 Thomas Carlyle, *The French Revolution* (1837), Book 5, ch. 6.

21 Francis Barker, 'The Tremulous Private Body', in *1642: Literature and Power in the Seventeenth Century* (Univ. of Essex, 1981), p. 9.

22 Malcolm Bradbury, *The History Man* (1976).

23 Terence Hawkes, *Structuralism and Semiotics* (1977), p. 17.

24 Ibid., p. 38.

25 Engels, *The Condition of the Working Classes*, p. 47.

26 Charles Kingsley, 'Preface Addressed to the Working Men of Great Britain', *Alton Locke* (1854 edition).

27 See for instance his speech to the Administrative Reform Association, 27 June 1855, in *Speeches of Charles Dickens*, ed. K.J. Fielding (1960), p. 197ff.

28 Elizabeth Gaskell, Letter to Catherine Winkworth, 23 Dec. 1848, in *Letters of Mrs Gaskell*, ed. Chapple and Pollard (1966), no. 35; and Letter to Mary Ewart, late 1848, ibid., no. 36.

29 R.G. Collingwood, *The Idea of History* (1946), part V, section 2, p. 246.

30 Ibid., p. 244.

31 Stendhal, *De l'Amour* (1822), ch. 24.

32 Roland Barthes, *Critique et Vérité* (1966), p. 15; *RB par Lui-même* (1975), p. 88.

33 George Eliot, *Adam Bede* (1859), ch. 15.

34 Barthes, *RB par Lui-même*, p. 123.

35 Emile Zola, *Le Roman expérimental* (1880), I.

36 Thomas Carlyle, *Chartism* (1839), ch. I.

Evangelicalism

1 Elie Halévy's *History of the English People in the Nineteenth Century* (1912–23; English trans. 1924–51) treats Evangelicalism in the opening volume, *A History of the English People in 1815*, Book 3, ch. 1, 'Religion', and in vol. 4, *Victorian Years*, ch. 7, 'Religious Beliefs'. Edward Quinlan's *Victorian Prelude* (1941) is about the origins of nineteenth century respectability and prudery, in which the Evangelical movement played a central role. E.P. Thompson's *Making of the English Working Class* (1963) discusses Methodism in great detail in order to explore its part in the growth of working-class movements. Owen Chadwick's two volumes on *The Victorian Church* (1966) in *An Ecclesiastical History of England* has a chapter on Dissent, two chapters on the church of England, and scattered discussions of particular issues.

2 Halévy, *History*, vol. I, Book III, ch. 1 (Penguin edition: *England in 1815*, III. p. 33).

3 See Thompson, *Making of the English Working Class*, ch. II, pp. 44–5.

4 Halévy, *History*, vol. I, Book III, Conclusion, p. 219.

5 Eric Hobsbawm, 'Methodism and the Threat of Revolution in Britain', in *Labouring Men* (1964).

6 Robert Southey, *Life of Wesley*, quoted by Thompson, *Making of the English Working Class*, 42. Coleridge made remarks to the same effect.

7   Thompson, *Making of the English Working Class*, ch. XI(i), p. 367.
8   Owen Chadwick, *The Secularisation of the European Mind in the Nineteenth Century* (1975), ch. 8(2).
9   Percy Bysshe Shelley, Notes to *Queen Mab* (1813), VII:13.
10 Thompson, *Making of the English Working Class*, ch. XI(i), p. 367.
11 George Eliot, *Felix Holt* (1866), ch. 3.
12 Halévy, *History*, vol. I, Book III, ch. 1, p. 13.
13 George Eliot, *Felix Holt*, Introduction.
14 Mark Rutherford, *The Revolution in Tanner's Lane* (1887), ch. 20.
15 Eliot, *Felix Holt*, ch. 3.
16 Thompson, *Making of the English Working Class*, ch. XI(ii), p. 398.
17 Rutherford, *The Revolution in Tanner's Lane*, ch. 10.
18 Ibid., ch. 1.
19 Ibid., ch. 5.
20 Valentine Cunningham, *Everywhere Spoken Against: Dissent in the Victorian Novel* (1975), Introduction.
21 Ibid., I:2, p. 23.
22 Anthony Trollope, *Barchester Towers* (1857), ch. 5. John Newton's remark is taken from Ian Bradley, *The Call to Seriousness: the Evangelical Impact on the Victorians* (1976), ch. 5, p. 103.
23 Dickens, *Bleak House* (1852–3), ch. 25.
24 Trollope, *Barchester Towers*, ch. 4.
25 Trollope, *Phineas Redux* (1874), ch. 31.
26 Michel Foucault, *The History of Sexuality* (1976; trans. 1978), IV:2, p. 92ff.
27 Ernst Troeltsch, *The Social Teaching of the Christian Churches* (1911; trans. 1931), Introduction and ch. II, section 9, esp. pp. 331–43, 'The Sect-type Contrasted with the Church-type'.
28 Mrs Oliphant, *Salem Chapel* 1863.
29 Rutherford, *The Revolution in Tanner's Lane*, ch. 23.
30 George Eliot, *Middlemarch* (1872), ch. 51.
31 Several of George Eliot's critics have remarked on her fondness for the image of the web to designate the complex range of human relationships. See Bernard Paris, *Experiments in Life: George Eliot's Quest for Values* (1965), and H.S. Kakar, *The Persistent Self: an Approach to Middlemarch* (1977), ch. 5.
32 George Eliot, *Romola* (1863), ch. 64.
33 W.E.H. Lecky, *History of England in the Eighteenth Century* (1878–90), vol. III, p. 77.
34 George Eliot, *Adam Bede* (1859), ch. 2.
35 George Eliot, *Janet's Repentance*, in *Scences of Clerical Life* (1858), ch. 18.

36 Ludwig Feuerbach, *The Essence of Christianity* (1841: translated by George Eliot 1846), ch. 4.
37 Rutherford, *The Revolution in Tanner's Lane*, ch. 7.
38 George Eliot, *Felix Holt*, ch. 4.
39 Trollope, *Barchester Towers*, ch. 5.
40 Thompson, *Making of the English Working Class*, ch. XI(i), p. 372.

Chapter 2   Crying

Expressing Emotion

1   Anne Sexton, Letter to Tillie Olsen, 14 Feb 1965; in *Anne Sexton: A Self-portrait in Letters* (1977), p. 256.
2   William Wordsworth, *Preface to Lyrical Ballads* (1800).
3   Plato, *Ion*, sections 533–5, tr. D.A. Russell (text from *Ancient Literary Criticism*, ed. Russell and Winterbottom (1972), 2:A.
4   Diderot, *Paradoxe sur le comedien* (1773).
5   The phrase is originally from the elder Cato; it is taken up and defended at length by Quintilian, *Institutio Oratoria* (*c*.95 AD), 12:i, in Russell and Winterbottom, (ed.), *Ancient Literary Criticism*, 9:6.
6   John Milton, *Apology for Smectymnuus* (1641), in Milton's *Prose Works* (Everyman edition), p. 121.
7   Ben Jonson, *Timber, or Discoveries* (1641), section XCCC.
8   John Keats, Letter to J.H. Reynolds, 21 Sept 1819.
9   William Shakespeare, *Coriolanus* (1608), V.iii.181ff.
10 Shakespeare, *Othello* (1604), V.ii.274ff.
11 Henry James, *The Portrait of a Lady* (1881), ch. 54.
12 J. Middleton Murry, *The Problem of Style* (1925), ch. 2.

Confession and Poetry

1   Nathaniel Hawthorne, *The Marble Faun* (1859), ch. 39.
2   A. Alvarez, *Beyond All This Fiddle: Essays 1955–67* (1968), p. 20.
3   Sylvia Plath, Interview for the British Council; Alvarez, *Beyond All This is Fiddle*, p. 50.
4   Alvarez, *Beyond All This Fiddle*, p. 17.
5   Donald Davie, 'Sincerity and Poetry', in *The Poet in the Imaginary Museum* (1977), pp. 140–6.
6   Thomas Hood, 'I remember, I remember', from *The Plea of the Midsummer Fairies and other poems* (1827).
7   Philip Larkin, 'I remember, I remember', from *The Less Deceived* (1955).

8 Robert Lowell, 'St Marks 1933', from *Day by Day* (1977).

9 Anne Sexton, 'The Double Image', from *To Bedlam and Part Way Back* (1960).

10 W.D. Snodgrass, 'Heart's Needle', in *Heart's Needle* (1960).

11 Anne Sexton, 'Imitations of Drowning', from *Live or Die* (1966).

12 'Walking in Paris', ibid.

13 'Protestant Easter', ibid.

14 'Consorting with Angels', ibid.

15 'The Addict', ibid.

16 Charles Gullans, 'Poetry and Subject-matter', *Southern Review*, 7:2 (Spring 1970). Taken from *Anne Sexton: the Artist and her Critics*, ed. J.D. McClatchy (1978), p. 131.

17 P.M. Spacks, '45 Mercy Street', *NY Times Book Review* 30 May 1976; from McClatchy, *Anne Sexton*, p. 189.

18 Anne Sexton, 'Two Sons', in *Live or Die*.

19 Anne Sexton, Letter to W.D. Snodgrass, 26 Nov 1958, in *Anne Sexton: A Self-Portrait in Letters* (1977), p. 43.

20 John Berryman, Prefatory note to the complete edition of the *Dream Songs* (1969).

21 Adrienne Rich, 'When we Dead Awaken: Writing as Re-vision', in *Lies, Secrets and Silences* (1969).

22 D.H. Lawrence, 'Mutilation', from *Look! We have come through* (1917).

23 W.B. Yeats, 'Crazy Jane Talks with the Bishop', in *Words for Music Perhaps* (1933).

24 Christina Rossetti, 'Twice' (written 1864, posthumously published).

25 P.M. Spacks in McClatchy, *Anne Sexton*, p. 189.

26 Anne Sexton, 'Music Swims Back to Me' from *To Bedlam and Part Way Back*.

27 Maxine Kumin, 'A Friendship Remembered', in McClatchy, *Anne Sexton*, 103ff.

28 Elizabeth Barrett, Letter to Robert Browning, 30 March 1846.

29 Elizabeth Barrett Browning, *Sonnets from the Portuguese* (1850), no. 20.

30 Edmund Gosse, *Robert Browning: Personalia* (1890). These are variants on the story (e.g. that Browning found the poems in his desk) but Gosse claimed to have got his version from Browning himself.

31 Anne Sexton, 'Menstruation at Forty', in *Live or Die*.

32 Shakespeare, Sonnet 110 (1609).

Expressing and Betraying

1 Alfred, Lord Tennyson, *In Memoriam* (1850), no. 50.

2 Tennyson, 'Supposed Confessions of a Second-rate Sensitive Mind' (1830).

3 R.G. Collingwood, *The Principles of Art* (1938), ch. VI, section 7, p. 121.
4 Ibid., ch. VI, section 3, p. 112.
5 Alexander Smith, 'Barbara' (1857) opening three stanzas: the rest of the poem can conveniently be found in *The Oxford Book of English Verse* (1910), though it was removed in later editions; or in Leavis's essay, note 7 below.
6 The first two lines are by Smith; the rest is, I must confess (or boast?), even more full of cliché than the original.
7 F.R. Leavis, 'Reality and Sincerity', *Scrutiny*, vol. XIX (1952–3), pp. 90ff.
8 Robert Lowell, 'The Withdrawal'.
9 Anne Sexton, 'Music Swims Back to Me'.
10 Sylvia Plath, 'Amnesiac'.
11 Wordsworth, 'Surprised by Joy' (1815).
12 Wordsworth, 'Composed upon Westminster Bridge, 3 Sept 1802'.
13 Samuel Taylor Coleridge, Letter to Southey, 7 August 1803.

Expressing the Dispersed Subject

1 See Michel Foucault, *The Order of Things* (1970; trans. of *Les Mots et les choses*, 1966), Preface, p. xxiii; and 'Truth and Power' in *The Foucault Reader*, ed. Paul Rabinov (1984), p. 59, and 'On the Genealogy of Ethics', ibid., p. 369.
2 Antony Easthope, 'Towards the Autonomous Subject in Poetry: Milton on his Blindness', in *1642: Literature and Power in the Seventeenth Century*, ed. Barker and others (1981), p. 301.
3 Antony Easthope, *Poetry as Discourse* (1983), ch. 8, p. 123.
4 Robert Browning, 'Cleon', from *Men and Women* (1855).
5 Irving Howe, 'Writing and the Holocaust', *The New Republic*, 27 Oct. 1986.
6 Jacques Derrida, *Positions* (1972; trans. 1981), p. 63.
7 John Donne, 'A Valediction Forbidding Mourning', (publ. 1633).

Chapter 3   Persuading

Literature as Didactic

1 Thomas Wilson, *The Art of Rhetoric* (1553): see Gregory Smith, *Elizabethan Critical Essays* (1904), Introduction, p. xxiv; Milton, *Paradise Lost* (1667), I, 34; Wordsworth, *Preface to Lyrical Ballads* (1800), in *Wordsworth's Literary Criticism*, ed. W.J.B. Owen (1974), p. 77.

2   See, for instance, G.M. Trevelyan, *British History in the Nineteenth Century* (1927), ch. 23.

3   F.R. Leavis, *D.H. Lawrence, Novelist* (1955), p. 17.

4   F.R. Leavis, *The Great Tradition* (1948), ch. 4, p. 193.

5   See George Steiner, *Language and Silence: Essays 1958–66* (1967). Steiner has pointed out this fact more eloquently than any other modern critic, but I must add that he does not advance much hard evidence for it.

Sermon and Poem

1   Romans I 15–16 (see Horton Davies, *Worship and Theology in England, 1603–1690* (1975), ch. 4.

2   Richard Hooker, *Treatise on the Laws of Ecclesiastical Polity* (1594–71), V:22.

3   John Donne, Sermon preached at Lincoln's Inn, 1618, in *Sermons*, ed. Potter and Simpson (1955), vol. II, pp. 95ff.

4   Donne, Holy Sonnet IX. The Holy Sonnets were published in 1633, and probably written (according to Helen Gardner) in 1609. This poem is in her edition of the *Divine Poems* (1952), p. 8, but I use the traditional numbering, not hers, and (as with all quotations in this book) modernized spelling.

5   Holy Sonnet XVII. Gardner, ibid., p. 14.

6   Preached at Whitehall, 19 April 1618. In *Sermons*, ed. Potter and Simpson, I, p. 293.

7   Sir Philip Sidney, *An Apology for Poetry* (*c.*1583). In (e.g.) Gregory Smith, *Elizabethan Critical Essays* (1904), vol. I, p. 154.

8   Preached upon the Penitential Psalms, 1623. In *Sermons*, ed. Potter and Simpson, VI, p. 56.

9   'Death's Duel', preached at Whitehall . . . 25 February 1630. Ibid., X, p. 229.

10 Donne, 'The Triple Fool', lines 8–11, in *Elegies & Songs and Sonnets*, ed. Helen Gardner (1965), p. 52.

11 Holy Sonnet XIII. In *Divine Poems*, ed. Helen Gardner, p. 10.

12 Gardner, ibid., pp. 1–5.

13 Preached at Lincoln's Inn, 1618. In *Sermons*, ed. Potter and Simpson, II, p. 119.

14 Preached to the Earl of Carlisle . . . at Sion, ?1622. Ibid., V, p. 245.

15 T.S. Eliot, 'Lancelot Andrewes' (1926), in *Selected Essays* (1934), p. 335.

16 T.S. Eliot, 'Hamlet' (1919), ibid., p. 45.

17 Helen Gardner, Introduction to Donne's *Divine Poems* (1952); L.L.

Martz, *The Poetry of Meditation* (1954); J.H. Summers, *George Herbert, His Religion and Art* (1954); John N. Wall, jr, 'Donne's Wit of Redemption', *Studies in Philology* 73 (1976), pp. 189ff; Patrick Grant, *The Transformation of Sin* (1974); Barbara K. Lewalski, *Protestant Poetics and the Seventeenth Century Religious Lyric* (1979).

18 Lewalski, ibid., ch. 1.
19 John Stachniewski, 'The Despair of Donne's Holy Sonnet's, *ELH* (1981), pp. 600ff.
20 Donne, Holy Sonnet VI, in *Divine Poems*, ed. Gardner, p. 7.
21 Lewalski, *Protestant Poetics*, p. 268.
22 William Empson, *Milton's God* (1961), ch. 4, p. 93.
23 Ibid., p. 98.
24 'Death's Duel', in *Sermons*, ed. Potter and Simpson, X, p. 229.
25 'A Hymn to God my God in my Sickness', lines 1–5, in *Divine Poems*, ed. Gardner, p. 504.
26 'Death's Duel', in *Sermons*, ed. Potter and Simpson, X, p. 229.
27 Preached to the King . . . at Whitehall, 18 April 1626. Ibid., VII, p. 118.
28 Preached at St Dunstan's upon Trinity Sunday 1627. Ibid., VIII, p. 37.
29 A Sermon of Valediction at my going into Germany, preached at Lincoln's Inn, 18 April 1619. Ibid., II, p. 235.
30 Donne, *The First Anniversary* ('An Anatomy of the World') (1611), 204ff.
31 Preached at the funeral of Sir William Cockayne, 12 Dec. 1626. In *Sermons*, ed. Potter and Simpson, VII, p. 257.
32 Ibid.
33 'A Hymn to God my God, in my Sickness', lines 26–30, in *Divine Poems*, ed. Gardner, p. 50.

Politics

1 *The Freedom Charter*: the Revolutionary Programme of the African National Congress. From *Apartheid*, ed. Alex La Guma (1972), pp. 229ff.
2 Nadine Gordiner, 'A Correspondence Course', in *Something out There* (1984)
3 Sara Gertrude Millin, *God's Stepchildren* (1924), Book II, part IV, ch. iv(7).
4 Ibid., Book II, part IV, ch.xii(1).
5 Doris Lessing, *The Grass is Singing* (1950), ch. 5.
6 Ibid., ch. 10.

7   Ibid., ch. 5.
8   Ben Turok, 'South Africa: the Violent Alternative', *Socialist Register* (1972), pp. 257ff.
9   Barry Feinberg, 'Ten Targets Reel under Rage of Vision', from *Apartheid*, ed. Alex La Guma.
10 Julian Grenfell, 'Into Battle' (1915). See Nicholas Mosley, *Julian Grenfell: his Life and the Times of his Death* (1976), p. 256.
11 Oswald Mtshali, 'The Birth of Shaka', from *To Whom it may Concern: an Anthology of Black African Poetry*, ed. Robert Royston (1973), p. 80.
12 Plutarch, *Life of Marius* (2nd C. AD), 37–9.
13 Alex La Guma, *In the Fog of the Season's End* (1972), ch. 18.
14 Alex Le Guma, *The Stone Country* (1964), part I, ch. 2.
15 *Quartet: New Voices from South Africa*: Alex La Guma, James Matthews, Richard Rive, Alf Wannenburgh; ed. Richard Rive (1963).
16 Nadine Gordimer, 'A Writer in South Africa', *London Magazine*, May 1965.
17 M. Ratcliffe, 'A South African Radical Exulting in Life's Chaotic Variety', Interview with Nadine Gordimer, *The Times*, 29 Nov. 1974.
18 Anthony Sampson, 'Love among the Madness', Interview with Nadine Gordimer, *The Observer*, 29 March 1987.
19 Michael Wade, *Nadine Gordimer* (1978), Conclusion.
20 Abdul R. JanMohamed, *Manichean Aesthetics* (1983), ch. 4.
21 John Cooke, *The Novels of Nadine Gordimer: Private Lives / Public Landscapes* (1985).
22 Stephen Clingman. *The Novels of Nadine Gordimer: History from the Inside* (1986).
23 Nadine Gordimer, *The Conservationist* (1974), p. 8.
24 Wade, *Nadine Gordimer*, p. 208.
25 Cooke, *The Novels of Nadine Gordimer*, p. 30.
26 Alan Paton, *Cry the Beloved Country* (1948)
27 Ezekiel Mphahlele, 'Mrs Plum', in *In Corner B* (1967), ch. 4.
28 Brian Bunting, Introduction to Alex La Guma, *And a Threefold Cord* (1964).

Chapter 4   Play

What is a Game?

1   Johan Huizinga, *Homo Ludens* (1944), ch. 7 (Paladin edition 1970, p. 154).
2   Sigmund Freud, *Beyond the Pleasure Principle* (1920, trans. 1922).

3 Freud, *Jokes and their Relation to the Unconscious* (1905). This was first translated as 'Wit and its Relation to the Unconscious': 'Witz' could mean either wit or jokes, but the later rendering describes the book more accurately. See esp. concluding pages of chs 6 and 7 (1960 edition of James Strachey's trans., pp. 137–9, 178–80).

4 Freud, 'The Relation of the Poet to Day-dreaming' (1908) in *Collected Papers*, vol. 4, no. ix.

5 *Mother Goose's Melody*, date uncertain, 1760–6; compiler uncertain, quite probably John Newbery, possibly helped by Oliver Goldsmith. See I. and P. Opie, Introduction to the *Oxford Dictionary of Nursery Rhymes* (1951), pp. 33ff.

6 I have mostly used Ernst Kretschmer, *Christian Morgenstern* (Sammlung Metzler, 1985). This remark from a letter to an editor in 1910 (*Briefe* 402) is quoted p. 112.

7 *Saemtliche Dichtungen* (henceforth *SD*) 8/7, Kretschmer, ibid., p. 84. In my attempts to capture at least a touch of Morgenstern's *Wahnwitz* I have of course had to abandon literal translation.

8 First stanza of 'Das grosse Lalula', *SD* 6/20, Kretschmer, ibid., p. 92.

9 *SD* 6/20–1, Kretschmer, ibid., p. 93.

10 Edward Lear, Letter to Evelyn Baring, n.d. Text from Vivien Noakes, *Edward Lear* (Fontana, 1968), p. 197.

11 Lewis Carroll, 'Jabberwocky', lines 1–4 (1855). See *Alice's Adventures in Wonderland & Through the Looking Glass*, ed. Roger Lancelyn Greene (World's Classics), text p. 134, notes pp. 266–9.

12 *SD* 6/76.

13 *SD* 6/41, Kretschmer, *Christian Morgenstern*, p. 107.

14 *SD* 8/8, Kretschmer, ibid., p. 84.

15 'Das Nasobem', *SD* 6/64, Kretschmer, ibid., p. 109.

16 *SD* 6/18, Kretschmer, ibid., p. 77.

17 *Briefe 406*, Kretschmer, ibid., p. 118.

Form as Play

1 Schiller, *Wallensteins Lager* (1798), *8er Auftritt*: as well as the Rhine turning into a stream of suffering, bishoprics have turned to deserts ('Die Bistuemer sind verwandelt in Wuesttuemer'), and so on.

2 George Puttenham, *The Art of English Poesie* (1589), in *Elizabethan Critical Essays*, ed. Gregory Smith, vol. 2. See esp. Book II, ch. 12.

3 Ibid., Book III, ch. 1.

4 Sir Philip Sidney, *Astrophil and Stella* (1591), no. 49.

5 Quoted by Freud in *Jokes*, ch. II (1960 trans., p. 35): I have simplified Schleiermacher's double word-play.

6 William Shakespeare, *Richard II* V.V.1–66.
7 Puttenham, *The Art of English Poesie*, Book III, ch. 3.
8 Ibid., Book III, ch. 5.
9 J. Middleton Murry, *The Problem of Style* (1925), ch. 1.
10 W.H. Auden, 'Making, Knowing and Judging', in *The Dyer's Hand* (1963), p. 47.
11 Milton, 'How soon hath time the subtle thief of youth' (1631)'; 'To the Lord General Cromwell, May 1652' (first published 1694).
12 Shakespeare, Sonnet 95 (1609).

Everything is Play?

1 Charles Lamb, 'In Praise of Chimney Sweeps'. *Essays of Elia* (1823); William Blake, 'The Chimney Sweeper', *Songs of Innocence* (1789).
2 Mark Twain, *Tom Sawyer* (1876), ch. 2.
3 A.D. Nuttall, *A New Mimesis: Shakespeare & the Representation of Reality* (1983), ch. 1 (p. 29)
4 Jacques Derrida, 'Signature, Event, Context', first published in *Marges* (1972), translation publ. in *Glyph* 1 (1976); John Scarle, 'Reiterating the Differences: a Reply to Derrida', also in *Glyph* 1.
5 Jacques Derrida, *Limited Inc* (1977).

Chapter 5 The Body of Literature

The Book

1 There are no footnotes to this section: because of its nature, they could only repeat material already in the text. A reference is however necessary to *Seuils*, by Gerard Genette (1987), which covers some of the same ground with the magisterial thoroughness for which Genette is justly renowned. The book only became available after I had finished mine, and it was at first tempting to take over lock, stock and barrel Genette's division of *paratexte* into *péritexte* and *épitexte* (what is part of and what is outside the actual book), as well as his systematic treatment of title, author's name, blurb, dedication, epigraphs, notes and the various kinds of preface. Thoroughness, however, has its drawbacks too, in particular the difficulty of separating the important from the trivial; although Genette declares that function is the most important point in all the elements of the paratext, he does not concentrate on function in the same cavalier fashion as I have done. I therefore hope that my more fragmentary and amateurish treatment adds something to his book.

Titles

1 Jonathan Culler, *Structuralist Poetics* (1975), ch. 8.

2 Three studies of titles have, in their very different ways, given much to this section: John Hollander, 'Haddocks Eyes', in *Vision and Resonance (1975); Michel Butor, Les Mots dans la peinture* (1980), and Harry Levin, 'The Title as a Literary Genre', *Modern Language Review*, 72 (1977), pp. xxziii–xxxvi.

3 Francis Bret Harte, 'What the Bullet Sang', *Complete Poetical Works*, p. 256.

4 Gerard Manley Hopkins, 'Heaven-Haven' (1866; publ. 1918).

5 Theodore Roethke, 'Child on Top of a Greenhouse', *Words for the Wind*, Collected Verse (1961).

6 Andrew Marvell, 'An Horatian Ode upon Cromwell's Return from Ireland', (1650), from *Miscellaneous Poems* (1681).

7 Charles Wolfe, 'The Burial of Sir John Moore after Corunna'. Text from *Oxford Book of English Verse*, 1923.

8 Denise Levertov, 'What were they like? (Questions and Answers)', *Where is Vietnam: American Poets Respond*, ed. Walter Lawenfels (1967), p. 73.

9 W.B. Yeats, 'Leda and the Swan', first published in *The Dial*, June 1924, reprinted in *The Cat and the Moon* (1924), then in *A Vision* (1925), and included in *The Tower* (1928). The note appeared in the first two publications. The remark about the 40 pages of commentary was made to L.A.G. Strong, see variorum edition, ed. Allt and Alspach (1968), p. 828, and John Unterecher, *A Reader's Guide to WBY* (1959), pp. 187–9.

10 Edwin Muir, 'The Annunciation' (1951), *Collected Poems*, p. 185.

11 Sylvia Plath, 'The Burnt-out Spa' (1959), *Collected Poems*, p. 185.

12 Sir Philip Sidney, Charita's Song from *Arcadia* (1580).

13 Denis de Rougemont, *L'Amour et l'Occident* (1938), trans. as *Passion and Society* (enlarged ed. 1956); and 'The Crisis of the Modern Couple' (first publ. 1949) in *The Anatomy of Love*, ed. A.M. Krich (1960), pp. 107ff. I have discussed the question more fully in *Love and Marriage* (1979), ch. 4.

14 Bernard Berenson, 'The Venetian Painters' (1894) in *Italian Painters of the Renaissance*.

15 John Wilmot, Earl of Rochester (?), 'Impromptu on Charles II', date unknown. See *Complete Poems*, ed. D.M. Vieth (1968), p. 134.

16 Thomas Carew, 'Epitaph on Lady Mary Villiers' (publ. 1640).

17 Matthew Arnold, 'The Function of Criticism at the Present Time', *Essays in Criticism*, First Series (1865).

18 Jonathan Dollimore and Alan Sinfield, eds *Political Shakespeare: New*

Essays in Cultural Materialism (1985), Introduction, p. viii.

19 Stephen Greenblatt, 'Invisible Bullets: Renaissance authority and its subversion. Henry IV and Henry V', ibid., p. 33.

Exploring the Edges

1 Alexander Pope, *The Dunciad* (1728), I, 38–39.
2 Pope, *The Dunciad* (1729), II, 54, note.
3 Pope, 'Epilogue to the Satires', Dialogue II, 14–19; 22–23.
4 Donald Davie, *Ezra Pound: Poet as Sculptor* (1965), p. 218; see also pp. 127–9.
5 Spenser, Dedicatory Sonnets to *The Faerie Queene* (1590, 1596). To the Earl of Oxenford, To the Earl of Essex, To the Lord Gray of Wilton.
6 Commendatory verses to ibid.: To the Learned Shepherd, by Hobynoll; 'A Vision upon this conceipt of the Faerie Queene' (by Walter Raleigh).
7 Milton, 'The Passion' (1630?, publ. 1645), note.
8 Shelley, 'On Love', prose fragment (*c*.1815, publ. 1880).
9 Shelley, *A Defence of Poetry* (1821).
10 Shelley, *Prometheus Unbound* (1820), II.i.90ff.
11 Shelley, 'Fragment: Thoughts Come and Go in Solitude' (1817).
12 Gerard Genette, *Seuils* (1987), pp. 307, 375.
13 Samuel Richardson, Letter to Lady Bradshaigh, 15 December 1748.
14 Samuel Richardson, *Clarissa* (1747–8), Everyman edition, vol. I, letters 49, 50.
15 D.H. Lawrence, 'The Novel', from *Reflections on the Death of a Porcupine* (1925), in *Phoenix*, II, p. 416.
16 Baudelaire, 'Au Lecteur', 31–32, *Les Fleurs du Mal* (1857).
17 Thackeray, *Vanity Fair* (1848), ch. 32.
18 Thackeray, Letter to his mother, 2 July 1847.
19 Spenser, *The Faerie Queene* (1590 version), Book III, canto xi, stanza 45.
20 Ibid. (1986 version), III.xii.45.

Murdering the Text

1 The source of the story is Suetonius, *Life of Virgil*, 39–41. See *Virgilii Opera*, ed. Conington, Introduction, (I, xxvii.
2 Thomas Mann, *Dr Faustus* (1947; trans. 1949), ch. 17.
3 Andreas Capellanus, *De Arte Honesti Amandi* (*c*1185; trans. J.J. Parry 1941). See esp. pp. 187–8.

4   Geoffrey Chaucer, *Canterbury Tales* (1386–9), T 104.
5   Chaucer, *Troilus and Criseyde* (1383), V 1786–1869.
6   Spenser, *Four Hymns* (1596), Dedication.
7   Spenser, 'An Hymn in Honour of Beauty', 197–203.
8   Spenser, 'An Hymn of Heavenly Love', 260–6.
9   *Hesperides, or the Works both Human and Divine of Robert Herrick* (1648), 'Noble Numbers, or his Pious Pieces', no. 2.
10 Chaucer, *Troilus and Criseyde*, V 1828–34.
11 Ibid., V 1849–55.
12 George Herbert, 'Jordan II', from *The Temple* (1633).
13 Andrew Marvell, 'The Coronet', (*c.*1650), in *Miscellaneous Poems* (1681).
14 Edmund Waller, 'Of the Last Verses in the Book', *Poems* (1686).
15 Samuel Johnson, 'Waller', in *Lives of the Poets* (1779–81).
16 Jacques Derrida, 'Structure Sign and Play in the Discourse of the Human Sciences', in *Writing and Difference* (1967; trans. 1978).
17 G.M. Hopkins, 'The Habit of Perfection' (1866; publ. 1918).
18 Adrienne Rich, 'Translations', in *Diving into the Wreck* (1973).
19 Henrik Ibsen, *A Doll's House* (1879; English version 1889). For the bowdlerized ending see Michael Meyer, *Henrik Ibsen*, vol.II (1971), p. 268.
20 Israel Zangwill and Eleanor Marx Aveling, 'A Doll's House Repaired', *Time*, March 1891.
21 Walter Besant, 'The Doll's House – And After', *English Illustrated Magazine*, Jan. 1890.
22 G.B. Shaw, *The Quintessence of Ibsenism* (1891), and cf. 'Still after the Doll's House', *Time*, Feb. 1890.

Index

289